Insights to Performance Excellence in Education 2001

An Inside Look at the 2001 Baldrige Award Criteria for Education

Also available from ASQ Quality Press:

Improving Student Learning: Applying Deming's Quality Principles in Classrooms
Lee Jenkins

Living on the Edge of Chaos: Leading Schools into the Global Age
Karolyn J. Snyder, Michele Acker-Hocevar, Kristen M. Snyder

Total Quality for School: A Suggestion for American Education
Joseph C. Fields

Creating Dynamic Teaching Teams in Schools
K. Mark Kevesdy and Tracy A. Burich, with contributions from Kelly A. Spear

Tools and Techniques to Inspire Classroom Learning
Barbara A. Cleary, Ph.D. and Sally J. Duncan

Orchestrating Learning with Quality
David P. Langford and Barbara A. Cleary, Ph.D.

Quality Team Learning for Schools: A Principal's Perspective
James E. Abbott

Futuring Tools for Strategic Quality Planning in Education
William F. Alexander and Richard W. Serfass

To request a complimentary catalog of ASQ Quality Press publications, call 800-248-1946 or visit our web-site at http://qualitypress.asq.org .

Insights to Performance Excellence in Education 2001

An Inside Look at the 2001 Baldrige Award Criteria for Education

Mark L. Blazey

Karen S. Davison

John P. Evans

ASQ Quality Press

Milwaukee, Wisconsin

Insights to Performance Excellence in Education 2001: An Inside Look at the 2001 Baldrige Award Criteria for Education
Mark L. Blazey, Karen S. Davison, and John P. Evans

ISBN 0-87389-485-5

Acquisitions Editor: Annemieke Koudstaal
Project Editor: Craig Powell
Production Administrator: Gretchen Trautman
Special Marketing Representative: David Luth

Microsoft® is a registered trademark of Microsoft Corporation.

ASQ Mission: The American Society for Quality advances individual and organizational Performance Excellence worldwide by providing opportunities for learning, quality improvement, and knowledge exchange.

Attention: Bookstores, Wholesalers, Schools and Corporations: ASQ Quality Press books, videotapes, audiotapes, and software are available at quantity discounts with bulk purchases for business, educational, or instructional use. For information, please contact ASQ Quality Press at 800-248-1946, or write to ASQ Quality Press, P.O. Box 3005, Milwaukee, WI 53201-3005.

To place orders or to request a free copy of the ASQ Quality Press Publications Catalog, including ASQ membership information, call 800-248-1946. Visit our web site at www.asq.org. or http://qualitypress.asq.org .

Printed in the United States of America

 Printed on acid-free paper

American Society for Quality

Quality Press
600 N. Plankinton Avenue
Milwaukee, Wisconsin 53203
Call toll free 800-248-1946
Fax 414-272-1734
www.asq.org
http://qualitypress.asq.org
http://standardsgroup.asq.org
E-mail: authors@asq.org

Contents

Preface

This book examines systems and practices that enable organizations of all types to achieve optimum levels of Performance Excellence. This book grew out of many discussions centered on the Malcolm Baldrige Criteria and how education at all levels could benefit from applying this management system in educational organizations.

We have spent a substantial portion of our professional lives focused on two major endeavors. The first is education, and our brief biographies attest to our broad coverage of the field from early childhood to postgraduate institutions and from gifted and talented to business education. The second is performance management systems.

We wish to offer our readers some insights from experiences derived from our work with high-performing organizations, as well as those not performing to high levels. We recognize that every organization is unique. Each organization has its own people, culture, work, and customers that create unique challenges for leadership and management. The work of education must be managed more effectively at all levels—from the classroom teacher to top administrators—to enable our children to remain competitive in a global economy.

For many years, public schools in the United States enjoyed an enviable position at the K–12 and higher education levels. They faced very little competition. At the K–12 level, charter schools, home schools, distance delivery, and vouchers are beginning to challenge the current system. Now at the higher education level, competition for students has become global and has intensified accordingly. The most serious competition, however, may be the kind that our students face in this century. This will be for continued leadership in the global marketplace.

Our goal for this book is that leaders at all levels of education will understand how to improve their organizations and regain a competitive edge. To do this, they must understand the parts of a high-performance management system, but more importantly, they must know how these parts connect and align. We believe that readers need to understand fully what each area of the performance management system means for educational organizations and find the synergies among the seven major parts of the management system: leadership; strategic planning; student, stakeholder, and market focus; information and analysis; faculty and staff focus; educational and support process management; and organizational performance results.

Educational leaders have reported that this book has been valuable as a step-by-step approach to help identify and put in place continuous improvement systems. As this progresses, improvement efforts in one area will lead to improvements in other areas. This book will help identify areas that need immediate improvement, as well as areas that are less urgent but, nevertheless, vitally linked to overall improvement.

Acknowledgments

Curt Reimann, Harry Hertz, and the dedicated staff of the Malcolm Baldrige National Quality Award office have provided long-standing support and guidance in promoting quality excellence. This book would not be possible in a timely fashion without the design and layout expertise, dedication, and commitment of Enterprise Design and Publishing and the assistance of Jessica Norris in typing and collecting information on state award practices.

The chapter on site visits is used with permission of Quantum Performance Group, Inc. Material for the core values, performance excellence model, criteria, selected glossary terms, and background information in this book are drawn from the Malcolm Baldrige National Quality Award 2001 Education Criteria for Performance Excellence. Portions of the Organizational Assessment Surveys and Safety and Security Survey are used with permission from Quantum Performance Group, Inc.

The following people have been inspirational and pivotal to our educational development and insights: Carol Davison, a dedicated and creative teacher and role model/mother of an author; the late Trudy Watson, who was a mentor; professor Maurice Johnson, who introduced the concept of Intentionality in Education; Sandra Kessler, for early pioneering in Cooperative Learning; and John Michalko, an inspirational teacher and friend to his students. Special recognition is deserved for Lynn Erdle and her staff at Canandaigua Academy High School (New York) for demonstrating role model skills at leading student-focused change. Great educational leaders helped shape our concepts of leadership at all levels, including Lynn Erdle, Gary Jones, Stephen Uebbing, Richard Rose, Daniel Hayes, Dan Hogan, John O'Rourke, Susan Snyder, James Latham, and Paul Darnall. The research of authors Peggy Seigle and Sandra Byrne was important to our work. We thank William L. Smith, for focusing thoughtfully on multiculturalism and diversity. Special acknowledgment goes to Marshall "Mike" Smith, Marc Tucker, Janice Weinman, and the dedicated people at the Institute for Educational Leadership, including Mike Usdan, Betty Hale, and Joan Wills, for continual national leadership in education.

Two dedicated and very special students, Mark Harold Blazey and Elizabeth Rose Blazey, have helped our work with critical review and feedback based on their experience in the public schools.

The School System of Pinellas County, Florida has won the Florida Sterling Award and continues to be a pioneer and role model school system that holds great promise for our public education system. We especially recognize the efforts of those who helped that district achieve excellence: James Shipley and Marie Shipley, J. Howard Hinesley, Ken Rigsby, Jerry Goolsby, Marilyn Caldwell and Chris Collins, Brenda Clark, Shirley Lorenzo, Cathy Athenson, and John Leanes.

Mark L. Blazey, Karen S. Davison, and John P. Evans

Foreword

I first ran into Mark Blazey in Pinellas County, Florida in 1994. Mark was co-facilitating a Quality Boot Camp for Pinellas school teams on how to use a Baldrige-based assessment to frame their school improvement plans. We next hooked up a year later during Baldrige Examiner training on the education pilot. When Mark asked me to write the Foreword to *Insights to Performance Excellence in Education 2001*, I immediately said "yes," based on these two earlier encounters. I'll share my reasons, but first, some relevant context that articulates why I strongly believe that educators, perpetually strapped for time and resources, should read this book.

As educators, we are taught to define our work world in terms of the programs we run, the grade levels or academic disciplines we teach, or the job positions we hold. Today, we're being asked to take this familiar mindset and apply it to an entirely different concept of work, described by unfamiliar terminology, such as *customer/supplier relationships and management processes.*

The need to rethink what has become second nature in education did not emanate from some sadistic plot to make educators feel inadequate. It's based on what we have discovered about organizational transformation—initially inside U.S. companies, now within varied settings—and about what all organizations must do to confront and benefit from the pain of change. For business, the challenge was/is global competition. To succeed in an increasingly demanding and dynamic marketplace, our best companies literally had to reinvent themselves. During the mid-1980s, they had to build the systemwide capacity not only to meet higher performance standards, but also to improve continuously in order to meet future, unknown challenges.

Fast-forward 15 years. Today, education confronts its own pain of change. This time the challenge is what I'll call Accountability-Plus. Not only must educators meet state performance standards for all children, but they must also help every child to succeed in school and to *like it* (that's the "plus" factor) so that students develop both the skill and the will to continue learning throughout their lifetimes.

How do we meet this awesome challenge? That's where *Insights* enters the picture. Really good teachers, like Mark, have a unique skill. They simultaneously hold high expectations for all students while accelerating each student's capacity for self-discovery. During Pinellas and Baldrige Examiner training, Mark demonstrated a unique talent for taking the Baldrige Criteria, truly an engineer's paradise, and making the contents less intimidating for the rest of us mere mortals. He accomplished this task by enabling participants to focus on what Rummler and Brache[1] refer to as "manag[ing] the white space on the organization chart." Blazey, Davison, and Evans refer to this activity as "connecting the dots." They go to great lengths to describe the linkages and interrelationships among the Baldrige seven Categories, 19 Items, and 30 Areas to Address. Armed with this frame of mind and handy blueprint, educators will discover that the "whole" of Baldrige, as an assessment tool, is far more valuable in improving their organizations than the sum total of the individual pieces. (To restate an extremely rude, but highly appropriate phrase from our political world, the authors make it possible to understand that "it's the *system*, stupid!")

Consequently, this book should prove to be a valuable resource in helping educators use the Baldrige Criteria to meet ever-increasing performance standards and customer expectations. It should also assist all types of educators in numerous settings to design, document, and continually enrich their own rigorous and long-term improvement strategies.

Here's the real "What's in it for me?". *Insights* should enable educators to accomplish what first attracted most of them to the education profession; the joy of engaging students in the process (that word again) of learning. To quote a very wise former CEO, "Good work is the goal. Recognition is the consequence."[2] Stated as a Baldrige truism: continuous improvement is its own reward.

Enjoy this book!

—Peggy Siegel, Ph.D.
Director, Business/Education Leadership Initiatives
National Alliance of Business

References

1. Gaery A. Rummler and Alan P. Brache, *Improving Performance: How to Manage the White Space on the Organization Chart* (San Francisco: Jossey-Bass, 1991).

2. Max DePree, *Leadership Jazz: The Art of Conducting Business through Leadership, Followership, Teamwork, Voice, Touch* (New York, NY: Dell Publishing Company Incorporated, 1993).

Introduction

The Malcolm Baldrige National Quality Award Criteria for Performance Excellence in Education and related scoring guidelines are powerful new assessment instruments that will help leaders of educational organizations identify strengths and key areas for improvement. Leaders then need to use the information to achieve higher levels of performance.

This will not be an easy task for education organizations or their leaders. There are complex and ever-changing relationships, involving the community, parents, educational administrators, students and stakeholders, research facilities, teachers, and partners. These complex relationships provide a challenge to an effective educational management system that drives performance improvement, not the status quo.

Over the past decade, organizations of all types have made fundamental changes in the way they work, guided by the Baldrige Criteria. The results have been used to drive improvement to ever-higher levels. The criteria evaluate every key facet of activity and closely monitor organizational performance. Leaders of these organizations have high expectations, value employees and their input, communicate clear directions, and align the work of everyone to achieve organizational goals and optimize performance. As a result of the efforts of these organizations, Americans have enjoyed higher productivity and living standards.

There are now similar but customized criteria for education. To provide value, streamline operations, and meet student and stakeholder demands, the criteria and scoring guidelines presented in this book offer a new road map for educators. As Dr. Stephen Uebbing, superintendent of the Canandaigua City School District and New York State's 1999 Superintendent of the Year, said of the Performance Excellence Criteria, "The old system has taken us about as far as it's going to go. In order for us to make the jump to the next level of improvement in student achievement, we have to move away from the existing paradigms and look for a new vehicle. The quality principles, we believe, are the vehicle that will take us to the next level."

Because of the complexity of managing modern organizations, the continually increasing demands of customers and stakeholders, and the fast-moving, global competition, the criteria used to examine organizational management systems and processes are often complex and difficult to understand. This introduction outlines the framework, key concepts, and "lessons learned" by educational and other organizations that are beginning to get better at what they do.

The introduction includes the following information:

- A practical rationale for using the Baldrige Criteria to improve educational organizational performance.
- Education Award Criteria goals and core values that underlie the Baldrige Education Criteria.
- Key characteristics and themes of the 2001 Education Criteria.
- Practical insights and lessons learned—ideas on strategies to put high-performance systems in place and promote organizational learning. This section emphasizes themes driven by the criteria and the core values. It also includes suggestions about how to start down the path to systematic organizational improvement; how to go about "getting better at what you do."

A note about the language and terms used in this book. First, a detailed glossary is included in the back of the book that will clarify unfamiliar terms and terms used in specific ways. The terms used in the criteria attempt to make concepts from business more user-friendly for education. For example, "faculty and staff" instead of employees and "students and stakeholders" instead of customers. An attempt was made to not use or to minimize terms that are unfamiliar to educators. "School" and "organization" or "enterprise" are used interchangeably. "Teacher" is used generically and includes the classroom teacher, professor, instructor, and lecturer.

Special Note:

Each criteria Item is accompanied by a linkage diagram that depicts the relationships of Item requirements to each other. The major or primary linkages are designated using a solid arrow (————▶). The secondary linkages are designated using a dashed arrow (- - - - -▶). Also, for each criteria Item, we have included examples of effective practices that some organizations have developed and followed. We have also included samples of effective practices for teachers and administrators. We also invite readers to send us promising practices they know of, as well as comments about how we can make this book more useful to readers. E-mail may be sent to *Blazey@Quantum Performance.com*. These samples present some ideas about how to meet requirements. Examiners should not take these sample effective practices and convert them into requirements for organizations they are examining. *Sample practices for teachers were included for many but not all of the Items; the authors welcome examples of additional sample effective practices for the year 2002 book.*

Insights Into Education
Performance Excellence

This section provides information for educational leaders who are transforming their organizations to achieve substantially higher levels of Performance Excellence. This section presents:

- A "business case" or rationale for using the Baldrige Education Criteria to improve organization performance.
- The core values, themes, and concepts that drive organizational change to high levels of performance and underlie the Baldrige Criteria.
- Practical insights and lessons learned—ideas on transition strategies to put high-performance systems in place and promote organizational learning. It emphasizes themes driven by the 2001 Criteria and Core Values. It also includes suggestions about how to start down the path to systematic organizational improvement, as well as lessons learned from those who chose paths that led nowhere or proved futile despite their best intentions.
- A focused examination of safety and security in our schools over the last decade. An organizational assessment survey sample based on some requirements of the Baldrige Criteria is included in the "Self-Assessments of Educational Organizations and Management Systems" chapter, which begins on page 197.

A Practical Rationale for Using the Baldrige Performance Excellence Education Criteria

Education leaders know that change is tough. One of our wise professors once said, "It is easier to move a graveyard than to change curriculum." It is hard work to change an educational and learning system that has perhaps been relatively unchanged and unchallenged for decades. Because leaders know they will be asked and perhaps tempted to turn back many times, they appreciate improvement examples and encouraging results from organizations that are ahead of them on the journey and still progressing. Systematic processes based on the Baldrige Criteria to improve performance in education are relatively new and generally immature. Compared with the business sector, only a relatively small number of role model examples of best practices exist in education. However, the authors will draw examples and practices from organizations that have instituted or are in the process of instituting fundamental and systematic changes in the way they meet the demands of the future for more highly educated and skilled people.

What Schools and Students Can Do

The *New York Times Magazine* ran an article by James Traub entitled "What No School Can Do."[1] It is a thoughtful history of educational reform. He alleged, and rightly so, that we have "fiddled" with practically everything possible in education—from school facilities to curriculum to teacher training. His thesis is that schools *cannot produce* students whose achievement cannot be predicted by socioeconomic status. Indeed, in a survey and analysis of 24 major schoolwide reform models introduced between 1970 and 1994 aimed at increased performance, only one had strong evidence of positive effects on student achievement. The others failed to demonstrate any conclusive evidence of success.[2]

In contrast, David E. Drew's article "Tell Students Yes, You Can"[3] cites extensive research to the contrary. Drew, who is dean of the School of Educational Studies at Claremont Graduate University, cited studies that indicate Americans do a "massive disservice to our children by lowering…expectations…in math, science—or any other discipline." Based on his research, Drew believes that American teachers and parents erode students' achievement, self-confidence, and aspiration levels by blaming underperformance on poor schools, poor aptitude, bad teaching, and poor nutrition. In his work *Aptitude Revisited: Rethinking Math and Science Education for America's Next Century,* Drew contrasts our attitudes about children who underperform with those from other countries, such as Japan and China, who are outperforming American students. Whereas American teachers and parents assume the student cannot master the content and that is the reason for the poor performance, parents and teachers in Japan and China assume that the child has not worked hard enough. The Chinese assume that every child can master advanced math, for example, if they work hard enough. He cites research with African American and Latino students who went on to excel in advanced subjects such as calculus. Stretch goals, extra homework, study groups, positive expectations, and positive self-perception of ability made the difference for these students.

The National Assessment of Title I includes information and data that tracked progress of students in high poverty schools through 1999. Overall, there continued to be a substantial (several grade levels) achievement gap between high- and low-poverty schools and this widened between the late 1980s to 1999.[4]

The good news in this report is that several states (Connecticut, Maryland, North Carolina, Ohio, and Texas) went against this trend and actually increased achievement in mathematics and reading while lessening the achievement gap between its high- and low-poverty schools.[4]

Based on research and data, the guiding assumptions for success in *Lessons from the States,* by Robert Rothman[5], closely mirror the Baldrige themes and principles. These are the themes and principles to which this book will return throughout.

A Focus on Teaching and Learning, including High Expectations for All Students

Setting high expectations is a proven and powerful way to raise achievement for *all* students. It requires changing some deeply held and long-standing attitudes. This is the job of leaders at every level including classroom. For example, a junior high school in Texas serves a population of 90 percent "at risk" students who are Hispanic and poor. The principal was serious about raising performance and setting high expectations. She abolished remedial courses and substituted solid academic coursework and eventually even advanced placement courses. The results were that the school eliminated the performance gap and all groups have a better than 90 percent passing rate on state tests in all areas.

Standards Development and Alignment, including Use of Data to Drive Improvements

In addition to setting high expectations, schools and systems that have shown success have maintained high expectations over a long period of time and have thus kept the expectations consistent. They have not "fiddled" and "tinkered" incessantly with the course they have set according to the current reform "program of the month."

Successful schools, systems, and states use data to determine where they are successful, and where to allocate resources needed for areas in need of improvement. The use of data is the "way of doing business" for schools and school systems that have adopted the Baldrige Criteria as a reform strategy.

Flexibility and Accountability

Accountability is a powerful and feared tool for leaders to use to insist high standards are set for all students, including specially labeled groups. Unless there are real goals and positive and negative consequences, accountability will be meaningless. For example, in Chicago, schools and individuals are held accountable for performance. The district has placed 100 schools on probation and more than 70 percent of those on probation have improved. Jobs of staff, faculty, and administrators depend on performance. About 250 have been fired or resigned for reasons linked to academic performance. The accountability measures have raised student performance. While still low, academic achievement since 1995 is significantly better than before the account-ability thrust and shows a trend of improvement that includes the lowest performers. The dropout rates have declined three years in a row.

Linkages Among Schools, Families, and Communities

Students at all levels have health and social service needs that will interfere with academics if not addressed. Schools need to ensure that health needs such as eye glasses, vaccinations, and nutrition are met, and coordinate with appropriate agencies when they are not.

Targeted Resources, including Improving Teacher Quality

In trying to understand gains on both the National Assessment of Educational Progress and the state tests, *Lessons From the States* found consistently that teaching quality made the difference. This focus on teacher quality included restructuring and raising teacher salaries that were then linked to performance, and targeting resources to professional development of faculty. Some schools have even given teachers a financial stake in the success of the school, thus making them true "stakeholders." The professional development was part of a detailed accountability system in successful efforts.

U.S. schools *can* institute fundamental change in every level and type of educational organization by following the example of successful businesses and industries that use the Malcolm Baldrige Criteria to assess and improve their management system. They can be flexible in an effort to engage all students in active learning and in choosing courses of studies that interest and challenge them. They can involve students in teams solving real problems to give them a greater sense of responsibility, ownership, and control. What schools *can* do is the subject of this book.

Differences in the way stakeholders view the value of the high school diploma compared to public school teachers may, in part, account for the lack of true structural and substantive change to K–12 public schools. In public opinion surveys, teachers in K–12 schools view schools very differently from key stakeholders— professors in higher education and business leaders. For example, a survey conducted October to November, 1998,[6] reported that only 27 percent of college professors and 39 percent of employers thought a high school diploma meant that the typical student had at least learned the basics. Seventy-six percent of public school teachers, on the other hand, thought the typical high school diploma meant the student had at least learned the basics.

The tenth anniversary of the first National Education Summit, a meeting between former President George Bush and the nation's governors, occurred in 1999. The focus a decade ago was on how to improve educational performance in the United States. At that time, high school students' average scores on most standardized achievement tests were lower than scores in the 1960s and on a downward spiral. Scholastic Aptitude Tests (SATs) scores were also declining. U.S. students were not competitive on international science and mathematics assessments. In 1990, the National Center for Education Statistics described the condition of elementary and secondary education as "poor" relative to student performance in other countries. American students performed poorly on assessments of mathematics and science. On both assessments, they were in the lowest group of industrialized countries, and in mathematics, they ranked last. Results from science assessments were similar. In an international assessment, U.S. students placed in the lowest group of nations and second-to-last overall. Since *A Nation at Risk* was published in 1983 by the U.S. Department of Education, student achievement has been flat or headed downward. A 1998 report indicates, "Not much has changed in terms of educational achievement—we are still a nation at risk educationally."[7]

Although there are many valid and serious concerns with the "fairness" of international comparisons, such as the Third International Mathematics and Science Study (TIMSS), the real question for American education is: Are we or are we not achieving at a level that will enable our children and our country to be successful in the future? Despite lots of monies, attention, tinkering, and experiments, on the latest round of international science and mathematics tests, American students still lagged behind students in nearly half the countries that gave the uniform quiz—including Australia, Canada, and several European and Asian nations. American student performance seemed to decline in comparison to foreign students as they move through the school system. "American students continue to learn," Richard Riley, former Secretary of the United States Department of Education stated, "but their peers in some other nations have been learning at a faster rate." Learning at a slower rate places our students at as dramatic a disadvantage as a racing sports car with an economy car's engine. The half-life of useful knowledge (how long knowledge is retained before half of the learning is obsolete) is rapidly decreasing, especially in leading-edge fields such as microelectronics and bioengineering. Intel estimates that the half-life of knowledge for a microelectronics engineer decreased from 18 to 11 months between 1989 to 1999. This means rate of learning can be a critical advantage or disadvantage to technical leadership.

Lower skills at the elementary and secondary levels have a direct effect on higher education and eventually the workforce. Secondary school graduates entering college with lower skill levels means more time must be spent on remedial or lower levels of instruction. Many students are not prepared to read, compute, and write at the college level. Remedial instruction to correct deficiencies adds costs and diverts resources from college-level instruction. When surveyed, 88 percent of business, government, and academic leaders viewed the greatest problem for higher education as too many students needing remedial education.[6] Policy discussions in several states, including New York, are currently underway to limit the amount of resources public institutions of higher education may use for academic rework.

We failed to reach the goal of U.S. governors that U.S. students would be first in the world in science and mathematics achievement by the year 2000. We were not even close. Worse, we are far from attaining it in the foreseeable future. Clearly, relying on minor adjustments to the current system will not enable us to achieve that goal or to move up in the worldwide ranking of student knowledge and skills. The United States has also fallen to the bottom of the industrialized world for student graduation rates. Ranked against such nations as Japan and Belgium, our graduation rate has not kept up. We have not regressed, but our competitors have improved faster than us. We have not kept pace with the rate of improvement in this critical area around the world. In a competitive world, the failure to improve means we fall further behind.

According to recent studies, higher education is still well-regarded by the public. Although this is good news, it is alarming that our best universities and colleges are enrolling more and more non-American students, particularly in areas such as statistics, advanced mathematics, and the sciences. This trend, while strengthening the resources of higher education, will not promote U.S. leadership.

While describing American higher education as the best in the world, business executives have expressed dissatisfaction with the way colleges and universities are managed. They tend to view these institutions as inflexible, bureaucratic, and largely unresponsive to students and stakeholders.

Tuition rates in U.S. institutions of higher education have increased more rapidly than the cost of living. This indicates that colleges and universities are either making larger profits (or surplus revenue) or not improving performance effectiveness as quickly as the rest of the organizations that contribute to our economy and cost of living. Accordingly, these schools are under increasing pressure to be accountable for and improve the management of their resources and provide more educational value. In addition, global competition and information technology have created a number of challenges for higher education. Distance learning is beginning to challenge the traditional classroom.

Information technology has also created a new kind of competitive environment. The information technology revolution provides new and exciting ways to deliver learning experiences at all levels of education. With this new capacity comes increasing pressure to upgrade teaching methods that exploit the new technology's capabilities and match student enthusiasm for the technology. New ways of delivering instruction, such as long-distance and Web-based delivery, now compete with traditional "stand-up" lectures, which have been a mainstay of higher education institutions. New pathways for information technology have created thousands of virtual classrooms—even in the lower grades of schools. This increasing interdependency creates a special educational challenge to deal with entirely new competition. Excellent faculty are no longer confined to the four walls of their "home" institution. Students, more and more, are able to find the knowledge they seek from top-level faculty who may or may not be at their university or school.

Businesses have had to compete globally for some time. Education at all levels is now beginning to face the same tests. Brought together by webs and pathways that span the globe, the world is at the fingertips of our students. This means that information on schools at all levels is available to allow students to learn from other students about how their schools compare to others on test scores, food, grading policies, and so on. Our students will be competing for jobs and market share in a global marketplace. Unfortunately, given their performance on standardized tests, it seems too many will be easy to beat.

The rationale for using the Baldrige Education Criteria is simple: The United States cannot maintain its economic, political, and moral leadership without superior skills and competencies of all of its citizens. It is the job of schools, colleges, and universities to develop these skills, and they are not improving fast enough to meet the challenge.

U.S. students now compete in the world economy, not just their region and state. To be realistic, their performance must be judged globally, not locally. Accordingly, U.S. schools at all levels must set their standards higher and improve teaching, learning, and the management of education in order to continue our standard of living.

Competition for the existing structure of schools in the form of charter schools, home schools, and long-distance and Web-based learning are here. The educational establishment must deal with the reality of both competitive threats and growing student/stakeholder demands.

The Malcolm Baldrige Criteria for Performance Excellence in Education outline effective practices and core values that have helped U.S. businesses, government agencies, and several school systems and institutes of higher education improve their performance. Schools of all types will find that these criteria, if applied systematically, will improve their performance and the academic achievement of their students. Both are needed to help us meet the challenges of the new millennium.

Practical Insights

Connections and Linkages

Connect the dots, a popular children's activity, helps kids understand that, when properly connected, apparently random dots create a meaningful picture. In many ways, the seven Categories, 19 Items, and 30 Areas to Address in the Baldrige Education Criteria are like the dots that must be connected to reveal a meaningful picture. This is part of the systems approach mentioned as a key theme that underlies the criteria. With no paths to make the web, or join the dots, staff development is not related to strategic planning; information and analysis are isolated from process management; and academic performance improvement efforts are disjointed, fragmented, and do not yield robust results. This book describes the linkages and interrelationships among the Items of the criteria. The exciting part about having them identified is that you can look for these linkages in your own organization and, if they don't exist, start building them.

Transition Strategies

Putting high-performance school management systems in place is a major commitment that will not happen quickly. At the beginning, you will need a transition strategy to get you from management by opinion, power, or intuition to more fact-driven management. The next part of this section describes one approach that has worked for many organizations in various sectors: driving performance improvement through an existing top management structure.

Performance Improvement Council

The performance improvement council is usually the administrative cabinet or its equivalent—the primary policy-making body for the organization. The name change is significant and brings with it a new role and renewed focus on shared goals and mission with a focus on continuous improvement. It should spawn other groups at different levels in the school system to take on roles as performance improvement councils.

The major role of the performance improvement councils is to be a conscience for the strategic plan and mission of the organization. Council members must communicate; share practices and policies; and involve faculty, staff, and stakeholders. All faculty and staff and, when appropriate, students and stakeholders, must know the mission and goals and how their work contributes to achieving the goals. Members of the performance improvement council become leaders for major improvement efforts and sponsors for several process or continuous improvement teams throughout the organization. The council structure can effectively align the work and optimize performance at all levels and across all functions of the school.

Selecting new members for the performance improvement council should be done carefully. Each member should be essential for the success of the operation, and together they must be sufficient for success. Partnerships with the school community, including unions, parents, faculty, staff, and students, should be forged using these councils. The most important member is the senior leader of the school, college, or educational entity seeking to optimize performance. This person must participate actively, demonstrating the kind of leadership that all should emulate. Improvement can be led from the top, but it cannot be "dictated and delegated." Of particular importance is a commitment to consensus building as the *modus operandi* for the council. This tool, a core of performance improvement programs, is often overlooked by leadership. Other council members selected should have leadership responsibility for broad areas of the organization, such as faculty and staff resources, operations planning, curriculum, and data systems.

The Use of Champions

Members of the performance improvement council should each lead a major category across the system. They need to be the "champion" of this category. For example, the Category 3 champion would focus upon disciplines, departments, and other units of students and stakeholders. He or she, for example, may gather information from key student groups and share concerns and perspectives from students on their needs and expectations. If major complaints are identified, they would be shared with other category champions and corrective actions agreed upon. In this way, major initiatives include perspectives and requirements from all categories.

Performance Improvement Council Learning and Planning

The performance improvement council will eventually become extremely knowledgeable about high-performance management systems. Council members are among the first in the organization to learn about continuous improvement tools and processes.

To be effective, every member of the council (and every member of the organization) needs to understand the Baldrige Criteria because the criteria describe the components of the entire management system. Participation in carefully designed training focused on the criteria and the importance of performance improvement for educational enterprises has proven to be the best way to understand the complexities of the system needed to achieve Performance Excellence. Any additional training should be carried out in the context of planning—that is, learn tools and use them to plan the performance improvement implementation, practices, and policies.

The following are suggested actions for the performance improvement council:

- Develop one integrated strategic performance improvement plan.
- Create the communication plan and infrastructure to transmit performance improvement policies throughout the organization.
- Define the roles of faculty and staff, including new recognition and reward structures to support needed behavioral changes.
- Develop a master training and development plan. Involve team representatives in planning so they can learn skills close to when they are needed. Define what training is provided to whom, and when and how success will be measured.
- Launch improvement projects that will produce both short- and long-term successes. Improvement projects should be clearly defined by the performance improvement council and driven by the strategic plan. Typical improvement projects include important faculty and staff processes, such as career development, performance measurement, and diversity, as well as improving operational education programs and services in the line areas.
- Develop a plan to communicate the progress and successes of the organization. Through this approach, the need for performance improvement processes is consistently communicated to all faculty and staff.

Lessons Learned

Ongoing training will be necessary in the context of performance improvement teamwork and councils. All faculty, staff, and most importantly, students need the knowledge and skills on which to build a learning organization that continually improves. Such training typically includes team building, leadership skills for the classroom and organization, consensus building, communications, and effective meeting management. These are necessary for effective teams to become involved in solving critical problems in a disciplined and systematic way.

An important competency involves using a common process to define student and stakeholder requirements and determine the ability of the organization to meet those requirements. Measuring success and determining the extent to which stakeholders are satisfied is critical. Stakeholders may include parents of students, businesses, or the next level of education (such as grade three as the stakeholder for grade two, high school English teachers as stakeholders for middle school English teachers, or college professors as stakeholders for high schools). Students also have roles as stakeholders when they purchase food from the cafeteria or ride the bus. When a problem arises, staff and faculty close to the problem must be able to define the problem correctly, isolate the root causes, generate and select the best solution to eliminate the root causes, and implement the best solution.

It is also important to be able to understand data and make decisions based on facts, not merely intuition or feelings. Students, faculty, and staff need to share a common culture of fact-based decision making, particularly when making decisions about programs and student learning. Guessing that an instructional approach is or isn't working cannot be part of the culture. Familiarity with statistical and decision-making tools to analyze student and staff work and performance data is important. With these tools, processes can be analyzed and vastly improved. Reducing unnecessary steps in processes, variability, and cycle time and increasing process consistency are powerful ways to improve quality and reduce cost simultaneously.

Knowledge of techniques for acquiring comparison and benchmarking data, curricular and instructional process improvement, leadership strategies and roles, strategic planning, and student and stakeholder satisfaction will help faculty and staff expand their optimization and high-performance thrust across the entire organization.

Today's students, the same ones who are scoring poorly academically against the rest of the developed world, are going to be in charge of our corporations, schools, and government in the coming years (unless we relinquish leadership to students from other countries who are better prepared). Those who are calling for home schools, vouchers, or charter schools are sending our current schools a clear message—we want leading, not lagging, skills and capabilities. Those ideas that used to be radical are now in the editorials of major mainstream newspapers under such banners as "School Board Associations, instead of rejecting charter schools, should welcome them." Education, a constitutionally established responsibility of the states, was a national determinant in the 2000 presidential election. Demands for Performance Excellence to move into our schools are widespread.

Performance improvement has permeated major sectors of the American economy, from manufacturing and service industries to professional services, health care, public utilities, and government. Education has pioneered some efforts as well. All of these segments have contributed valuable lessons to the performance improvement movement and have played an important part in our recovery from the economic slump caused by the poor service and products of the 1970s. Relying on the Baldrige model, we will share some of the insights and lessons learned from leaders of high-performing organizations.

An Assessment Comes to Life

I. Background

The professor had been at the school for approximately one year, but he had just agreed to take the position of Associate Dean for the MBA Program. Almost immediately, his colleagues began to offer their advice about what his immediate priorities should be. The professor wasn't sure who had solid information, who might be speaking from too narrow a perspective, and who might have an axe to grind. He reflected that his situation was much like that of the new general manager of a business unit for which he understood the work in broad terms, but he knows he doesn't know all of the subissues and subtleties that might be lurking.

After reflecting over a long weekend, he concluded that he wanted some sort of broad assessment of the MBA Program as a basis for setting his own priorities. On the pad of paper that he was using for note taking, he finally wrote down three reasons for doing this. First, he wanted to build a base of facts. Second, he knew he needed to draw on the knowledge of others. Third, he wanted to do this in such a way as to create some ownership of the results, priorities, and directions that would emerge. He was familiar with the Baldrige framework because he was then serving as a senior examiner in that process. He understood the strengths of the framework, but he also had a realistic sense of how much work it took to prepare a Baldrige application.

II. Preparing

He did not automatically assume that the Baldrige framework was the way he wanted to go. First, and before he announced his intentions to anyone, he made a list of planning questions that he knew he would have to answer.

- What framework to use for an assessment?
- How many people (and who) to involve?
- How to organize them?
- How much time to spend?
- How to set the improvement priorities and how many to select?

He also knew that he would face questions about how to define action items for the improvement priorities that emerged, but he thought he would wait to let that be determined by what the assessment produced.

Framework

The professor knew he wanted some organizing set of concepts to establish the scope of the assessment. The Baldrige framework was certainly a candidate, and he was thoroughly familiar with that. However, he realized that a good argument could be made to organize the work in a common sense way around the primary functional elements of the MBA Program. This would produce a miniassessment of each of the following elements: admissions, student support, career services, curriculum, and teaching. People were generally familiar with this structure, and lots of people even thought they were experts about the elements! After some reflection, however, he decided to use the Baldrige framework. One of the key reasons for this was the experience of having seen how the Baldrige evaluation process helped one to get beyond activities that were apparent on the surface to issues that were more deeply buried and fundamental, and also to issues that crossed functions.

Now, however, he had a new set of problems. He was going to be relying on the volunteer labor of a number of his colleagues, virtually all of whom were unfamiliar with the Baldrige framework. He needed some kind of core team, but this was not an easy decision. The smaller the team, the more work there would be per team member. The larger the team, the greater the challenge of orienting everyone and coordinating the work. He also had to consider whether the assessment could be done in one intensive activity or whether it had to be spread over time. He also knew that he had to strike the right balance among the complexity, thoroughness, and depth of the assessment. This was the first attempt to do anything like this, in this way, in this MBA Program, and he certainly wasn't going to ask a team of a few colleagues to try writing the equivalent of a 50-page Baldrige application! Yet he also knew that the assessment had to probe carefully and deeply enough to produce results that would serve as guidance for future work.

Approach

He finally decided to form a small team of people for each Baldrige Category. Each team contained faculty and staff and consisted of three or four members. He recognized that it would have been desirable to include students on teams, but he was doing this during the summer and the students who would be returning for their second years in the fall were all away doing internships. He found a way to capture student input, as we will see later in this account. In order to make that amount of work manageable, he decided that the assignment would be for each team to produce two slides—one page (slide) of strengths and one page of opportunities for improvement—for the assigned category. In this way, he hoped to get each team to concentrate on the primary elements of each category without the burden of spending an uncomfortably large amount of time generating results that could not all be used. These assessment slides were to be presented in a one-day feedback retreat that he scheduled so as to allow each team a reasonable period of time in which to do its work. So, the approach consisted of the following elements:

- One small team of faculty and staff was assigned to each of the seven Baldrige Categories.
- Each team was responsible for producing one slide each of strengths and opportunities for improvement.
- Each team would have approximately three weeks to complete its work.
- The teams would convene for a one-day feedback retreat, present their results, and confer about the issues that should be selected for action.

Execution

First, our leader had to form the teams. With a combination of appeal to institutional spirit and forceful persuasion, he recruited a faculty member to lead each team. He then filled out the teams with enough faculty and staff to permit some division of the work. Next, he faced the task of providing some orientation for the teams regarding the Baldrige framework. For this he involved a colleague who was also familiar with the Baldrige framework. The colleague scheduled an orientation meeting with each team leader to discuss the category for which that individual was responsible. These discussions produced a scaled down interpretation of the category that was suitable for a first assessment of an organization that had not used this particular approach previously. The teams then went to work, but a number of followup questions arose for discussion during the ensuing three weeks.

The feedback retreat occurred close enough to the opening of the school year that most of the students had returned. Taking advantage of this, the associate dean invited the officers of the MBA student association to participate in the retreat. This provided a legitimate student perspective in the process, even though it occurred later than would have been preferable. It also served the end purpose of creating some student understanding and ownership of the results. While there was certainly some variation across the teams in the diligence and thoroughness with which the assignment were completed, each team produced its two slides for a report. Not surprisingly, one innovative team leader found a way to break through that limitation, however. The leader of the team assigned to the Results Category used a PowerPoint presentation that may have contained only two slides. However, each bullet on each slide had a hyperlink to an expanded body of information. Even now, two years later, that faculty member kids the associate dean about the result.

Results

Five themes were distilled from the discussion that followed the team reports. They are reported here, along with a brief statement about the actions that followed. The improvement priorities from the first assessment are listed below:

- Clarify the strategic direction for the MBA Program.
- Identify and articulate the school's core values.
- Reexamine student demographics.
- Redesign the MBA curriculum.
- Increase the international content of the curriculum.

The first two actions became the focus of work by a team of faculty, staff, and students over the next year. The eventual result was a statement of direction and values that were widely discussed and eventually adopted. They have been woven into the orientation for each entering class and they have influenced the way in which the program is executed during the academic year. The program has constructed a multidimensional scorecard with several metrics and a list of improvement strategies for each dimension. This scorecard is now online and available to anyone who has Internet access.

Enrollment levels for women and minority students had declined in recent years. Through active recruitment and attention to these issues when prospective students visited the school, both of these trends have been reversed.

A team with faculty, staff, and student participation undertook a review of the first year of the curriculum. Recommendations for changes in required courses were defined, evaluated, debated, adopted, and implemented. Another team undertook study of the second year of the curriculum and restructured it around a series of concentrations based on extensive discussion inside the school and with representatives of corporations who hire the program's graduating students. These concentrations now provide an organizing framework for courses in the second year of the program.

III. Follow-Up

The first assessment occurred in 1998. Some of the improvement actions were completed in the following year, but it was only at the conclusion of the 1999-2000 academic year that the final work on the second year of the curriculum was essentially completed. A follow-up assessment was conducted during the summer of 2000, this time with student involvement from the beginning of the process. The approach was based on the Baldrige framework, but once again the depth and scope were tailored in order to produce results of value within an amount of time and effort that was practicable for a volunteer assessment team.

The theme that excellence demands continuing refinement became part of the MBA Program as a result of the ongoing assessment. Even the very best people, programs, and processes can become stale if not refined. They can become second-rate as they are surpassed by those programs and processes that do refine, revitalize, and reinvent themselves.

Leading the Change to High Performance

There is no lonelier, more challenging, yet critical and rewarding job than that of the school leader. The authors work with many, many leaders who listen to advice carefully. They really want to know the best approaches to use for their organizations. Yet what they do with the advice and counsel is always interesting. This section is intended to help those leaders go resolutely down the right path.

Neither leader exists in real life, but both leader profiles are based on actual events and observations of different people in leadership positions.

A Tale of Two Leaders

It was a time of turbulence; it was a time of peace. It was a time of growth and streamlining. It was the happiest of times; it was also the most painful of times. Most of all it was a time of change… although it was also considered a time for the status quo.

The following tales are of two school leaders—one is consistent and persistent in communicating the direction and message that will bring about excellent results and high performance. You may know these people or someone who reminds you of them. If so, you will understand the reason for this section.

Background

M.J. was the new principal of City High, a public high school in a school system where she had previously held various staff, faculty, and administrative positions. For the most part, parents, the school board, and the community supported education and had a long tradition of pride in the community and its institutions, including City High. However, as with many American high schools, City High had a history of a "turn of the century" structure and schedule, coupled with "command and control" governance. Mistrust was rampant at all levels, based in part on constant power brokering at the expense of students, parents, and other stakeholders.

In addition to a dictatorial management style and school environment problems, the previous principal had a history of basing policy and budget decisions on the whims of the moment—even those with major impacts on students and faculty. His faculty and school meetings had no agendas and were controlled solely by the school principal. He was challenged by no one, having held the position and wielded all its power for over 20 years.

In short, this was a school where administrators tried to increase their power and influence by "intimidating and punishing faculty and staff," and faculty and staff behaved the same way toward students. There was a clear and compelling case for establishing a different kind of leadership, especially instructional leadership, as M.J. entered City High as the new principal.

The first message to the faculty and staff

Establishing leadership and setting the tone for a new culture in the school was the "hidden agenda" for the first all-staff meeting. The message was delivered passionately, from M.J.'s heart—so much so that at times M.J. was almost close to tears. She talked about what she stood for and what was important to her. High on the list were trust and honesty. She shared her vision for City High—to be the best high school in the state and that the school had the students, parents, school board, and faculty and staff to succeed. There was a promise made to take this improvement agenda in "baby steps" that would not overwhelm the school. Part of her message was that she would be involved in helping faculty to improve their teaching and instruction. Included was a challenge for them to stretch and push themselves to improve.

In contrast to her predecessor, her building was to have a "personal wellness and family focus" that began at the school level. Faculty and staff were urged to focus on their health, well-being, and own family as their number one priority, notwithstanding that their job in the school was of critical importance. In giving permission and encouragement to focus on their health, wellness, and families, a major obstacle to trust was removed. Many times in the past, faculty and staff were forced to tell less than accurate accounts of absences that were actually due to personal matters such as concerts, sports events, sick children, or problems that needed attention. These were simply not seen as valid priorities by the prior principal.

The Next Steps

The priority of the first year, after "walking the talk" of the initial meeting, was to empower faculty and staff. The high school at a glance consisted of 100 closed doors behind which stood 100 people "doing their own thing" (usually consisting of highly directive teaching). The school had no history of the principal providing instructional assistance to teachers. In fact, the prior principal was usually in his office, behind the desk, facing the wall and his computer—never in any classroom. He did not visit teacher classrooms at all and did not value his role in the classroom. This changed quickly. M.J., and then the instructional leadership team composed of administrators and supervisors, began allocating a large portion of their time to instructional leadership, including hands-on classroom observations and feedback. At first, this was done by dropping into classrooms unannounced and then providing positive feedback on what was observed. Gradually, teachers began to ask for and welcome suggestions for improvement and feedback because it was not a "catch teachers being bad" effort. Soon formal observations, goal setting, and reflection and dialogue conferences were the norm.

The budget process was used to further create an empowered staff and faculty. Each department supervisor was provided a budget for the first time, and guidelines to accomplish their priorities. They were not second guessed or overridden by M.J. This was an important signal of trust and responsibility commensurate with the authority that was sent to department supervisors.

Faculty meetings, which previously had been the sole province of the principal's interest, had a new tone of interconnectivity and communication. There were agendas sent out prior to meetings with openings for information from all stakeholders, including school improvement teams and the teachers' professional association. Other meeting management skills were slowly introduced, such as positive feedback, timeframe limits, action planning, and follow-up dates.

At each faculty meeting, a certain portion of time was used to create a "learning and improvement culture" that aligned with the goals and priorities of the school. A piece of the vision for the school was shared at each faculty meeting in order to reinforce and continue the messages of trust, honesty, and excellence. Faculty meetings included "minisessions" focused on teaching strategies and techniques, such as modeling, active participation (instead of directive teaching), and guided participation.

Messages to faculty and staff that stated, "I care and I appreciate you" were sent in multiple ways and made an important difference in the school climate. These were simple, handwritten notes to faculty and staff on various occasions to welcome them back to school after a recess; brunches prepared and served by the administrative staff for the instructional faculty and staff; and other informal "get-togethers" where communication, trust, and fun were permitted and encouraged.

Training and the Change Process

Teachers at City High were asked by M.J. to set one stretch goal that would improve their ability to teach. The first year, the teachers did not need to share their goal. There was no formality such as documentation or measurement. Teachers did not feel threatened. The second year, teachers were again asked to set a stretch goal but this time they were also asked to formalize goals that could be measured. M.J. observed that teaching and administrative staff lacked core skills to improve their teaching, such as analyzing and using test data, employing reading and study skills strategies in their content area, and giving constructive feedback to students. Determining teaching effectiveness by using in-process measures were also lacking.

Training was provided on effective feedback and teaching to all principals and administrative staff, who then coached their department supervisors, master teachers, and teachers in these skills. M.J. and her fellow assistant principals used and role modeled these skills daily in their formal and informal classroom visits and at each faculty meeting.

Training and coaching in use of data was a priority. Because administrators had used data to "punish" and alarm staff previously, there was a deep reluctance to collect and/or share data of any kind. Since tracking improvement without data is impossible, this was an obstacle to overcome. M.J. first modeled data use by publishing her own measurable goals on the school Web site and tracking progress. Slowly, it became acceptable to share assessment data to look at trends, such as gender differences in performance or course selections, and finally, standardized test score differences between students, teachers, and subjects. The use of data was a major improvement thrust of the next few years.

As M.J. and her staff began to use data more and more to assess what was effective and what was not among the many programs and services the school supported, they began to "clean out the cupboard" to discontinue outdated programs and develop new ones. Training became an ongoing activity, part of planning every new program, so the skills and expertise to be successful were part of the school's competencies. For example, academic performance in several subjects was low, in part, because students could not read at the level required for the assignments and examinations. High school teachers were not necessarily proficient reading teachers. All teachers were "refreshed" in reading instruction so they could assist students in reading assignments as necessary.

Opening the Doors

In touring City High 18 months after the new leadership began, there were only a few classroom doors that remained closed. There was a new environment of trust, cooperation, and fairness that permeated the relationships between teachers, administrators, students, and parents. There was a common focus in the school on teaching and learning. This environment, necessary and conducive to teaching and learning had begun to yield results in student and stakeholder satisfaction, faculty and staff satisfaction, and most importantly, student performance. Because there is an earnest desire to be the best and improve performance, not to "catch teachers being bad and punish them" there has been real change in the way students are treated in City High and in the teaching/learning process itself.

Leadership Summary

The above tale helps to illustrate that changing culture is not easy. It requires dedicated and unwavering consistency in support of the "new way" of behaving and believing. The following actions, part of the above tale, are critical to changing culture in a school environment.

Establish clear goals and a clear direction. Explain clearly what will be required and how the new requirements are different from the old. If you do not know what new behaviors are required, find out. Talk to those leaders who have successfully engineered this kind of improvement in the past. Leaders who are not clear invite confusion and inaction.

Show unwavering commitment. Leaders are pivotal to the success of the enterprise—faculty and staff watch them closely. Don't blink in the face of setbacks—quitting is easy and doing so will make faculty and staff more cynical and demoralized. When leadership commitment and support is seen as tentative, faculty and staff will perceive the changes as "optional," take-or-leave suggestions. Considering the profound ability most people have to resist change, this creates more support for doing nothing.

Prove you will change. If leaders do not "walk the talk" and demonstrate their eagerness to operate differently, others once again conclude that the leaders are not serious and the new requirements are optional.

Keep energy levels high and focused on both process improvements and better performance outcomes. Select improvements that are easy as well as difficult. Small successes are needed to keep the energy and support for performance excellence high. Larger improvement projects take longer to carry out but usually bring greater benefit. Celebrate process improvements as well as better performance outcomes.

Encourage people to challenge the status quo. Do not tolerate system craziness—break old bureaucratic rules and policies that prevent or inhibit work toward goals. Free your people from bureaucratic silliness and you will find great energy and support from faculty and staff.

Change rewards. Make following the new culture and achieving goals worthwhile by rewarding desired behaviors and making the continued use of the old ones unpleasant. All faculty and staff need to understand recognition and rewards are issued for achieving results. They are not to be treated as an entitlement of employment. It is important to test the effectiveness of rewards and recognition. Remember, just because you value a reward does not mean that faculty or staff will do the same.

Measure Progress. What gets measured gets done. When leaders use measurements to track progress, people think they are serious about tracking and improving. If you do not bother measuring, productivity is usually lower. In addition, measurements help identify those who are to be rewarded, and those who are not. Finally, keep measurements simple and efficient. Do not allow the process of measurement to divert energy and focus.

Communicate, communicate, communicate. Communication cannot replace an inspiring vision and sound goals, but poor communication can scuttle them. People need to understand the logic and rationale behind the vision and goals. Leaders need to tell them what's coming; how they will be affected; what's expected of them. Remember to take every opportunity to communicate your desires—once is not enough. The opponents of change will work nonstop to undermine the new goal, vision, and culture. Communicate consistently to overcome this resistance. Also remember that even motivated and supportive people forget—remind them often of the vision and new expectations. Leaders that do not communicate effectively invite the rumor mill to fill in the blank spaces. Bad news, bad rumors, and outright lies frequently fill the communication gap leaders might inadvertently leave.

Involve everyone. People who do not actively support change inadvertently oppose it. Insist on full involvement and define a role for everyone. Find ways to make everyone accountable for transforming the culture and improving performance. Remember that if a supervisor fails to support the changes needed to improve performance, it is probably a good idea to encourage that person to work for another school.

Start fast, then go faster. Slow progress, which the opponents of change like to see, creates a self-fulfilling prophecy—that the proposed changes will not be effective. However, speed creates a sense of urgency that helps overcome organizational inertia, achieve stunning results, and defeat the gloom and pessimism of naysayers.

Change Dynamics

Change Will Take Place When It Can No Longer Be Resisted

As an organization moves forward with performance improvement, the first reaction of faculty and staff may be that they are not businesses—they deal with human learning. The business of education, indeed, centers around student learning. However, as with any other business, achieving excellence is essential to ensure success. To achieve excellence, schools need the best management practices at the organization and classroom levels. Good leaders, both teachers and administrators, in the right place make a significant difference in performance.

Products of education are unique to the business of education just as the production of cars is unique to the auto industry. Skills, competencies, techniques, and research results are structures to support their business. However, the requirements of students and stakeholders are similar to those of any business—on-time delivery, reliability, professional treatment, responsiveness, and good value for the money. To satisfy students and other stakeholders and optimize student learning, the best management practices need to be put in place.

Research and scholarship in particular raise an important issue for the interpretation and application of the Baldrige Criteria for educational organizations. The 2001 Criteria allow organizations for which research and outreach are core aspects of their mission to address these elements as Education Design and Delivery Processes.

Resistance to Change Is Likely to Come First and Strongest from the Best People

We observed a middle school that encountered a difficult experience when a small committee enthusiastically planned its first all-school quality training. Two days before the session was to be held, a letter signed by about twenty teachers was delivered to the school administrator. It basically said that the training was ill timed and not needed. It was signed by the best teachers in the school. Administrators did not know how to handle this letter but they did the right thing. They discussed openly the need for the training with the group and built more debriefing time into the training session. They also stuck to the plan of performance improvement they had promised to the community.

There are many excellent faculty and staff on board who have pushed the envelope of excellence as far as they can with traditional methods. They represent the best of the traditional school structure and methodology. They typically have difficulty understanding why change is needed when they have always been in the forefront of achievement. It is critical that dialogue with these excellent contributors continue so they do not create a barrier to moving forward. The best and brightest need to understand the limits of the paradigms that made them successful, in order to change to become even more successful.

Category Lessons

Category 1: Leadership

Great Educational Leaders Lead by Example and Message

The National Education Goals Panel Policy Finding Number One is that schools with demonstrated success in raising student achievement typically have strong leaders. One characteristic of a high-performance educational organization is outstanding academic results. How does an organization achieve such results? How does it become world-class? While no scientific studies have been able to document a single road that leads to such success, we have found unanimous agreement on the critical and fundamental role of leadership. There is not one example of an organization or unit within an organization that achieves profound improvement without the personal and active involvement of its top leadership. Top leaders in these organizations create a powerful vision that focuses and energizes the workforce. Everyone is pulling together toward the same goals. Frequently, an inspired vision is the catalyst that overcomes the organizational status quo.

During the transition of your organization, sending the right signals can be pivotal in getting your message across. Following are some powerful examples that have worked:

- Canceling your own administrative meetings when the agenda does not include substantive issues of policy that are critical to the mission and key goals.
- Defining your role as the conscience of the mission and strategic plan of the organization. Ask repeatedly how any request for resources relates to the organization's teaching and learning priorities.
- Redrawing reporting relationships so that administration is seen as the support for the instruction rather than the "big boss." One school renamed their administrative cabinet the College Support Council.
- Promoting and rewarding those who demonstrate advanced performance management leadership skills. One community college only promoted those who had successfully completed its very rigorous "Quality Academy," consisting of Baldrige-based criteria training and studies of various quality principles.
- Delivering presentations in person (by the president, superintendent, or board members) of key goals and mission to schools, colleges, or other units of the organization.

Great educational leaders are great communicators. They identify clear objectives and a game plan so the organization succeeds in its mission of producing student learning. They assign accountability, ensure that faculty and staff have the tools and skills required, and create a work climate where transfer of learning occurs. They reward teamwork and data-driven improvement. While practicing what they preach, they serve as role models for continuous improvement, consensus building, and fact-based decision making, and push authority and accountability to the lowest possible levels.

One lesson learned from great leaders is to minimize the use of the word *quality*. Too often, when skilled, hard-working, dedicated faculty and staff are told by leaders, "We are going to start a quality effort," they conclude that their leaders believe they have not been working hard enough or producing quality work. The faculty and staff hear an unintended message—"We have to do this because we are not good." They frequently retort, "We already do quality work!" Unfortunately, the use of the word quality can create an unintended barrier of mistrust and negativism that leaders must overcome before even starting on the road to Performance Excellence.

As an alternative, we advise leaders to create a work climate that enables faculty and staff to develop and use their full potential, to improve continually the way they work—to seek higher performance levels and reduce activities that do not add value or optimize performance. Most readily agree that there is always room for improvement. This leads to our second lesson learned.

Leaders will have to overcome two organizational tendencies: (1) rejection of any management model or theory "not invented here," and (2) the idea that there are many equally valid models. Most traditional awards and certifications are either not Baldrige-based or based on a very low level of Baldrige achievement. This includes such processes as various accreditation reviews and blue ribbon organization awards. The Baldrige model—including the many national, state, and organization assessment systems based on it—is accepted worldwide as the standard for defining Performance Excellence in organizations. Its criteria focus on validated, leading-edge practices for managing an organization. A decade of extraordinary performance results shown by Baldrige Award winners and numerous state-level, Baldrige Award–based winners (including schools) have helped convince those willing to listen and learn.

To be effective, leaders must understand the Baldrige model and communicate to the workforce and leadership system their intention to use that model for assessment and improvement. Leaders need to understand the system and realize that it is their responsibility to share the knowledge and set the direction. This brings us to our third leadership lesson learned.

A significant portion of senior leaders' time—as much as 60 to 80 percent—should be spent in visible Baldrige-related leadership activities, such as goal setting; planning; reviewing academic performance and improvement; recognizing and rewarding high performance; and spending time understanding and communicating with faculty, staff, stakeholders, and students, rather than micromanaging faculty and staff work. The senior leaders' perspective in goal setting, planning, and reviewing performance must look at the inside from the outside. Looking at the organization through the critical eyes of external stakeholders is a vital perspective.

The primary role of the effective senior leader is not to manage internal operations, but to be visionary and focus the organization on satisfying students and stakeholders through an effective leadership system. Leaders must role model the tools of consensus building and decision making as the organization focuses on its vision, mission, and strategic direction to keep stakeholders loyal.

Falling back on command-and-control behavior will be self-defeating. The leadership system will suffer from crossed wires and mixed messages. Using the consensus approach to focus the organization on its mission and vision will take time, of course. However, this is similar to taking more time during the course and curriculum design phase to ensure that learning problems are prevented later. The additional time is necessary for organizational learning, support, and buy-in, particularly around two areas—the competitive environment, and the requirements of stakeholders. The resulting vision will have more depth. The leadership system will be stronger. Finally, the deployment of the vision and focus will take a shorter time because of the buy-in and support created during the process.

Teachers/Instructors Are Leaders of the Classroom Learning System

Educational organizations are made up of many interconnected systems. The leader of the most fundamental system is in the classroom—the leader, instructor, professor, teacher, or lecturer. *Classroom* can mean any classroom form—four walls with one teacher and a class, a doctoral tutorial, or a virtual classroom where students learn long-distance. It is leadership that will determine whether the students are engaged or just "filled with stuff;" whether parents and stakeholders are involved in the process or seen as only taxpayers, field trip chaperones, and cookie makers. For this reason, under sample effective practices is included a section for classroom leaders on their role in each of the seven categories. It is not an exhaustive list, but it provides examples of what classroom leaders should be considering under each category.

L Is for Listen

Successful leaders know the power in listening to their people—those they rely on to achieve their goals. One vital link to the pulse of the organization is faculty, staff, and student feedback. To find out whether what you have said has been heard, ask for feedback and then listen carefully. To know whether what you have outlined as a plan makes sense or has gaping faults, ask for feedback and then listen. Your system cannot improve without leadership that listens to and acts on feedback from faculty, staff, students, and stakeholders. Improvement on goals and action plans depends on this process of listening and refining.

Lead and Drive Change

Educational leaders can count on relentless, rapid change being part of the academic world. The rate of change confronting business today is far faster than that driven by the industrial revolution. Skills driven by the industrial revolution carried our parents through a 40-year work cycle. Today, our children are told to expect five career (not job) changes during their work life. Human knowledge now doubles every five to seven years, instead of the 40 years it took in the 1930s.

There are several lessons in this for leaders today. Change may not occur on the schedule they set for it. It is difficult to predict. Also, change is often resisted not only by those entrenched in the *status quo*, but by those most successful because they have difficulty seeing the need to change.

Leaders who hold the values of high performance will need to drive change to make the necessary improvements. Embracing the concepts of organizational learning (not just individual) will facilitate change in the organization. Leaders will need to promote organizational learning as a tool to manage change and drive it through the organization.

Category 2: Strategic Planning

Deploy through People, Not Paper

Strategic planning is performance improvement planning, deployment, and implementation. The organization's strategic plan is also its business, human resources, and performance improvement plan. Easily enough said, but trying to get agreement on exactly what strategic planning is will result in a variety of ideas. Therefore, the planning process should begin by ensuring that all contributors agree on terminology. Otherwise, the strategic plan may be a curriculum plan, a budget plan, or a master building plan, depending on who is leading the effort.

Leaders should concentrate on the few critical improvement goals necessary for organizational success, such as improving academic performance and reducing rework and learning cycle time. The well-developed strategic plan does the following:

- Documents the impact of achieving these few goals.
- Details actions and resources needed to support the goals.
- Discusses the competitive environment that drives the goals.

One highly successful organization simplified this document to a single electronic page, to which senior leaders referred each month by computer during academic progress and performance review meetings.

The most critical lesson learned when it comes to strategic plans is that there can be no rest until every person in the organization knows the strategic plan and can describe how he or she contributes to achieving the plan's goals and objectives.

Imagine this test in your organization: A visitor meets with the superintendent or dean to gain an understanding of the personal vision and plan for the organization. Suppose the visitor then interviews teachers, research faculty, support staff, students, and many others at all levels, asking them to explain the organization's vision and plan and their role in achieving the plan. In high-performance organizations, a consistent story emerges from people at all levels. In addition, the visitor gets a sense that the vision and plan are real and attainable. The visitor could be any stakeholder: a parent, a prospective student, a trustee, a legislator, or any taxpayer or donor. The visitor could also be an examiner for the Baldrige Award, because the test suggested here is an actual process used by these examiners. It can also be used effectively by any organization to assess itself.

In any case, ensure two things:

1. That the strategic plan does not merely rest in a prominent position on the bookshelves of top administrators.
2. That it is used to drive and guide actions and is understood by all. That means all decisions must consider the impact on achieving strategic goals and objectives.

If these actions are not taken, work will not be aligned. People may work hard but are likely to pull in many directions. This scenario leads to nonproductive pet projects and programs competing for time and other resources. It is critical to get all faculty and staff pulling in the same direction. At the same time, alignment does not require or even suggest conformity and standardization across units as diverse as different departments in a college of arts and sciences, or different grade levels in a school. There is, however, a need to create clear understandings about priorities and the actions needed to achieve them. If a faculty member is hired by a department in which research is a primary part of the mission and that individual expects to be rewarded primarily for teaching and student advising, both the organization and the individual have made mistakes that will be costly in human terms and in organization productivity.

Category 3: Student, Stakeholder, and Market Focus

Students Need To Be Involved in School Improvement

It is interesting that often students are the last people asked about ways to improve education. A strong source of resistance to performance management has come from faculty and staff who do not fully understand the value of student feedback. They are rightly concerned that students, if seen as primary customers, might have requirements that would be contrary to sound education or, more generally, might wish to apply a "consumerist" view to education. For example, students may make the unreasonable requirement that they should all receive grades of A, or students might favor entertainment over challenge. Clearly, this is not consistent with management of high-performance organizations. The focus of this discussion needs to address one prominent issue: How can we best engage students in their learning to optimize it?

Student feedback on the attributes of the learning process and environment can be very valuable in identifying opportunities for improvement without undermining the responsibility of the instructor to select content and establish the level of challenge. Harry Roberts, now retired from the Graduate School of Business at the University of Chicago, said: "Students know when they're confused by a presentation. Yet, because students can feel intimidated about asking questions, an instructor may not be aware of the problem without a mechanism for obtaining feedback."

All students have certain requirements of their instructors and teachers, including: expectations of fairness and consistency; clear directions for assignments; classes that begin and end on time; respectful treatment; and a safe, secure environment. In other kinds of businesses, these kinds of expectations generally are included in basic faculty and staff requirements, without which the organization cannot be successful. In education, these issues are central to creating a constructive learning environment, without which education cannot be successful.

At all levels of education, kindergarten through postgraduate, students need to be engaged in planning and evaluating their learning. Tools and techniques for assessment, such as using rubrics and student portfolios, have helped instructors engage students in planning and evaluating their learning. Students need to have a much higher degree of involvement in planning their curriculum, assessments, and class projects as they move on in their education.

Students as customers or stakeholders in schools are more easily defined at higher levels when employment, admission to college or graduate school, and certain levels of competency are clear customer requirements. At lower levels, it is easy to see students as customers with specific expectations as they buy their food from the cafeteria, ride the bus, receive homework instructions, and attend dances or fun nights at school.

As students progress from kindergarten through graduate school and beyond, they take on different roles and have differing requirements. There is an invisible continuum of increasing responsibility for their own education and learning as they mature. To optimize learning requires more involvement of the student in their own learning and more student engagement as they mature. Not engaging students in their learning will suboptimize programs and waste time and resources.

For example, a school district chose the character development of its students as one of its key goals. This was a goal of the school board and the community. Many businesses and individuals in the community contributed funds and support for this program. As the planning team developed the curriculum, a parent suggested that students needed to be involved in planning, and faculty needed to be trained with students. This did not happen, and students saw the program as "something done to them." Further, they noted many discrepancies between the promises of their teachers and what was delivered. Although they were being asked to take personal responsibility for keeping promises and turning in homework on time, teachers were not grading and returning papers when they said they would. Their coaches were telling students that if they worked hard and attended practices they would play during games, yet only a few players were playing, and this had more to do with natural skill than hard work. This tended to make the message of the program, "Do as I say, not as I do." This was a sure recipe for the program's failure, particularly among teenagers.

Engaging students in the educational planning and decisions that affect them will have the largest payback in terms of performance and a positive organizational climate. There are numerous examples of how institutions that are "focused on student learning" ignore students when planning their learning experiences.

A middle school decided to improve its efficiency by banning students from carrying book bags from class to class. Students were never involved in this decision and did not appreciate the unwelcome and burdensome rule. The net result of this policy was that more students arrived at class late and unprepared. They had to go to their lockers, which were located all over the building, before every class. Students routinely arrived at class without their homework because it was in their lockers. This policy adversely affected student learning, and grades suffered because students were marked down for not bringing homework to class—homework that was complete but left in the locker.

A college decided to send out student transcripts in batches of 20 for convenience instead of when students needed them. Some students missed deadlines for financial aid for transfer credits while waiting for the 20th transcript to be requested, even though their requests were made weeks ahead of time.

Involving students in solving problems and in making decisions that affect them will increase the solution's likelihood of success. It also will give students a message that they have some control over their educational lives. Studies, including Coleman's famous landmark study from the 1960s, have identified perception of control as a major difference between middle class, successful students and poor students who fail. Poor students, especially minority students, do not see themselves as having any control over their lives. Educational organizations would help such students to gain a more positive sense of self by involving them in solving problems that affect them.

Another lesson has to do with external customers and stakeholders, such as parents, businesses, and taxpayers. Organizations that make it easy for customers to complain are in a good position to hear about problems early so that they can fix them and plan ahead to prevent them. If organizations handle customer complaints effectively at the first point of contact, positive referral and satisfaction will increase, and the organization will learn about its processes more quickly.

The next lesson has to do with educating the organization's leadership in the fundamentals of student and stakeholder satisfaction research models before beginning to collect student and stakeholder satisfaction data. Failure to do this may affect the usefulness of the data as a strategic tool. At the very least, it will make the development of data-collection instruments a long, misunderstood effort, creating rework and unnecessary cost.

Do not lose sight of the fact that the best student and stakeholder feedback method, whether it is a survey, focus group, or one-on-one interview, is only a tool:

- Make sure the data gathered are actionable.
- Aggregate the data from all sources to permit complete analyses.
- Use the data to improve planning and operating processes.

Finally, be aware that students and other stakeholders are not interested in the organization's problems, just as you are not interested in the problems of your grocer or mechanic. Your interest is in receiving the product or service as required. Similarly, students and other stakeholders merely want products or services delivered as promised.

Category 4: Information and Analysis

Focus on the Power of Measures

One of the six major findings of the National Education Goals Panel Study was that successful schools have used a wealth of information from student assessments and community outreach (beyond student scores and rankings) to guide decisions on policy, practice, and resource allocation. Educational organizations are very committed to collecting information. Unfortunately, the facts and information they collect do not always relate to key goals and priorities. The first lesson is to design what you collect to answer the questions that you want answered (and must answer due to local, state, and national requirements), and then make sure the information is available to all who need it to make decisions.

For example, schools around the country have been running an expensive ($6 billion) and popular program to help students avoid drugs. It is funded by the Safe and Drug-Free Schools and Communities Act. Elementary and secondary schools partner with local police departments to learn about the perils of drug use and hand out T-shirts and trinkets to students when they "graduate." If the program's goals were goodwill or effective partnerships in the community, the program would be an overwhelming success. The goal of the program, however, is to reduce the number of students taking drugs. Evidence suggests that students who participate and graduate from this program are not any more likely to avoid drugs than other students.

What Gets Evaluated Gets Done; What Gets Rewarded Gets Done First

Key goals need to be measurable in clear and understandable ways. The following are lessons learned that can help educational organizations make their measures truly powerful. Because not everything is subject to counting or quantification, we include under the heading of "measurement" many valuable concepts that require careful judgment in the context of approaches to assessment and evaluation.

Data-Driven Management and Avoiding Contephobia

The high-performance organization collects, manages, and analyzes data and information to drive excellence and improve its overall performance. Said another way: in the best organizations and classrooms, information is used to drive actions. Using data and information as strategic weapons, effective leaders use comparisons aggressively. First, they compare actual performance within the organization to goals or plans. In addition, they compare their organization constantly to competitors, similar educational service providers, and world-class organizations. They uncover Performance Excellence and performance problems.

While people tend to think of data and measurement as objective and hard, there is often a softer by-product of measurement: the basic human emotion of fear. This perspective on data and measurement leads to the next lesson learned about information and analysis. Human fear must be recognized and managed in order to practice data-driven management. This fear can be found in two forms. First, there are those who have a simple fear of numbers—those who hated mathematics in school and may simply practice avoidance behavior when faced with anything quantitative. These individuals are uncomfortable in discussions of numerical data. When asked to measure or when presented with data, they can become fearful, angry, and resistant. Their reactions can undermine improvement efforts.

A second form of fear may be present in one who understands numbers and realizes that numbers can impose higher levels of accountability. The fear of accountability, *contephobia* (from fourteenth-century Latin "to count," modified by the French "to account"), is based on the fear of real performance failure that numbers might reveal or, more often, an overall fear of the unknown that will drive important decisions. Power structures can and do shift when decisions are data driven. The power of the loudest voice or last person leaving the boss's office erodes in the face of reliable information and data.

Fearful individuals can undermine effective data-driven management systems. In managing this fear, leaders must believe and communicate through their behavior that the purpose of data is to promote better decision making, not punishment. It is important for leaders at all levels to demonstrate that system and process improvements are the objective, not mechanisms for punishment or sanction.

A mature, high-performance organization will collect data on competitors and similar providers and compare itself against world-class leaders. Some individuals may not be capable of seeing the benefit of using this process. Benchmarking data are a means of identifying, learning from, and adopting best practices or methods from similar processes, regardless of industry or product similarity. Adopting the best practices of other organizations has driven quantum leap improvements and provided great opportunities for breakthrough improvements.

Organizations that are new to the experience of making systematic improvement aimed at excellent performance may choose to postpone benchmarking processes against known superior performers within the education arena or against other world-class performers. Eventually, however, only by using valid and reliable data from outside the organization can leaders confirm that performance is good or excellent. Benchmarking serves that purpose.

This lesson relates to not being a DRIP. This refers to a tendency to collect so much data (which contributes to contephobia) that the organization becomes "Data Rich and Information Poor." This reflects inadequate planning of the measurement system. Avoid wasting resources, and stretch the resources available for managing improvement by asking this question: Will these data help make improvements for our students, faculty, and staff, or in other top-result areas, such as reducing drug use or increasing science test scores? If the answer is no, do not waste time collecting, analyzing, and trying to use the data (unless required by law or regulation).

Category 5: Faculty and Staff Focus

In high-performing organizations, faculty and staff are the most valuable asset of the organization—investment and development are critical to optimizing performance. Faculty and staff should be perceived as internal stakeholders and a vital part of the chain. They provide a valuable service—helping to produce students and graduates with enhanced knowledge, skills, thinking abilities, and competencies, who become motivated workers and responsible citizens. A large disconnect in all levels of education is the distance of one grade level to the next, one building to the next, and one system to the next. Said another way, the distance between high school and kindergarten, the high school and college, and the social studies department and the mathematics department, creates a disconnect in the student learning experience.

The Big Challenge Is Trust

The high-performing organization values its faculty and staff and demonstrates this by enabling people to develop and realize their full potential while providing them incentives to do so. Focusing on faculty and staff excellence maintains a climate that builds trust. Trust is essential for faculty and staff participation, engagement, personal and professional growth, and high performance. Without it, the relationship in the classroom also suffers. Student-faculty relationships, in turn, will not be based on trust, and students will not be meaningfully engaged in their learning.

A new principal of a troubled middle school with many safety and drug issues tried to forge new relationships built on trust with his faculty and staff. He sent them signals that he was prepared to forge new relationships with faculty. For example, teachers and faculty were treated like "adults" and allowed to leave the building for emergencies and appointments without his permission. He did not make decisions and take the role of parent of the school, but let faculty and staff work with him on a new mission, to make new rules and a governance structure based on data and consistency. This helped produce much higher levels of trust with students and, subsequently, higher performance.

A community college empowered a committee of faculty and staff to make decisions about funding projects based on institutional priorities. The president and trustees were impressed that the committee did not allocate all the funds because they did not think many projects were actually based on institutional priorities. Imagine the message this sent about next year's projects—focus them on our common goals and institutional priorities. Stronger alignment and focus resulted.

A college for the deaf selected a cross-college faculty/staff/student committee to survey students and stakeholders and prepare for market changes. The committee enacted faculty and student recruitment, program, and curriculum recommendations. The college's entrance into the next 10 years was significantly enhanced in many measurable ways.

Schools need to take a critical look at their current reward and recognition systems. Leaders must be willing to revise—overhaul, if necessary—recognition, compensation, promotion, and feedback systems to support whatever constitutes high performance for that institution. Promotion, compensation, recognition, and reward must be tied to the achievement of educational results, including student and stakeholder satisfaction, innovation, academic performance improvement, and where applicable, effective research. Promotion/compensation is a powerful tool in aligning, or misaligning, the work of the organization. Most organizations have the authority to provide effective rewards and recognition, but few leaders have either the courage or energy to make the necessary changes. A community college took two years to convince a sponsor that it needed a program to reward outstanding performance with additional compensation.

A second human resource lesson learned relates to training and development. Training is not a panacea or a goal in itself. The organization's direction and goals must support training, and training must support organization priorities. Empowered and skilled people are the competitive edge of a high-performing organization. Training must be aligned with overall strategy. If not, money and resources are probably better spent on a memorable holiday party.

Timing is critical. Overall awareness training for entire faculties and groups that work together with common goals can be very effective in educational organizations. However, broad-based workforce skill training should not come until needed. Many organizations rush out and train their entire faculty and staff on tools and techniques only to find they have to retrain months or years later. Key participants should be involved in planning skill training so that important skills are developed just in time for them to use in their assignments. Many organizations have had great success with just-in-time training that is delivered shortly before the recipients are expected to need or be asked to apply it.

For example, there are dozens of decision-making and group process tools that will be useful for classroom use. Learning them all at once will not result in their use. Rather, it makes more sense for teachers to look at their goals and decide how to engage students more in the learning process—perhaps in the selecting of a project. They may then learn how to use rubrics or fishbone diagrams. This will require the use of several tools, and an internal expert to teach them how to use these tools, to engage students more fully in their studies.

Continuous skill development requires that administrators support, reinforce, and strengthen skills on the job. Leadership development at all levels of the organization must be built into faculty and staff development. New technology has increased training flexibility so that all knowledge does not have to be transferred solely in a classroom setting. Consider many options when planning how best to update skills. After initial awareness training occurs, high-performing organizations emphasize organizational learning where faculty and staff take charge of their own learning, using training courses as only one avenue for skill upgrading. Transferring learning to other parts of the organization, such as departments, levels, or projects, is a valuable organizational learning strategy and reinforcement technique. Training must be offered when an application exists to use and reinforce the skill. Otherwise, most of what is learned will be forgotten. The effectiveness of training must be assessed based on the impact on the job, not merely the entertainment value of the instructor or the clarity of course materials.

Faculty and staff surveys are often used to measure and improve satisfaction. Surveys are especially useful to identify key issues that should be discussed in open forums. Such forums are truly useful if they clarify perceptions, provide more in-depth understanding of faculty and staff concerns, and open communication channels with leaders. Schools have success in improving faculty and staff satisfaction by conducting routine satisfaction surveys, meeting with them to plan improvements, and tying improvements in satisfaction ratings to promotion and recognition. The chapter on assessment contains several examples of surveys that may be effective for your organization.

Two final faculty and staff excellence lessons have to do with engaging and involving faculty in decisions about their work, because then they better understand the importance of involving and engaging their students. Involving faculty, staff, and students in decision making without the right skills or a sense of direction produces chaos, not high performance. The two lessons are:

- First, leaders who empower faculty and staff before ensuring that a sense of direction has been fully understood will find that they are managing chaos.

- Second, not everyone wants to be empowered. There may be teachers/faculty and staff members who truly seek to avoid responsibility for making improvements, claiming "that's the administration's job." These individuals do not last long in a high-performing organization. They begin to stick out like lone birds in the winter. Most responsible administrators and faculty who want the organization to thrive and excel do not want such people to drag down the organization.

The bigger reason why individuals fail to "take empowerment and run with it" is the administration's mixed messages. In short, administrators must convince faculty and staff that they really believe faculty, staff, and students are in the best position to improve their own work processes. Consistent leadership is required to help faculty and staff overcome legitimate, long-standing fear of traditional administrative practices used so often in the past to control and punish.

Remember, aligning compensation and reward systems to reinforce performance plans and core values is one of the most critical ways to enhance organizational performance; however, getting faculty and staff to believe their leaders really trust them to improve their own processes is difficult but vital. Training and development should be done not just to accumulate training hours, but to ensure that knowledge and skills needed for improvement are acquired. Finally, just as feedback from students is important to instructors, feedback from faculty and staff is important for administrators.

Category 6: Process Management

Involve Faculty and Staff Closest to the Work

High-performance organizations identify key processes and manage them so that student and stakeholder requirements are met consistently and performance is continuously improved.

The first lesson learned has to do with the visibility of processes. Many processes are highly visible, such as counseling, tutoring, serving a meal, or purchasing equipment. However, many educational processes are hard to observe, such as course design or student responses. It cannot be assumed that everyone will see the organization as a collection of processes. The simple exercise of drawing a process flow diagram with people involved in an invisible process can be a struggle, but it can also be a valuable revelation. With no vantage point from which to see work as a process, many people never think of themselves as engaged in a process. Some even deny it. The fact that all work—visible and invisible—is part of a process must be understood throughout the organization before faculty and staff can begin to manage and improve key processes.

Educational organizations often succeed at making their internal processes better, faster, and (perhaps) cheaper for them. However, this may or may not actually improve student performance. When analyzing internal processes, someone must stubbornly play the role of advocate for the student and stakeholder perspective. Ensure that the improved processes will help meet key organizational goals, such as improving student learning or providing the key researcher an opportunity to be more creative and productive. Process improvement should reduce unnecessary costs or work steps, and/or boost performance results. Avoid wasting resources on process improvements that do not benefit stakeholders, students, staff, or faculty.

A fourth lesson involves design processes, an important but often neglected part of process management. The best organizations have learned that improvements made early in the process, beginning with design, save more time and money than those made farther "downstream." To identify how design processes can be improved, it is necessary to include ongoing evaluation and improvement cycles. Reducing the time for designing new curriculum not only reduces costs, but can return the teacher to student-centered activities more quickly.

Category 7: Organizational Performance Results

Encourage Activities that Lead to Desired Performance Results

Student learning results are based upon mission-related factors and assessment methods. Student performance should reflect mission-related results; current levels and trends should be reported; and data should be segmented by student group. This is an important Item for all educational organizations because it looks at student achievement over time, related to comparable organizations and/or student populations.

Student and stakeholder satisfaction is a critical and ongoing result that every successful organization must achieve. Educational systems must ensure that the data from student and stakeholder satisfaction and dissatisfaction are used at all levels to plan and make improvements. When students and stakeholders are asked their opinion, an expectation is created in their minds that the information will be used to make improvements that benefit them—even in kindergarten.

Some organizations have found it beneficial to have their students and other stakeholders analyze some of their academic performance results with the idea of learning from them, as well as building and strengthening relationships. This may or may not be appropriate for your organization, but many successful organizations have shared results with key groups at a level appropriate for their specific organization.

Budgetary, financial, and market results focus on expenditures, budget, and income. It is important that these results, with a Baldrige score maximum of 40 points out of 1000, be viewed in the context of the other results areas, especially student learning (200 points) and student and stakeholder satisfaction (70 points). Profits, market share, and meeting budget are the results, not the driver, of improved performance. This is not to say that inefficiencies are to be tolerated, but student learning is the primary driver of learning and curricular decisions.

Faculty and staff results provide an early alert to problems that may threaten success. Absenteeism, turnover, accidents, low morale, grievances, and poor skills or ineffective training suboptimize organization effectiveness. By monitoring performance in these areas, educational leaders can adjust quickly and prevent little problems from growing and overwhelming the organization.

Organizational effectiveness results provide useful information on key measures of the program, offering, or service itself. This information allows an organization to predict whether students and other stakeholders are likely to be satisfied—usually without asking them. For example, the likelihood that student satisfaction would be high with a given teacher would increase if the teacher knew and behaved consistently with factors students want in their teachers. These factors might include the following:

- Being knowledgeable about content
- Using relevant examples
- Returning assignments promptly
- Showing relationships between unknown content and known content
- Being fair
- Being genuinely interested in learning and teaching

One important lesson in this area is to select measures that correlate with, and predict, student and other stakeholder preference, satisfaction, and loyalty.

Organizational effectiveness results pertain to measures of internal effectiveness that may not be of immediate interest to students and stakeholders. Examples include cycle time (how long it takes to administer a test and return the grades), waste (how many tests or test items have to be rewritten or thrown out because of faulty wording or mistakes), and test-reporting accuracy (which may affect programs, students, and faculty). Ultimately, improving internal work process efficiency can result in reduced cost, rework, waste, and other factors that affect performance, whether academic results-driven or budget-driven. As a result, students and stakeholders benefit indirectly. To remain competitive, or to meet increased performance demands with fewer resources, organizations will be required to improve processes that enhance operational and support service results.

Effective performance management is as much a key to survival for educational organizations as for any other organization. This is true for both private sector and public sector schools. It is important to avoid overreliance on financial results. Financial results are the most lagging indicators of all school performance measures. Leaders who focus primarily on financials often overlook or cannot respond quickly to changing needs. Focusing on budgets and finances to run educational enterprises—to the exclusion of more leading indicators, such as operational performance and student and stakeholder satisfaction—is like driving your car by looking only in the rearview mirror. You cannot avoid potholes and turns in the road, and eventually you crash.

Do Not Tolerate System Craziness

An example of system craziness generally involves many layers. For example, in New York and many states, schools are motivated in part by state aid formulas which allocate funds based on student attendance and days of operation. Therefore, schools often prefer to hold planning and conference days for half days rather full days, especially for elementary school students. From the school's perspective, this is logical. From the student learning and student safety perspective, it is crazy. The learning is disrupted in the same subjects for multiple half days and compromises these subjects. Many students, especially older students, return to empty homes because of parental working hours, and this is when most troubling behavior occurs—when students are unsupervised. So, we have a state aid formula that has been in effect for several decades that doesn't take into effect the impact on learning or safety.

Another example of this: A student was so accelerated in mathematics that the high school arranged for him to take a course at a nearby college. However, the student had to miss every other physical education class because of the travel time involved. The parents petitioned the school to waive the requirement based on his varsity sports involvement for all three seasons, which was allowable by the state. The school denied the request and the student, who was admitted to an ivy league college with an overall 3.7 average, had to spend the summer making up the physical education requirement to earn the diploma.

Another example comes from the student services area. A parent asked her child why he was not eating the lunches the school provided. He replied that he would not eat peanut butter and cheese sandwiches. The parent went to school and asked the cafeteria manager why she was serving peanut butter and cheese sandwiches. The manager acknowledged that these were not eaten but in fact thrown out by the majority of students. She said that federal guidelines for nutrition required a certain number of grams of protein and that if they put on enough peanut butter to satisfy the requirement, it would literally be so thick as to choke the student. So they added a slice of cheese to make up the protein requirement. Of course, students have to actually eat the sandwich to get any protein at all, but this apparently was not figured into the menu design. This is a perfect example of "crazy compliance," but not Performance Excellence.

Stakeholders' requirements are of two types: (1) requirements based on student needs reflected in the organization's educational services, and (2) personal needs of stakeholders themselves. For example, parents might request services related to their children's educational program (Type 1), and the parents might also request special meeting times with the organization to accommodate their work schedules (Type 2). Many of the employer and other stakeholder needs must be addressed in the organization's educational services to students. The Education Criteria place primary emphasis upon such needs because the organization's success depends heavily upon translating these needs into effective educational services and experiences.

School Safety and Security

School safety and security concerns are tearing at the fabric of educational organizations and their communities. Crisis planning and violence prevention are diverting attention and resources from teaching and research. School activities are being modified or cancelled because of liability concerns and high insurance rates. Shop class, recess, science labs, field trips, and sports—including cheerleading—have been threatened by lawsuits. Schools report that they are being forced to spend more and more of their time documenting injuries, filling out Federal weapons forms, and reporting every scraped elbow (according to a National Association of Secondary School Principals 1999 survey). In response to awareness of the need for school safety improvement, The U.S. Department of Education and the U.S. Department of Justice recommended that school safety teams be formed and used to design, implement, and monitor comprehensive school safety plans. Web sites that offer information on school violence are springing up. School safety team training workshops are diverting teacher attention. The criteria for Performance Excellence in Education address school safety in many ways. This section:

- Links the seven Baldrige Categories to improving school safety and security;
- Describes, at the Item level, specific criteria requirements related to school safety and security; and
- Reports results on a nationwide survey, covering the last decade, on school safety and security.

[A sample survey for educational organizations to use to monitor safety and security, Organizational Self-Assessment for Education: Safety and Security, is available in the Self-Assessment section of this book on page 197. It is based on safety- and security-related requirements of the Baldrige 2001 Criteria.]

Linkages Between and Among Categories that Address School Safety

Each category has specific requirements that relate to or support school safety and security activities.

Leadership

Leaders consider the needs and expectations of all students and stakeholders for a safe school. They promote clear values, such as respect and tolerance, and create a school environment where all are safe and secure. They have a clear societal responsibility to consider all risks associated with school operations. Student safety is an increasingly serious issue.

Strategic Planning

The strategic planning process considers faculty, staff, student, and stakeholder needs and expectations. This includes potential threats (which may include safety concerns) that impact school performance.

Student, Stakeholder, and Market Focus

The organization uses a variety of listening and learning methods to determine and anticipate student and stakeholder needs and concerns. It involves and engages students in learning and solving problems. It builds and improves positive relationships with students and stakeholders through a variety of methods. It uses satisfaction and dissatisfaction data to monitor progress and target improvement strategies.

Information and Analysis

The organization uses data and information to improve the learning environment. It ensures data users (including students, staff, and faculty) have access to reliable, confidential, and user-friendly data. It provides data on safety and schoolwide performance.

Faculty and Staff Focus

The school's work systems promote faculty/staff cooperation and enhance their capability to respond to changing student needs. The organization provides training, education, and support for faculty and staff. It assesses and systematically improves safety, health, and well-being through a variety of methods and indicators. It maintains a safe, healthful, and secure work environment.

Process Management

The organization's educational support systems address student well-being needs. The school provides programs to ensure faculty and staff are prepared to deal with special situations that may involve safety and security. The school's plants and facilities, information services, and other support services promote safety and security.

Organizational Performance Results

The school tracks trends and results related to safety and security and well-being of students and faculty and staff. It uses data on satisfaction and dissatisfaction and well-being to improve the school climate. Specific improvements in school safety are reported and tracked.

Requirements at the Item Level that Address School Safety

1.1—The school's leadership system (such as administrators, school boards, or trustees) and senior leaders should guide the school in setting directions and in developing and sustaining effective leadership throughout the organization. This includes establishing *a climate conducive to learning that promotes ethical values, equity for all students, empowerment, innovation, and safety.*

1.2(a)—Senior leaders should address responsibilities to the public and ensure the school practices good citizenship. The school should address the current and potential affects on society of its operations, such as *risks associated with operating schools.* Schools should also anticipate public concerns with its operations, examine potential problems, and address them.

2.2—The schools should develop strategy and action plans for accomplishing *key objectives,* such as school safety improvement. Measures, objectives, and plans used to drive improvements must be developed. The school should target improvement in safety and security.

3.1—The school should determine longer-term requirements, expectations, and preferences of current and future students. The school uses this information to understand and anticipate needs and to create *an overall climate conducive to learning for all students. It identifies student needs and expectations, including those relating to safety.* It also works to engage students in active learning.

3.2—The school determines and enhances the satisfaction of its students and stakeholders to build relationships, to improve current educational services, and to support planning.

Student and stakeholder satisfaction and dissatisfaction are determined using techniques such as surveys, formal and informal feedback from students and stakeholders, and complaints. Student and stakeholder dissatisfaction indicators might include dropout rates, complaints, student conflict, safety/security, and absenteeism.

4.1—The schools should develop a fact-based measurement system, which includes selecting and tracking indicators of school safety and educational climate. The organization uses these data to set and put in place improvement priorities, including, for example, school safety and overall organizational health.

4.2—The school must ensure that data and information are kept secure, confidential, and accessible, as appropriate, to support decision-making throughout the organization.

5.2—Faculty and staff education, training, and development are systematically provided, in part, to strengthen their ability to solve problems and deal with school safety and security issues.

5.3—The school should maintain a safe, healthful work environment and climate that supports the well-being, satisfaction, and motivation of faculty and staff. Health, safety, and ergonomic issues are addressed in improvement activities. Key measures and targets for each of these environmental factors should be defined. Faculty and staff should take part in establishing these measures and targets. Measures and/or indicators of well-being, satisfaction, and motivation (5.3c) might include safety, absenteeism, turnover, grievances, strikes, other job actions, and worker's compensation claims, as well as results of surveys.

6.1—Educational programs and offerings should be designed and implemented to ensure they address student educational and *well-being needs.* These may include a focus on safety, treatment of fellow students, ridicule, and other good citizen values.

6.2—Key student services such as security, health services, and housing are designed and delivered. Schools should ensure student safety at all times. They may develop partnerships with other schools and community organizations to ensure effective transitions as students leave or enter school.

6.3—The school should provide support programs that may address *safety and security* concerns. These may include counseling, advising, tutoring, facilities management, transportation, security, and health services.

7.2—Summarizes student and stakeholder satisfaction and dissatisfaction results, which include safety and security issues.

7.4—Summarizes faculty and staff-related results, including faculty and staff well-being, satisfaction, and development that include safety and security.

7.5—Summarizes key performance results that contribute to enhanced learning and/or operational effectiveness, as well as public responsibility and citizenship. This includes indicators of *school safety, student engagement and active learning, school responsiveness, and educational climate.*

The Nation's Education Goals Report Addresses Safety and Security in the Schools

The Nation's Education Goals Report [8] provides some information on how schools are doing nationwide in addressing the criteria Items previously listed. *The Nation's Education Goals Report* was developed by a panel charged with reporting on national and state progress toward the National Education Goals established in 1989 by the first National Education Summit. This was convened by President George H. Bush and the nation's governors. The summit led to the adoption of goals targeted for the year 2001. According to the report's Foreword, "We still have far to go before we attain the level of success envisioned by the President and governors ten years ago. . . . We must redouble our efforts to ensure our schools are free of drugs, alcohol, and violence."

The goal that specifically addresses safety and security is National Education Goal #7: Safe, Disciplined, and Alcohol- and Drug-free Schools. It states: "Every school in the United States will be free of drugs, violence, and the unauthorized presence of firearms and alcohol and will offer a disciplined environment conducive to learning." Needless to say, we failed miserably.

The following is a summary of indicators, in an order based on their probable impact on student learning—the primary educational result. These indicators were used to determine the extent of progress (if any) toward the goals:

- Between 1991 and 1994, no state significantly reduced the percentage of public secondary school teachers reporting that student *disruptions interfere with learning* (p. 64).

- Between 1993 and 1997, one state significantly reduced the percentage of students reporting that they did not go to school at least once during the past 30 days because *they did not feel safe* (p. 62).

- Between 1991 and 1994, no state significantly reduced the percentage of public school teachers reporting that *lack of parental involvement* in their schools is a serious problem (p. 65).

- Between 1991 and 1997, no state significantly reduced the percentage of public high school students who reported *using marijuana* at least once during the past 30 days (p. 56).

- Between 1991 and 1997, no state significantly reduced the percentage of public high school students who reported having *five or more drinks in a row* at least once during the past 12 months. (p. 57).

- Between 1993 and 1997, only the Virgin Islands significantly reduced, and 15 states *increased,* the percentage of public high school students who reported that someone offered, sold, or gave them an *illegal drug on school property* at least once during the past 30 days (p. 58).

- Between 1993 and 1997, only American Samoa significantly reduced the percentage of public high school students who reported they were threatened or injured with a *weapon, such as a gun, knife, or club on school property* during the past 12 years (p. 59).

- Between 1993 and 1997, one state significantly reduced the percentage of public high school students who reported that they were in a *physical fight on school property* at least once during the past 12 months (p. 60).

- Between 1993 and 1997, four states significantly reduced the percentage of public high school students who reported they carried a *weapon, such as a gun, knife, or club on school property* at least once during the past 30 days (p. 61).

Fundamental change is needed to ensure that students feel they are in an environment where they are safe to learn and grow. If 10 years of thinking has not achieved desired results, is it reasonable to conclude that 10 more years of thinking will produce different outcomes? Samuel Clemens (Mark Twain) observed that one definition of insanity is doing the same thing over and over and expecting a different result. The Baldrige Criteria offer a guideline for meaningful, systematic, and structural change—our rational and sane hope for different outcomes to meet the needs and expectations of students, parents, employers, the community, and the nation as a whole.

References

1. James Traub, "What No School Can Do," *New York Times Magazine,* 16 January 2000.

2. Herman et al., *An Educator's Guide to Schoolwide Reform,* included in *High Standards for All Children: A Report from the National Assessment of Title I on Progress and Challenges Since the 1994 Reauthorization* (January 2001)

3. David E. Drew, "Tell Students Yes, You Can," *USA Today,* (February 7, 2001): 11A.

4. *High Standards for All Students: A Report from the National Assessment of Title I on Progress and Challenges Since the 1994 Reauthorization* (Washington, D.C.: ED Pubs, January, 2001). Order from: www.ed.gov/offices/OUS/eval/elem.html, or from ED Pubs, Educational Publications Center, U.S. Department of Education, P.O. Box 1398, Jessup, MD 20794-1398.

5. Robert Rothman, "Bringing All Students to High Standards: Report on National Education Goals Panel Hearings," in *Lessons From the States* (December 2000). Order from www.neap.gov or National Education Goals Panel, (202) 724-0015.

6. "Reality Check, Public Agenda," *Education Week* (January 1999).

7. "Standards Count," paper presented at the Tenth Anniversary Conference of the National Assessment Governing Board, (Washington D.C., November 19, 1998).

8. National Education Goals Panel, *The National Education Goals Report: Building a Njation of Learners,* 1999 (Washington, DC: US Government Printing Office, 1999).

Education Criteria Goals and Values

Education Criteria Purposes

The Malcolm Baldrige Education Criteria for Performance Excellence are the basis for assessment and feedback to education organizations. In addition, the criteria have three important roles:

1. To help improve educational performance practices, capabilities, and results.
2. To facilitate communication and sharing of best practices information among educational organizations of all types.
3. To serve as a working tool for understanding and improving performance and for guiding planning and opportunities for learning.

Education Criteria for Performance Excellence Goals

The criteria are designed to help organizations use an aligned approach to organizational performance management that results in:

- Delivery of ever-improving value to students and stakeholders, contributing to improved education quality;
- Improvement of overall organizational effectiveness and capabilities; and
- Organizational and personal learning.

Core Values and Concepts

The Baldrige Education Criteria are built on a set of interrelated core values that characterize all types of high-performing organizations and are present in the best schools in the nation. This section presents the 11 core values that underlie the criteria. These values bind an organization together and are the foundation upon which success is built. These core values are critical for successful educational organizations of any size and in any sector—from rural schools to city universities to private academies. By integrating these values into the everyday life of education as schools engage students in their own learning, educators can convert their institutions into improving organizations.

For maximum learning to take place, students need much more from their teachers, professors, and schooling than just knowledge. They need to be fully engaged in seeking and interpreting knowledge and facts. All of the following core values are linked with this underlying need to engage students in the learning process.

These core values and concepts follow.

Visionary Leadership

An organization's senior leaders should set directions and create a student-focused, learning-oriented climate; clear and visible values; and high expectations. The directions, values, and expectations should balance the needs of all your stakeholders. Your leaders should ensure the creation of strategies, systems, and methods for achieving excellence, stimulating innovation, and building knowledge and capabilities. The values and strategies should help guide all activities and decisions of your organization. Senior leaders should inspire and motivate all faculty and staff, encouraging them to contribute, to develop and learn, to be innovative, and to be creative.

Your senior leaders should serve as role models through their ethical behavior and their personal involvement in planning, communications, coaching, development of future leaders, review of organizational performance, and faculty and staff recognition. As role models, they can reinforce values and expectations while building leadership, commitment, and initiative throughout your organization.

In addition to their important role within the organization, senior leaders have other avenues to strengthen education. Reinforcing the learning environment in the organization might require building community support and aligning community and business leaders and community services with this aim.

Every successful educational organization, strategy, and method for achieving Performance Excellence is guided by effective leadership:

- Effective leaders convey a strong sense of urgency to counter the natural resistance to change that can prevent the organization from taking the steps that these core values for success demand.
- Such leaders serve as enthusiastic role models, reinforcing and communicating the core values by their words and actions. Words alone are not enough.
- Leaders at all levels of education needs to communicate clearly understood goals. Relationships must be built on trust and kept alive by open and honest communication. This includes leaders from boards and the top level of administration; school, college, building, and department level leaders; and significantly, classroom leaders—instructors and teachers. Whenever a link in the leadership chain is broken, the success of those being "led" usually becomes more random and uneven.
- Leaders must take steps to ensure that all systems and people, including leaders at all levels in the organization, and compensation, reward, and recognition pull together to support these values and goals.

Learning-Centered Education

In order to develop the fullest potential of all students, education organizations need to afford them opportunities to pursue a variety of avenues to success. Learning-centered education supports this goal by placing the focus of education on learning and the real needs of students. Such needs derive from market and citizenship requirements.

A learning-centered organization needs to fully understand these requirements and translate them into appropriate curricula and developmental experiences. For example, changes in technology and in the national and world economies are creating increasing demands on employees to become knowledge workers and problem solvers, keeping pace with the rapid market changes. Most analysts conclude that, to prepare students for this work environment, education organizations of all types need to focus more on students' active learning and on the development of problem-solving skills. Educational offerings also need to be built around effective learning, and effective teaching needs to stress promotion of learning and achievement.

Learning-centered education is a strategic concept that demands constant sensitivity to changing and emerging student, stakeholder, and market requirements and to the factors that drive student learning, satisfaction, and persistence. It demands anticipating changes in the education environment, as well as rapid and flexible responses to student, stakeholder, and market requirements.

Key characteristics of learning-centered education include the following:

- High developmental expectations and standards are set for all students.
- Faculty understand that students may learn in different ways and at different rates. Student learning rates and styles may differ over time and may vary depending on subject matter. Learning may be influenced by support, guidance, and climate factors, including factors that contribute to or impede learning. Thus, the learning-centered organization needs to maintain a constant search for alternative ways to enhance learning. Also, the organization needs to develop actionable information on individual students that bears upon their learning.
- A primary emphasis on active learning is provided. This may require the use of a wide range of techniques, materials, and experiences to engage student interest. Techniques, materials, and experiences may be drawn from external sources such as businesses, community services, or social service organizations.

- Formative assessment is used to measure learning early in the instructional process. Individual needs and learning styles are used to modify subsequent instruction.
- Summative assessment is used to measure progress against key, relevant external standards and norms regarding what students should know and should be able to do.
- Students and families are assisted in using self-assessment to chart progress and to clarify goals and gaps.
- There is a focus on key transitions, such as school-to-school and school-to-work.

Without fully engaging students in learning, optimum student performance cannot be achieved. Focusing on learning means:

- Setting standards and expectations of excellence, not mediocrity, for students.
- Recognizing that students differ in learning rates and styles and using information about learning preferences to enhance learning.
- Emphasizing that learners should be active in selecting their learning vehicles and engaged in the process as much as their maturity and the subject matter allow. It is important to recognize that most educators underestimate student capability.
- Using assessment formatively (during the learning process) and summatively (after the learning process) to improve the learning at all stages of the process.
- Providing rapid and immediate feedback to students on their performance so improvement cycles become shorter.

Students need faster feedback on their performance. This enables faster corrections and improvement in learning cycle time. Students are also motivated by immediate feedback to continue to do better. One of the biggest impacts on student performance appears to be the fairness and speed of instructor feedback. Variables, such as methods of instruction, instructor training, and even reduced class size, have produced uneven performance results. The variable that is having the most dramatic impact on student learning is reduction in the cycle time involved in teaching, assessing learning, and correcting mistakes. The quicker students get feedback, the more meaningful and specific the feedback, the larger the performance gains. This is an example of learning-centered education.

Basing decisions about support services, student services, and educational services on student learning have an impact. For example, teenagers are not usually at peak performance early in the morning. The vast majority of high schools begin substantive instruction at 7:35 A.M., and colleges make 8 A.M. classes an unwelcome freshman "right of passage." The hours of operation of the public high school are not based on preferences or needs of students or stakeholders—certainly not on student learning needs or working hours of the modern family. Mostly, they are based on bus schedules and faculty/staff preferences. A similar complaint has been looked at regarding instructional segments. Most classes in high school are all the same length—50 minutes—for the convenient of scholastics, not optimum student learning. Variable instructional segments of 50 to 130 minutes, depending on learning dynamics, focuses on learning needs, not scholarly convenience.

Organizational and Personal Learning

Achieving the highest levels of performance requires a well-executed approach to organizational and personal learning. *Organizational learning* includes both continuous improvement of existing approaches and adaptation to change, leading to new goals and/or approaches. Learning needs to be embedded in the way your organization operates. This means that learning: (1) is a regular part of the daily work of all students, faculty, and staff; (2) is practiced at personal, work unit/department, and organizational levels; (3) results in solving problems at their source ("root cause"); (4) is focused on sharing knowledge throughout your organization; and (5) is driven by opportunities to effect significant change and to do better. Sources for learning include faculty and staff ideas, education and learning research findings, student and stakeholder input, best practice sharing, and benchmarking.

Improvement in education requires a strong emphasis on effective design of educational programs, curricula, and learning environments. The overall design should include clear learning objectives, taking into account the individual needs of students. Design must also include effective means for gauging student progress.

A central requirement of effective design is the inclusion of an assessment strategy. This strategy needs to emphasize the acquisition of formative information—information that provides an early indication of whether or not learning is taking place—to minimize problems that might arise if learning barriers are not promptly identified and addressed.

Faculty and staff success depends increasingly on having opportunities for personal learning and practicing new skills. Organizations invest in personal learning of faculty and staff through education, training, and other opportunities for continuing growth. Such opportunities might include job rotation and increased pay for demonstrated knowledge and skills. Educational and training programs may benefit from advanced technologies, such as computer- and Internet-based learning and satellite broadcasts.

Personal learning can result in: (1) more satisfied and versatile faculty and staff who stay with the organization, (2) organizational cross-functional learning, and (3) an improved environment for innovation.

Thus, learning is directed not only toward better educational programs and services but also toward being more flexible, adaptive, and responsive to the needs of students, stakeholders, and the market.

> High-performing organizations create a culture of learning, evaluating, and improving everything they do. They strive to get better and get faster at getting better. In order to do this, educational organizations need to do the following:
>
> * Create a culture of continuous learning and change essential to establishing and sustaining true competitive advantage. They need to embed this culture into the everyday life of the organization. They need to make continuous improvement an automatic reflex, like an eye blink. It is truly embedded when it happens easily, automatically, and naturally. In fact, the absence of refinement ought to feel strange— not the other way around. Moreover, one of the greatest values to notice in students is the passion for continuous improvement.
> * Reward improvement of processes and performance as part of the culture change.
>
> With systematic, continuous improvement, time becomes a powerful ally. As time passes, the organization and its members grow stronger and smarter. Without continuous improvement, time becomes an enemy. Competitors gain, causing us to fall further behind.

Valuing Faculty, Staff, and Partners

An organization's success depends increasingly on the knowledge, skills, innovative creativity, and motivation of its faculty, staff, and partners.

Valuing faculty and staff means committing to their satisfaction, development, and well-being. Increasingly, this involves more flexible work practices tailored to faculty and staff with diverse workplace and home life needs. For faculty, development means building not only discipline knowledge but also knowledge of student learning styles and of assessment methods. Faculty participation might include contributing to the organization's policies and working in teams to develop and execute programs and curricula. Increasingly, participation is becoming more student-focused and more multidisciplinary. Organization leaders should work to eliminate disincentives for groups and individuals to sustain these important, learning-focused professional development activities.

For staff, development might include classroom and on-the-job training, job rotation, and pay for demonstrated skills. Increasingly, training, education, development, and organizational structure need to be tailored to a more diverse workforce and to more flexible, high-performance work practices.

Major challenges in the area of valuing faculty and staff include: (1) demonstrating your leaders' commitment to the success of your faculty and staff, (2) recognition that goes beyond the regular compensation system, (3) development and progression within your organization, (4) sharing your organization's knowledge so your faculty and staff can better serve your students and stakeholders and contribute to achieving your strategic objectives, and (5) creating an environment that encourages creativity.

Education organizations need to build internal and external partnerships to better accomplish overall goals. Internal partnerships might include cooperation among leadership, faculty, and staff, such as agreements with unions. Partnerships with faculty and staff might entail faculty and staff development, cross-training, or new organizational structure such as high-performance work teams. Internal partnerships also might involve creating network relationships among your work units to improve flexibility, responsiveness, and knowledge sharing.

External partnerships might be with other schools, suppliers, businesses, business associations, and community and social service organizations—all stakeholders and potential contributors. Strategic partnerships or alliances are increasingly important kinds of external partnerships, as they might offer entry into new markets or a basis for new programs or services. Also, partnerships might permit the blending of your organization's core competencies or leadership capabilities with the complementary strengths and capabilities of partners.

Successful internal and external partnerships develop longer-term objectives, thereby creating a basis for mutual investments and respect. Partners should address the key requirements for success, means for regular communication, approaches to evaluating progress, and means for adapting to changing conditions.

Valuing faculty and staff means providing the resources and support for faculty and staff to develop and learn continually. The organization as a whole learns if knowledge and learnings are shared. This value must be at the heart of the culture of any educational institution. Educational organizations need to reflect on the relationship between the board and its top administrators, and then between the top administrators and faculty and staff. The relationships at the top, if based on trust and common goals, will cascade down into the organizational structure. Trust will then be the basis for the relationship between teachers and students in most classrooms. If top administrators are valued by the board, college deans and principals valued by central administrators, and teachers valued by site administrators, then students are more likely to be valued by their instructors. If an organization values its members and provides support for development, initiative, and self-directed responsibility, it is able to create a workforce that is motivated to become continually better and fully use their capabilities. Unfortunately, the reverse is also true. Top leaders that micromanage send a message of arrogance and distrust. Messages of distrust and arrogance are then passed all the way to students and parents.

Agility

Agility is an increasingly important measure of your organizational effectiveness. It requires a capacity for faster and more flexible response to the needs of your students and stakeholders. Many organizations are learning that an explicit focus on and measurement of response times help to drive the simplification of the organizational structure and work processes. All aspects of time performance are becoming increasingly important and should be among your key process measures. Other important benefits can be derived from this focus on time; time improvements often drive simultaneous improvements in organization, quality, and cost.

Agility involves moving quickly to reduce cycle time and instructional time. Reducing cycle time to be more responsive often involves more than just the individual organization. New cooperative agreements need to be forged. For example, a community college may take over a year to launch (some have been as long as five years!) a new program that the community needs. The delay may be due to the state education department review process—a generally non-value-added step in the program development process. This kind of delay, which is ingrained into the process and appears "normal," needs to be eliminated directly through appropriate channels.

At the public school K–12 level, cycle time can be reduced in some instances by faster feedback to students on assignments and tests and letting students learn at different rates. Testing out of some subjects in middle school, high school, and college, such as "keyboarding" (a favorite prerequisite), is certainly worthwhile to save money and time.

Focus on the Future

In today's education environment, a focus on the future requires understanding the short- and longer-term factors that affect your organization and the education market. Pursuit of educational excellence requires a strong future orientation and a willingness to make long-term commitments to students and key stakeholders—the community, employers, faculty, and staff. Your organization's planning should anticipate many factors, such as changes in educational requirements, instructional approaches, resource availability, student/stakeholder expectations, new partnering opportunities, technological developments, the evolving Internet environment, new student and market segments, demographics, community/societal expectations, and strategic changes by comparable organizations. Strategic objectives and resource allocations need to accommodate these influences. A major longer-term investment associated with your organization's improvement is the investment in creating and sustaining a mission-oriented assessment system focused on learning. This entails faculty education and training in assessment methods. In addition, the organization's leaders should be familiar with research findings and practical applications of assessment methods and learning style information. A focus on the future includes developing faculty and staff, creating opportunities for innovation, and anticipating public responsibilities.

Every educational organization must be guided by its own set of measurable goals and its view of the future (based, of course, on student and stakeholder needs and requirements). For educators who are often immersed in institutions with a scholarly historical perspective, this may be more difficult. Our fast moving, ever-changing businesses today mean new skill requirements for students. Education, which largely relies on past history to guide it, needs to change its focus to anticipate and better prepare for emerging demands. Some of its tried-and-true required curricular offerings may need to be shelved. More relevant experiences need to take their place.

Examples are plentiful at all levels. Look at current course contact in home and career skills that require middle school boys and girls to learn the difference between pancake servers and spatulas and how to make sugar-laden soft drinks. Unfortunately, it is not the future that is driving these types of courses, it's the past—protecting the minority of teachers who do not possess relevant knowledge for today and tomorrow. College students who came to college with computer skills are required to take a course on "how to use a mouse." Community college students who are majoring in communications don't graduate because they fail their final exam on bowling. These same students have no laboratory experience or "office prep" courses to prepare them for the work environment. These are not isolated examples of the silliness educators perpetrate to ensure full employment. A staggering amount of time and resources are diverted from critical learning by these special interests.

What skills do these students need for their future? Educational organizations need to focus on this question and clean out their academic closets. With the current need for teachers growing and employment at an all-time high, it makes sense to retrain educators who are certified in outdated disciplines.

Managing for Innovation

Innovation means making meaningful change to improve an organization's programs, services, and processes and to create new value for the organization's stakeholders. Innovation should lead your organization to new dimensions of performance. Innovation is no longer strictly the purview of research; innovation is important for providing ever-improving educational value to students and for improving all educational and operational processes. Organizations should be led so that innovation becomes part of the culture and is integrated into daily work.

Many teachers speak of the need to innovate—but their actions may not support their words. Consider the following incident: A cartoon is entitled "Today we are making rainbows." The teacher asked a class of children to draw rainbows. A little girl (Elsa) is following directions and painting rainbows. Her friend (Lizzy) is talking to her about an abstract drawing she is painting with three-dimensional figures and wild colors. Lizzy is very excited about making a story to go with her drawing, publishing it on the Web, and translating it into Spanish. Elsa replies—"Are you crazy? The teacher told us to paint rainbows." Lizzy finishes her painting and illustrated story and goes up to the teacher beaming with pride and accomplishment. She comes back a few moments later with a clean sheet of paper. Lizzy looks at Elsa and says, "Today we're painting rainbows."

Well! We all know what would happen if we had a school full of such noncompliant students. By 4th grade, most of the innovation and relativity has been beaten out of the minds and hearts of students. Innovation is a value necessary for substantive change to occur.

Management by Fact

Organizations depend on the measurement and analysis of performance. Such measurements should derive from the organization's needs and strategy, and they should provide critical data and information about key processes and results. Many types of data and information are needed for performance management. Performance measurement should focus on student learning, which requires a comprehensive and integrated fact-based system—one that includes input data, environmental data, performance data, comparative/competitive data, data on faculty/staff, cost data, and operational performance measurement. Measurement areas might include students' backgrounds, learning styles, aspirations, academic strengths and weaknesses, educational progress, classroom and program learning, satisfaction with instruction and services, extracurricular activities, dropout/matriculation rates, and post-graduation success.

Analysis refers to extracting larger meaning from data and information to support evaluation, decision making, and operational improvement. Analysis entails using data to determine trends, projections, and cause and effect that might not otherwise be evident. Analysis supports a variety of purposes, such as planning, reviewing your overall performance, improving operations, change management, and comparing your performance with comparable organizations or with "best practices" benchmarks.

A major consideration in performance improvement and change management involves the selection and use of performance measures or indicators. *The measures or indicators you select should best represent the factors that lead to improved student, operational, and financial performance. A comprehensive set of measures or indicators tied to student, stakeholder, and/or organizational performance requirements represents a clear basis for aligning all activities with your organization's goals.* Through the analysis of data from your tracking processes, your measures or indicators themselves may be evaluated and changed to better support your goals.

Management by fact is the cornerstone value for effective planning, decision making, faculty and staff involvement, engaging students, and leadership. Educators make decisions every day that directly affect student performance and learning. Without data, the basis for decision making is intuition—gut feel.

Most drivers decide when to fill their fuel tanks based on data from the fuel gauge and get very uncomfortable if the gauge is broken. People routinely, however, make decisions of enormous consequence about learning methods, strategies, goals, and students with little or no data. This is a recipe for disaster, not one designed to ensure high performance. All participants in the organization, from top leaders and teachers to students, must have access to data to promote informed, effective decision making. Data must be relevant, accurate, accessible, and timely. In the absence of data, judgments are made based on intuition, opinion, and personal perspectives. Unfortunately, student perspectives and teacher perspectives do not always agree. The right data reduces guesswork and promotes consistently better, more reliable decision making at all levels.

Public Responsibility and Citizenship

An organization's leaders should stress its responsibilities to the public and the need to practice good citizenship. These responsibilities refer to basic expectations of your organization related to ethical practices and protection of public health, safety, and the environment. Planning should anticipate adverse impacts that might arise in facilities management, laboratory operations, and transportation. Ethical practices need to take into account proper use of public and private funds. Effective planning should prevent problems, provide for a forthright response if problems occur, and make available information and support needed to maintain public awareness, safety, and confidence.

Organizations should not only meet all local, state, and federal laws and regulatory requirements, but they should treat these and related requirements as opportunities for improvement "beyond mere compliance." This requires the use of appropriate measures in managing public responsibility.

Practicing good citizenship refers to leadership and support—within the limits of an organization's resources—of publicly important purposes. Such purposes might include improving education in your community, environmental excellence, resource conservation, community service, and sharing quality-related information. Leadership also entails influencing other organizations, private and public, to partner for these purposes.

> Public responsibility and citizenship is a strategic imperative—especially for students. After all, a key mission is to produce an educated citizenry. Schools, colleges, and universities serve at the center of their communities and need to role model ethical and data-driven decision making at all levels. These organizations are highly visible and under constant scrutiny. Schools are constantly being judged by their students, parents, and other stakeholders.
>
> Educational organizations must determine and anticipate any adverse effects to the public of their products, services, and operations. A strong focus on safety and security is needed to allay fears of students and parents. Failure to do so can undermine public trust. These are not altruistic principles, but minimum requirements for effective schools to demonstrate as they develop the minds and values of future generations.

Focus on Results and Creating Value

An organization's performance measurements need to focus on key results. Results should be used to create and balance value for your students and key stakeholders—the community, employers, faculty, staff, suppliers, and partners. By creating value for students and stakeholders, your organization contributes to improving overall education performance and builds loyalty. To meet the sometimes conflicting and changing aims that balancing value implies, organizational strategy should explicitly include student and key stakeholder requirements. This will help ensure that actions and plans meet differing student and stakeholder needs and avoid adverse impacts on any students and/or stakeholders. The use of a balanced composite of leading and lagging performance measures offers an effective means to communicate short- and longer-term priorities, monitor actual performance, and provide a clear basis for improving results.

> Results should include a balance of lagging indicators (such as student achievement, graduation rates, and financial measures), and leading indicators (such as attendance, learning rates, rework required, and time on task). Without a balanced results (outputs) focus, organizations can become fixated on processes (inputs) and lose sight of the important factors for success. Without a results focus, the activity becomes the goal, not the outcome of the activity. This is partly responsible for the tendency to be introspective and internally focused.
>
> Creating value means reviewing offerings to make sure they add real and desired value for students and stakeholders. For example, what is the value of a Drug and Violence Awareness program such as DARE if violence and drug use continues to increase over time? What is the value of an eighth grade graduation competency in mask making for art? Is it a proven predictor of high school success or a reasonable prerequisite for all students? What is the value of the physical education class for students who are active participants in a varsity sport and enduring two hours of strenuous training each day? Do all students on varsity sports teams need two or more hours of sports practice each day in addition to mandated attendance in physical education class three hours a week? Could the time be better spent?

Systems Perspective

The Baldrige Criteria provide a systems perspective for managing your organization to achieve performance excellence. The core values and the seven Baldrige Categories form the building blocks and integrating mechanism for the system. However, successful management of overall performance requires organization-specific synthesis and alignment. Synthesis means looking at your organization as a whole and builds upon key educational requirements, including your strategic objectives and action plans. Alignment means using the key linkages among requirements given in the Baldrige Categories, including the key measures/indicators.

Alignment is depicted in the Baldrige framework on page 47. Alignment includes your senior leaders' focus on strategic directions and on your students and stakeholders. It means that your senior leaders monitor, respond to, and manage performance based on your key results. Alignment includes using your measures/indicators to link your key strategies with your key processes and align your resources to improve overall performance and satisfy students and stakeholders.

Thus, a systems perspective means managing your whole organization, as well as its components, to achieve success.

Education is a very large system that generally begins with a preschool or kindergarten classroom. Each classroom and organization is also a system, and the Baldrige Criteria require this perspective be used to make decisions with the potential to benefit the entire system.

An often overlooked part of the system in education is the "supply chain" that starts at pre-school or kindergarten level. Harold L. Hodgkinson makes this point well in *All One System: A Second Look.*[9] Over a decade ago, Hodgkinson published *All One System*, which asserted that our graduate schools were dependent to some extent on the quality of pre-school students. In fact, he noted that education at the top level of mathematics, for example, depended upon, but was totally divorced from mathematics education at lower levels. There is very little dialogue across K–12 to higher education's hallowed halls. Truthfully, there is very little dialogue between elementary to middle to high schools in the same district. The likelihood of colleges and high schools communicating about student mastery or learning is even more remote.

Students often experience the disconnects and overlaps that this lack of communication and planning creates. Consider the high school teachers who tell students each year that they have been poorly prepared in middle school for a particular subject. However, no communication with the middle school teachers ever takes place so the problem continues year after year. Creating a meaningful dialogue to create a systematic way to address problems and challenges is a high priority for educational improvement.

There are always better ways to do things. The challenge for educators and organizations is to find them. Schools, colleges, and universities that base efforts on the core values that underlie the Baldrige Education Criteria are in a better position to build organizations that foster trust, effective learning, high performance, and steady improvement. They position the organization to optimize—and succeed, where others fail.

Reference

9 Institute for Educational Leadership and The National Center for Public Policy and ____ Education, 1999 (Washington, DC).

Key Characteristics of the Education Criteria

The Criteria Focus on Organizational Performance Results

The criteria focus on the key areas of organizational performance as indicated in the following list. Organizational performance results are a composite of the following:

- Student learning results
- Student- and stakeholder-focused results
- Budgetary, financial, and market results
- Faculty and staff results
- Organizational effectiveness results

The use of this composite of indicators is intended to ensure that strategies are balanced—that they do not inappropriately trade off among important stakeholders, objectives, or short- and long-term goals.

The Criteria Are Nonprescriptive and Adaptable

The criteria are a set of 19 basic, interrelated, results-oriented requirements. However, the criteria do not prescribe:

- Specific tools, techniques, technologies, systems, or starting points;
- That your organization should or should not have departments for quality, planning, or other functions;
- How your organization should be structured; or
- That different units in your organization should be managed in the same way.

These factors are important and are likely to change as needs and strategies evolve. Hence, the criteria do emphasize that such factors be evaluated as part of your organization's performance reviews.

The criteria are nonprescriptive because:

- The focus is on results, not on procedures, tools, or organizations. Schools are encouraged to develop and demonstrate creative, adaptive, and flexible approaches for meeting basic requirements. Nonprescriptive requirements are intended to foster incremental and major (breakthrough) improvement as well as basic change.
- Selection of tools, techniques, systems, and organizations usually depends on many factors, such as size, school type, the organization's stage of development, and faculty and staff capabilities and responsibilities.
- Focusing on common requirements within an organization, rather than on common procedures, fosters better understanding, communication, sharing, and alignment while supporting creativity and diversity in approaches.

The Criteria Support a Systems Approach to Organizationwide Goal Alignment

The systems perspective to goal alignment is embedded in the integrated structure of the core values and concepts, the criteria, and the results-oriented, cause-effect linkages among the criteria Items.

Alignment in the criteria is built around connecting and reinforcing measures derived from your organization's strategy. These measures tie directly to student and stakeholder value and to overall performance. The use of measures thus channels different activities in consistent directions with less need for detailed procedures, centralized decision making, or process management. Measures thereby serve both as a communications tool and a basis for deploying consistent overall performance requirements. Such alignment ensures consistency of purpose while also supporting agility, innovation, and decentralized decision making.

A systems perspective to goal alignment, particularly when strategy and goals change over time, requires dynamic linkages among criteria Items. In the criteria, action-oriented cycles of learning take place via feedback between processes and results.

The learning cycles have four, clearly defined stages (Figure 1):

1. **Plan.** Formulate plans, including design of processes, selection of measures, and deployment of requirements.
2. **Do.** Execute plans.
3. **Study/Check.** Assess progress, taking into account internal and external results.
4. **Act.** Revise plans based on assessment findings, learning, new inputs, and new requirements.

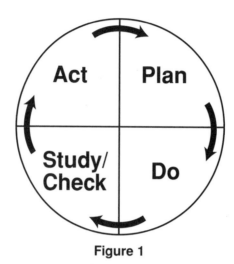

Figure 1

The Criteria Support Goal-based Diagnosis

The criteria and the scoring guidelines make up a two-part diagnostic (assessment) system. The criteria are a set of 19 performance-oriented requirements. The scoring guidelines spell out the assessment dimensions—approach, deployment, and results—and the key factors used to assess against each dimension. An assessment thus provides a profile of strengths and opportunities for improvement relative to the 19 basic requirements. In this way, assessment leads to actions that contribute to performance improvement in all areas. This diagnostic assessment is a useful decision tool that goes beyond most performance reviews and is applicable to a wide range of strategies and management systems.

Key Education Themes of the 2001 Criteria

Mission Specificity

Although education organizations typically share common aims, individual organizational missions, roles, and programs vary greatly. Use of a single set of criteria to cover all your organizational requirements means that these requirements need to be interpreted in terms of your own organizational mission. This is necessary because specific requirements and critical success factors differ from organization to organization. For this reason, effective use of the criteria depends on putting these mission requirements into operation consistently across the seven categories of the criteria framework. In particular, Strategic Planning (Category 2) needs to address your key mission requirements, setting the stage for the interpretation of your other requirements. For example, results reported in Organizational Performance Results (Category 7) need to reflect results consistent with your organization's mission and strategic objectives.

The Education Criteria are most explicit in the area of student learning, as this requirement is common to all education organizations regardless of their larger missions. Despite this commonality, the focus of student learning and development depends on your organizational mission. For example, results reported by trade schools, engineering schools, and music schools would be expected to differ because they would reflect each organization's mission. Nevertheless, all three types of organizations would be expected to show year-to-year improvements in their mission-specific results to demonstrate the effectiveness of their performance improvement efforts.

> The criteria take into account that specific requirements and critical success factors differ from organization to organization. For this reason, organizations need to use mission requirements to drive operations across the seven categories of the criteria. The strategic planning process must address all key mission requirements. Organizational Performance Results (Category 7) must report on the degree of attainment of strategic and operational initiatives, including the organization's mission objectives. The Education Criteria are most detailed in the area of student learning because this is a critical mission requirement of all educational organizations.

Customers

The Business Criteria for Performance Excellence use the generic term "customers" to describe the users of products or services. Although market success depends heavily on user preference, other stakeholders must be considered as well when setting overall organizational requirements. In the Education Criteria, the focus is on students and stakeholders, the key beneficiaries of educational programs and services.

As do businesses, education organizations must respond to a variety of requirements—all of which should be incorporated into responses to the Education Criteria. The adaptation of the Business Criteria to education includes a specific approach for defining key student requirements. This approach distinguishes between students and stakeholders for purposes of clarity and emphasis. Stakeholders include parents, employers, other schools, and communities. The requirements for current students differ from those for future students. Requirements for current students are more concrete, specific, and immediate; determining requirements for future students is part of the organization's planning and should take into account changing student populations and changing requirements future students must be able to meet. A major challenge organizations face is "bridging" current student needs and the needs of future students. This requires an effective organizational learning/change strategy.

Education organizations must also address the variety of requirements of their various stakeholders. Stakeholders' requirements are of two types: (1) requirements directly related to your organization's educational services, and (2) requirements of the stakeholders themselves. For example, parents might request services related to their children's educational program, such as integration of math and science curricula (Type 1), and the parents might also request special meeting times with the school to accommodate their work schedules (Type 2). Many of the needs of businesses and other stakeholders are actually needs that must be addressed in your organization's educational services for students. The Education Criteria place primary emphasis on such needs because your organization's success depends heavily on translating these needs into effective educational services and experiences. In addition, successful operation of an organization may depend on satisfying accreditation, environmental, legal, and other requirements. Thus, meaningful responses to the criteria need to incorporate all relevant requirements that organizations must meet to be successful.

The Education Criteria recognize many types of groups and persons who have a stake in their organization; they make demands and have requirements of organizations. The criteria distinguish between students and stakeholders in an effort to help distinguish the requirements of these two classes of customers. Stakeholders include parents, employers, other organizations, and communities. Students are further delineated into current students and future students. Requirements from current students are more specific and immediate, whereas requirements of future students take into account more long-range factors. Successful organizations must address both groups of customers to consistently achieve high levels of performance.

Concept of Excellence

The concept of excellence built into the criteria is that of "value-added" demonstrated performance. Such performance has two manifestations: (1) year-to-year improvement in key measures/indicators of performance, especially student learning; and (2) demonstrated leadership in performance and performance improvement relative to comparable organizations and/or to appropriate benchmarks.

This concept of excellence is used because: (1) it places the major focus on teaching/learning strategies; (2) it poses similar types of challenges for all organizations regardless of resources and/or incoming student preparation/abilities; (3) it is most likely to stimulate learning-related research and to offer a means to disseminate the results of such research; and (4) it offers the potential to create an expanding body of knowledge of successful teaching/learning practices in the widest range of organizations.

The focus on value-added contributions by your organization does not presuppose manufacturing-oriented, mechanistic, or additive models of student development. Also, the use of a value-added concept does not imply that your organization's management system should include documented procedures or attempt to define "conformity" or "compliance." Rather, the performance concept in the Education Criteria means that your organization should view itself as a key developmental influence on students (though not the only influence) and that your organization should seek to understand and optimize its influencing factors, guided by an effective assessment strategy.

In today's global competitive environment, excellence must be based on achievements, not inputs. Demonstrated performance, rather than intention, is vital. For decades, schools have taken pride and some solace in measures of success based on inputs—well-trained teachers, good facilities, and good curriculum and instructional techniques. However, when inputs do not produce desired outputs, excellence has been denied. This means year-to-year improvement in key measures and/or indicators of performance outcomes, as well as demonstrated leadership in performance and performance improvement, must be assessed relative to comparable organizations or benchmarks. This theme is important to all levels and types of education for the following reasons: It places the major focus on outcome measures of excellence to adjust teaching and learning strategies; it poses similar challenges to all organizations regardless of resources or student pool; it may stimulate teaching/learning research and dissemination of the results of such research; and it may create an expanding body of knowledge to share the best of teaching and learning practices.

Accreditation processes should be mentioned briefly here because they are so pervasive throughout education. The role of these processes as mechanisms for quality assurance to the public, frequently done via peer review as a form of self-governance, has been of considerable historical importance. However, the typical accreditation process starts primarily from a set of input-based standards and produces an evaluation of organizational compliance with those standards. The perspective of these processes is primarily oriented toward providing or renewing a "license to do business." These reviews evaluate conformity to the minimum standards necessary for the organization to exist. Any nonconformities found during the evaluation usually imply a requirement on the part of the organization either to implement an immediate correction or at least to provide a plan for achieving compliance. Important as this function is, it does not inherently produce a striving for excellence in performance, or even for continuous improvement.

The very title of the criteria that serve as the basis for this book suggests a different orientation. The underlying mindset is that every process can be improved. It is the continuing experience of the authors of this book that the leaders of high-performing organizations are justifiably proud of the progress their organizations have made; yet keenly interested in ways to take performance still higher. Compliance with a common denominator is not enough for these organizations and their people and stakeholders. They are hungry for mechanisms that will continually raise the bar by supporting, facilitating, and driving high performance. A section of this book on page 193, Comparing Assessment for Performance Improvement and Accreditation, discusses this topic in more depth.

Assessment Strategy

Central and crucial to the success of the concept of excellence in the Education Criteria is a well-conceived and well-executed assessment strategy. The characteristics of such a strategy should include the following:

- Clear ties should be established between what is assessed and your organization's mission and objectives. This means not only what your students know but also what they are able to do.
- There should be a strong focus on improvement—of your students' performance, your faculty's capabilities, and your organization's program performance.
- An embedded, ongoing assessment with prompt feedback should be an integral component.
- The assessment also should be based on curricula, reference appropriate criteria, and address your key learning goals and your overall performance requirements.
- Clear guidelines should be established regarding how your assessment results will be used and how they will not be used.
- There should be an ongoing evaluation of your assessment system itself to improve the connection between assessment and student success. Success factors should be developed on an ongoing basis based on external requirements such as those derived from your markets and from other organizations.

Assessment is central to the achievement of excellence. A sound assessment strategy provides the factual basis for improvement so decisions are not based on intuition or opinion. They may include the following: alignment between the organization's mission and goals and what is being assessed; a focus on improvement, not the status quo of student performance, faculty capabilities, and educational program performance; prompt feedback and ongoing assessment; a curriculum-based and criteria-referenced strategy; clear guidelines of how assessment results will and will not be used; and an ongoing evaluation and improvement cycle for the assessment system.

Primary Focus on Teaching and Learning

Although the Education Criteria framework is intended to address all organizational requirements, including research and service, primary emphasis is placed on teaching and learning. This is done for three main reasons:

1. Teaching and learning are the principal goals of education organizations. Thus, sharing successful teaching and learning strategies and methods would have the greatest impact on improving the nation's education organizations.

2. Those who encouraged the creation of a Baldrige Award category for education cited improvement in teaching and learning as their primary or only rationale for such an award.

3. Only a small percentage of education organizations engage in research. Peer review systems exist to evaluate research. Funding organizations and businesses provide avenues to channel the directions of much research. Numerous excellent forums and media already exist for sharing research results. Much of the research performed in education organizations involves students as part of their own overall education. Thus, the educational role of research is incorporated in the Education Criteria as part of teaching and learning. Other important aspects of research—faculty development and student/faculty recruitment—are also addressed in the criteria.

The criteria are intended to address all organizational requirements, including those mainly focused on research and service. The primary emphasis is on teaching and learning. The criteria are intended to have the greatest possible impact on educational system improvement, and the percentage of schools that engage in research is small compared to teaching and learning institutions.

Schools that have research, service, and/or other scholarships as part of their core missions must ensure these activities achieve optimum performance. In other words, if research, for example, is critical to organization success (as at a research university), the effective design and execution of research must be a part of the core operations, evaluated, and continually improved. This activity would not be required of organizations for which research is not critical to organization success.

Performance Excellence for Education Criteria Framework

Organizations must position themselves to respond well to the environment within which they compete. They must understand and manage threats and vulnerabilities as well as capitalize on their strengths and opportunities, including the vulnerabilities of competitors. These factors guide strategy development, support operational decisions, and align measures and actions—all of which must be done well for the organization to succeed. Consistent with this overarching purpose, the award criteria contain the following basic elements: Driver Triad, Work Core, Brain Center, and Outcomes. (See Figure 2).

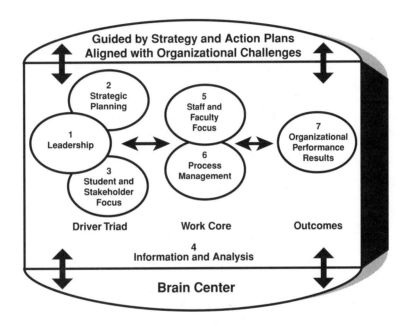

Figure 2

Strategy and Action Plans

Strategy and action plans are the set of student- and stakeholder-focused organization-level requirements, derived from short- and long-term strategic planning, that must be done well for the organization's strategy to succeed. Strategy and action plans set the context for action in high-performing organizations, drive the alignment of measures for all work units, guide overall resource decisions, and provide the vehicle through which leaders drive the organization to ensure student and stakeholder satisfaction and overall success.

The Driver Triad

The Driver Triad (Figure 3) consists of the categories of Leadership, Strategic Planning, and Student and Stakeholder Focus. Leaders use these processes to set direction and goals, monitor progress, make resource decisions, and take corrective action when progress does not proceed according to plan. The processes that make up the Driver Triad require leaders to set direction and expectations for the organization to meet student, stakeholder, and market requirements, and fully empower faculty and staff (Category 1); provide the vehicle for determining the short- and long-term strategies for success, as well as communicating and aligning the organization's work (Category 2); and produce information about critical student and stakeholder requirements and levels of satisfaction, and strengthen student and stakeholder relationships and satisfaction (Category 3).

Figure 3

The Work Core

The *Work Core* (Figure 4) describes the processes through which the primary work of the organization takes place and consists of Staff and Faculty Focus (Category 5) and Process Management (Category 6). These categories recognize that the people of an educational organization are responsible for doing the work. To achieve performance excellence, these people need to possess the right skills and must be allowed to work in an environment that promotes initiative and self-direction. The work processes provide the structure for continuous learning and improvement to optimize performance.

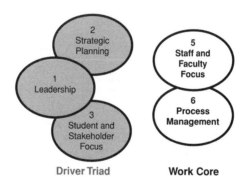

Figure 4

Outcomes

Outcomes (Figure 5) are comprised of the Organizational Performance Results, and are a composite of student performance results; student and stakeholder satisfaction; faculty partnerships and internal operating effectiveness; and include such measures as productivity and operational effectiveness; innovations; research; and safety, legal, and regulatory compliance.

The processes defined by the Driver Triad, Work Core, and Brain Center produce the Organizational Performance Results, which reflect the organization's actual performance and serve as the basis for leaders to monitor progress against goals and make adjustments to increase performance.

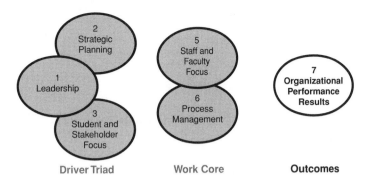

Figure 5

Information and Analysis

The foundation for the entire management system is Information and Analysis (Category 4). Information and Analysis (Figure 6) processes capture, store, analyze, and retrieve information and data critical to the effective management of the organization and to a fact-based system for improving organization performance and competitiveness. Rapid access and reliable data and information systems are especially critical to enhance effective decision making in an increasingly complex and fast-paced, competitive environment.

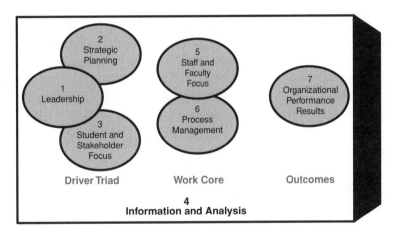

Figure 6

Information and analysis is also called the *Brain Center* (Figure 7) of an effective management system.

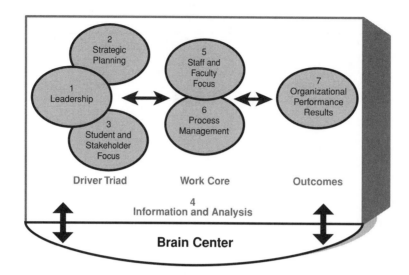

Figure 7

Organizations develop effective strategic plans to help set the direction necessary to achieve future success. Unfortunately, these plans are not always communicated and used to drive actions. The planning process and the resulting strategy are virtually worthless if the organization does not use the plan and strategy to guide decision making at all levels of the organization (Figure 8). When decisions are not guided by strategy, supervisors, administrators, and faculty and staff tend to substitute their own ideas for the correct direction. This frequently causes teams and individuals to work at cross-purposes, suboptimizing performance and making it more difficult for the organization to achieve desired results.

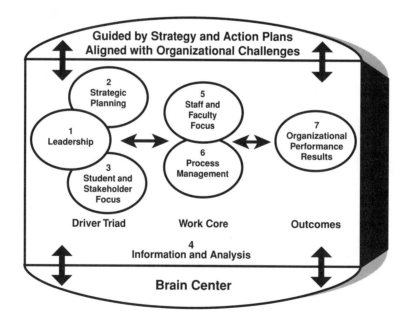

Figure 8

Taken together, these processes define the essential ingredients of a complex, integrated management system designed to promote and deliver performance excellence. If any part of the system is missing, the performance results suffer. If fully implemented, these processes are sufficient to enable organizations to achieve winning performance.

Award Criteria Organization

The seven criteria Categories are subdivided into Items and Areas to Address. Figure 9 demonstrates the organization of Category 1.

Items

There are 19 Items, each focusing on a major requirement. Item titles and point values are listed on page 64.

Areas to Address

Items consist of one or more Areas to Address. Information for assessment is prepared in response to the specific requirements of these areas. There are 30 Areas to Address.

Subparts

There are 88 subparts in 2001. Areas consist of one or more subparts where numbers are shown in parentheses. A response should be made to each subpart.

Notes

In 2001, there are 74 notes. Notes provide a better explanation of the Item requirements and identify some of the more obvious linkages. *Notes do not add requirements.* Do not interpret the explanations in the notes as if they were criteria requirements.

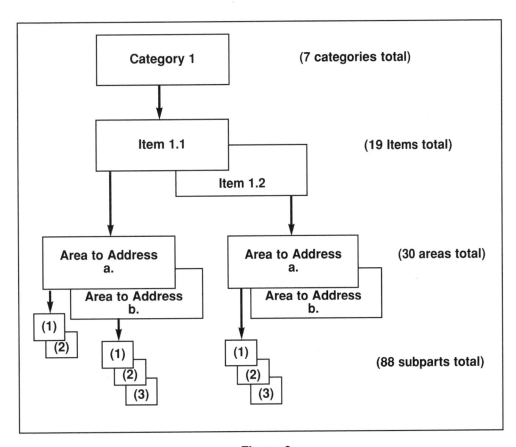

Figure 9

Baldrige Education Criteria Categories and Point Values

P Preface: Organizational Profile

P.1 Organizational Description

P.2 Organizational Challenges

Examination Categories/Items	Maximum Points
1 Leadership (120 points)	
1.1 Organizational Leadership	80
1.2 Public Responsibility and Citizenship	40
2 Strategic Planning (85 points)	
2.1 Strategy Development	40
2.2 Strategy Deployment	45
3 Student, Stakeholder, Market Focus (85 points)	
3.1 Knowledge of Student, Stakeholder, and Market Needs and Expectations	40
3.2 Student and Stakeholder Relationships and Satisfaction	45
4 Information and Analysis (90 points)	
4.1 Measurement and Analysis of Organizational Performance	50
4.2 Information Management	40
5 Faculty and Staff Focus (85 points)	
5.1 Work Systems	35
5.2 Faculty and Staff Education, Training, and Development	25
5.3 Faculty and Staff Well-Being and Satisfaction	25
6 Process Management (85 points)	
6.1 Education Design and Delivery Processes	50
6.2 Student Services	20
6.3 Support Processes	15
7 Organizational Performance Results (450 points)	
7.1 Student Learning Results	200
7.2 Student- and Stakeholder-Focused Results	70
7.3 Budgetary, Financial, and Market Results	40
7.4 Faculty and Staff Results	70
7.5 Organizational Effectiveness Results	70
Total Points	**1000**

Changes From the 2000 Education Criteria for Performance Excellence

The Education Criteria for Performance Excellence, like their health care and business counterparts, evolved with changing performance requirements. For 2001, there are a number of key changes in the Education Criteria, intended to improve their usefulness in organizational self-assessment and learning, and for national role model determination in the award process. In addition, the 2001 Education Criteria are brought into closer alignment with the Business Criteria (2001 Criteria for Performance Excellence), and the 2001 Health Care Criteria, thus enabling better communication and cooperation among education and health care organizations and businesses—a major goal of the Baldrige National Quality Program.

The 2001 changes reflect the increasing importance of electronic communication and the use of Internet-based learning and offerings. The criteria continue to emphasize the role of data, information, and knowledge management in improving performance.

The Organizational Profile (new in 2001), the criteria Items, and the Scoring Guidelines are aligned so that the educational service needs (doing the right things) and ongoing improvement of key processes (doing things better) are both addressed in the assessment.

The most significant changes in the Education Criteria are summarized as follows:

- The number of Areas to Address has been increased from 27 to 30.
- A new Preface, entitled Organizational Profile, replaces the Organization Overview from the 2000 Education Criteria. Its placement at the front of the criteria sets your organizational context for responding to the criteria Items.
- The Glossary of Key Terms continues to be revised and expanded.
- Category 4, Information and Analysis, now includes an Item on information management. The category has been rewritten to recognize the growing importance of the Internet and electronic communication and your dependence on reliable information from these communication vehicles.
- Category 6, Process Management, now specifically addresses all aspects of your organization's process management, including learning-focused education design and delivery, key student services, and support processes.

There have been some changes in all criteria Items; the most significant changes are highlighted and discussed below.

Preface: Organizational Profile

- This new section, to be completed before addressing the criteria Items, sets a basis for your Baldrige assessment. It is written in the same question format as the criteria Items.
- The Organizational Profile is the starting point for self-assessment and for writing an application. It also may be used by itself for an initial self-assessment; if you identify topics for which conflicting, little, or no information is available, it is possible that your assessment need go no further and you can use these topics for action planning.

Category 1: Leadership

- Item 1.1, Organizational Leadership, has been modified to better emphasize the senior leaders' role in creating and setting the current and future environment and in reviewing organizational performance.

Category 2: Strategic Planning

- You now are asked to respond in terms of your short- and longer-term planning time horizons, recognizing that these horizons differ among various education organizations.

- In Item 2.1, Strategy Development, you now are asked how your strategic objectives align with challenges identified in your Organizational Profile.

Category 3: Student, Stakeholder, and Market Focus

- In Item 3.1, now Knowledge of Student, Stakeholder, and Market Needs and Expectations, you are asked to address requirements, expectations, and preferences in the markets your educational programs will address.
- Item 3.2, now Student and Stakeholder Relationships and Satisfaction, places greater emphasis on the key aspects of relationship building: attracting and retaining students, satisfying students and stakeholders, enhancing student learning, and developing new educational services.

Category 4: Information and Analysis

- Item 4.1, now Measurement and Analysis of Organizational Performance, combines Items 4.1 and 4.2 from the 2000 Criteria. This Item continues to stress measuring, analyzing, aligning, and improving performance throughout the organization.
- Item 4.2, Information Management, is a new Item addressing the availability, quality, and accessibility of data and the quality of software and hardware.

Category 5: Faculty and Staff Focus

- Item 5.1, Work Systems, now includes succession planning and a stronger focus on organizing and managing for improved cooperation, communication, and knowledge sharing.

Category 6: Process Management

- Item 6.1, now Education Design and Delivery Processes, allows organizations for which research and outreach are core aspects of their mission to address these elements.
- Item 6.2, Student Services, is a new Item that asks you to identify and describe your key student services that lead to student success. This Item has been created by combining elements of Items 6.2 and 6.3 from the 2000 Education Criteria that emphasized student-focused services.
- Item 6.3, now Support Processes, is based on portions of Item 6.2, Education Support Processes, in 2000. It asks you to identify and describe your key processes that support daily operations and faculty and staff in delivering educational programs and offerings and student services.
- Item 6.3 from the 2000 Criteria, Partnering Processes, has been discontinued, allowing each organization to address partners as appropriate to its operations.
- Partnerships with other education organizations to facilitate transitions into or out of your school may be addressed in Item 3.2. For some education organizations, partnering is an aspect of student services and, therefore, needs to be included in Item 6.2.

Category 7: Organizational Performance Results

- Item 7.1, now Student Learning Results, has been renamed to emphasize the core mission and focus on learning in education organizations.
- Item 7.3, now Budgetary, Financial, and Market Results, has been expanded to include "market" in recognition of the changing education environment. Education organizations must remain aware of how changing and emerging markets contribute to budgetary and financial results.
- Item 7.5 now has two Areas to Address—7.5a (Organizational Effectiveness Results) and 7.5b (Public Responsibility and Citizenship Results)—to better differentiate the results for organizational effectiveness. If research and outreach processes are a part of your mission, results should be reported in 7.5a.

Scoring Guidelines

Descriptors for the Approach-Deployment scoring ranges have been modified to highlight the importance of addressing evaluation and improvement, as well as changing educational service needs.

P Preface: Organizational Profile

The Organizational Profile is a snapshot of your organization, the key influences on how you operate, and the key challenges you face.

The Organizational Profile

This new section is the starting point for self-assessment and for completing a written narrative. It will help identify gaps in key information. It focuses on key performance requirements and results. It will be used by examiners and judges in every stage of application review for the Baldrige Award, including the site visit. The profile may also be used for an initial self-assessment. If topics are identified in the profile for which information is conflicting, not available, or limited, these topics may be used for action planning as a first step in performance improvement.

The profile is limited to five pages for Baldrige Award applicants. These five pages are not counted in the overall application page limit of 50 pages.

P.1 Organizational Description

Describe your organization's environment and your key relationships with students, stakeholders, suppliers, and other partners.

Within your response, include answers to the following questions:

a. Organizational Environment

(1) What are your organization's main educational programs and/or services? Include a description of how they are delivered to students.

(2) What is your organizational context/culture? Include your purpose, vision, mission, and values, as appropriate.

(3) What is your faculty and staff profile? Include education levels, workforce and job diversity, bargaining units, use of contract employees, and special safety requirements, as appropriate.

(4) What are your major technologies, equipment, and facilities?

(5) What is the legal/regulatory environment under which your organization operates? Include mandated standards, curricula, programs, and assessments; occupational health and safety regulations; accreditation requirements; and environmental and financial regulations. Also include district boundaries and service offering restrictions, as appropriate.

b. Organizational Relationships

(1) What are your key student and stakeholder groups and/or market segments? What are their key requirements for your programs and services? Include how these requirements differ among student and stakeholder groups and/or market segments, as appropriate.

(2) What are your key supplier and partnering relationships and communication mechanisms?

Notes:

N1. Student and stakeholder groups and market segment requirements (P.1b[1]) might include special accommodation, customized curricula, reduced class size, customized degree requirements, student advising, and electronic communication.

N2. Communication mechanisms (P.1b[2]) should be two-way and might be in person, electronic, by telephone, and/or written. For many organizations, these mechanisms might be changing.

P.1 Organizational Description Item Linkages

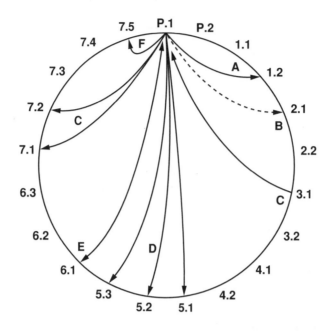

Nature of Relationship

A   The legal/regulatory environment described in P.1a(5) sets the context for the review of the management systems for public responsibility citizenship [1.2a(1)].

B   Faculty and staff educational levels, diversity, and other characteristics [P.1a(3)] may affect the determination of faculty and staff strengths and weaknesses as a part of the strategic planning process [2.1a(2)].

C   The student, stakeholder, and market groups reported in P.1b(1) were determined using the processes described in 3.1a(1 and 2). The information in P.1b(1) helps examiners identify the kind of achievement and satisfaction results, broken out by student, stakeholder, and market segment, that should be reported in Items 7.1 and 7.2.

D   Faculty and staff characteristics [P1a(3)] such as educational levels, workforce and job diversity, the existence of bargaining units, the use of contract faculty and staff, and other special requirements help set the context for determining the requirements for knowledge and skill sharing across work units, jobs, and locations [5.1a(1)]; determining appropriate training needs by faculty and staff segment [5.2a(1)]; and tailoring benefits, services, and satisfaction assessment methods according to various types and categories of faculty and staff [5.3b(1, 2, 3)].

E   The information in P.1a(1) derives from the delivery processes described in 6.1a and helps set the context for the design and examiner review of those processes [6.1b(1)].

F   The regulatory requirements described in P.1a(5), and the key suppliers and dealers listed in P.1b(2) create an expectation that related performance results will be reported in 7.5b and 7.5a respectively.

P.2 Organizational Challenges

Describe your organization's competitive environment, your key strategic challenges, and your system for performance improvement.

Within your response, include answers to the following questions:

a. Competitive Environment

(1) What is your competitive position? Include your relative size and growth in the education sector and the number and types of your competitors.

(2) What are the principal factors that determine your success relative to the success of your competitors and other organizations delivering similar services? Include any changes taking place that affect your competitive situation.

b. Strategic Challenges

What are your key strategic challenges? Include education and learning, operational, human resource, and community challenges, as appropriate.

c. Performance Improvement System

How do you maintain an organizational focus on performance improvement? Include your approach to systematic evaluation and improvement of key processes and to fostering organizational learning and knowledge sharing.

Notes:

N1. Factors (P.2a[2]) might include differentiators such as program leadership, services, e-services, geographic proximity, and program options.

N2. Challenges (P.2b) might include electronic communication with key stakeholders, reduced educational program introduction cycle times, student transitions, entry into new markets or segments, changing demographics and competition, student persistence, and faculty/staff retention.

N3. Performance improvement (P.2c) is an assessment dimension used in the Scoring System to evaluate the maturity of organizational approaches and deployment. This question is intended to help you and the Baldrige Examiners set a context for your approach to performance improvement.

P.2 Organizational Challenges Item Linkages

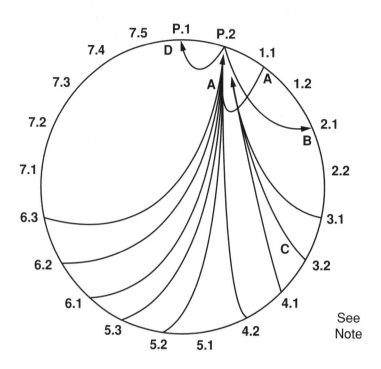

Nature of Relationship

A   Leaders [1.1a(2)] are responsible for creating an environment that drives organizational learning, which in turn contributes to the overall focus on performance improvement [P.2c]. The overall approaches to systematic evaluation and improvement, organizational learning, and knowledge sharing identified in P.2c should be consistent with overall requirements for improvement specifically required in Items 1.1b(3) leadership effectiveness; 3.1a(2) student and stakeholder requirements definition; 3.2a(4) building relationships and providing easy student/stakeholder access; 3.2b determining student/stakeholder satisfaction; 4.1a(3) and 4.1b(4) producing analyses to support continuous and breakthrough performance improvements; 4.2a(3) keeping data availability current, especially in a volatile work environment; 4.2b(2) keeping software and hardware current; 5.2 training and education effectiveness; 5.3a improving workforce health, safety, and well-being; 6.1a(6) transfer of learning; 6.1b(5) improve programs and delivery processes; 6.2a(5) improve student services; and 6.3b(7) improve support services.

B   The competitive environment defined in P.2a should be examined as part of the strategy development process [2.1a(2)].

C   Information about competitors, which is needed to create the description for P.2a, uses processes discussed in Items 3.1a(1), 3.2b(3), and 4.1a(3).

D   Progress in achieving strategic challenges, as described in P.2b, should be reported in Item 7.5a(2). In addition, the strategic challenges identified in P.2b should be consistent with the strategic objectives in 2.1b(1).

1 Leadership—120 Points

The Leadership Category examines how your organization's senior leaders address your organizational values, directions, and performance expectations, as well as a focus on students and stakeholders, student learning, empowerment, innovation, and organizational learning. Also examined is how your organization addresses its responsibilities to the public and supports its key communities.

The leadership system is responsible to promote core values; set high-performance expectations; and promote an organizationwide focus on students and stakeholders, student learning, empowerment, organizational learning, and innovation. The Leadership Category looks at how senior leaders guide the organization in setting directions for today and into the future. They also need to review organizational performance. Senior leaders need to communicate clear values and high-performance expectations that address the needs of all students and stakeholders. The category also looks at the how the organization meets its responsibilities to the public and how it practices good citizenship.

The category is broken into two Items.

Organizational Leadership

- Communicating and reinforcing clear values, short- and longer-term directions, performance expectations, and a focus on student learning and development.
- Reinforcing an environment for ethical values and equity for students; empowerment and innovation and faculty/staff and organizational learning.
- Reviewing organizational performance and capabilities, organizational health, and progress relative to goals, and setting priorities for improvement.
- Evaluating and improving the effectiveness of senior leadership and management throughout the organization, including faculty and staff input in the process.

Public Responsibility and Citizenship

- For regulatory and other legal requirements in areas such as safety and accreditation; anticipating public concerns and addressing risks to the public; ensuring ethical practices in all student and stakeholder interactions.
- For strengthening and supporting key communities.

1.1 Organizational Leadership (80 Points)
Approach/Deployment Scoring

Describe how senior leaders guide your organization and review organizational performance.

Within your response, include answers to the following questions:

a. Senior Leadership Direction

(1) How do senior leaders set and deploy your organizational values, short- and longer-term directions, and performance expectations, including a focus on creating and balancing value for students and stakeholders? Include how senior leaders communicate values, directions, and expectations through your leadership system and to all faculty and staff.

(2) How do senior leaders create an environment that promotes ethical values, equity for all students, empowerment, innovation, safety, organizational agility, and organizational and faculty/staff learning?

b. Organizational Performance Review

(1) How do senior leaders review organizational performance and capabilities to assess organizational success; performance relative to competitors, comparable schools, and/or other appropriately selected organizations; progress relative to short- and longer-term goals, including student achievement goals; and the ability to address changing organizational needs? Include the key performance measures regularly reviewed by your senior leaders. Also, include your key recent performance review findings.

(2) How are organizational performance review findings translated into priorities for improvement and opportunities for innovation? How are they deployed throughout your organization and, as appropriate, to your feeder and/or receiving schools and suppliers/partners to ensure organizational alignment?

(3) How do senior leaders use organizational performance review findings to improve both their own leadership effectiveness and your leadership system?

Notes:

N1.   The term *organization*, as used in the criteria, refers to the unit being assessed. The unit might be a school, a school district, a post-secondary institution, or a major academic unit within a college or university.

N2.   The term *stakeholder*, as used in the criteria, might include faculty, staff, parents, parent organizations, social service organizations, boards, alumni, businesses, and local/professional communities.

N3.   The term *supplier/partners*, as used in the criteria, refers to those who provide student services such as social services, before-/after-school day care, external bookstores, and transportation; partners such as future employers of students; and suppliers of goods for operations such as computing, photocopying, and grounds maintenance.

N4.   Organizational directions (1.1a[1]) relate to strategic objectives and action plans described in Items 2.1 and 2.2.

N5.   Senior leaders' organizational performance reviews (1.1b) should be informed by organizational performance analyses described in 4.1b and strategic objectives and action plans described in Items 2.1 and 2.2.

N6.   Leadership effectiveness improvement (1.1b[3]) should be supported by formal and/or informal faculty and staff feedback/surveys.

N7.   Your organizational performance results should be reported in Items 7.1, 7.2, 7.3, 7.4, and 7.5.

The first part of this Item [1.1a] looks at how senior leaders create and sustain mission and core values that promote high performance throughout the organization. In promoting high performance, leaders develop and implement systems to ensure values are understood and consistently followed. An organization's failure to achieve high levels of performance can usually be traced to a failure in leadership:

- To consistently promote high performance, leaders clearly set direction and make sure everyone in the organization understands their responsibilities. Success requires a strong future orientation and a commitment to improvement and the disciplined change that is needed to carry it out. This requires creating an environment for learning and innovation, as well as the means for rapid and effective application of knowledge.

- Leaders also ensure that organizational values actually guide the behavior of administrators, faculty, and staff throughout the organization or the values are meaningless. To enhance Performance Excellence, the "right" values need to be adopted. These values include a focus on students and other stakeholders. The failure to ensure a student and stakeholder focus usually causes the organization and its faculty and staff to focus internally. The lack of a student and stakeholder focus forces faculty and staff to default to their own ideas of what students and stakeholders really "need." This increases the risk of becoming arrogant and not caring about the requirements of students and stakeholders. It also increases the potential for creating educational services that no one wants or values. That, in turn, increases failure, rework, waste, and added cost/lower value.

- In addition, it is the responsibility of top leadership to create an environment that fully engages students and promotes faculty and staff innovation, learning, and knowledge sharing.

The second part of this Item [1.1b] looks at how senior leaders review organizational performance in a disciplined, fact-based manner. This organizational review should cover all areas of performance and provide a complete and accurate picture of the "state of health" of the organization. This includes not only how well the organization is currently performing, but also how well it is moving to secure future success:

- Key performance measures focus on and reflect the key drivers of success leaders regularly review. These measures relate to the strategic objectives necessary for success.

- Leaders use these reviews to drive improvement and change. These reviews provide a reliable means to guide the improvement and change needed to achieve the organization's key objectives.

- Leaders create a consistent process to translate the review findings into an action agenda sufficiently specific for deployment throughout the organization and to partners and key stakeholders as appropriate.

- In addition, leaders at all levels must evaluate their personal effectiveness. To ensure the evaluation is accurate, faculty and staff provide feedback to the leaders.

- Finally, leaders at all levels need to take action, based on the feedback, to improve their effectiveness.

1.1 Organizational Leadership

How senior leaders guide the organization in setting direction and developing and sustaining an effective leadership system throughout the organization.

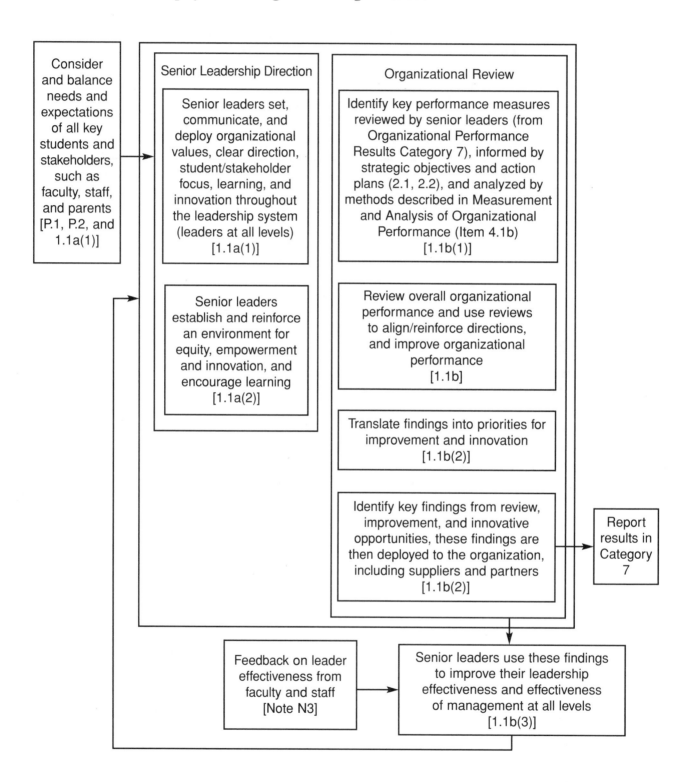

1.1 Organizational Leadership Item Linkages

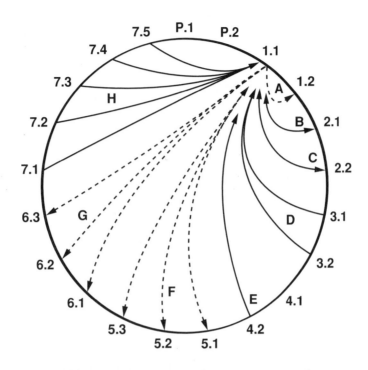

Nature of Relationship

A   Leaders [1.1], in support of organizational values, role model and support responsibility [1.2a] and practice good citizenship [1.2b].

B   To effectively set organizational direction and expectations, leaders [1.1a(1)] participate in the strategic planning process [2.1]. As a part of this effort, leaders [1.1a(1)] ensure strategic objectives balance the needs of key students/stakeholders [2.1b(2)]. Leaders also use the timelines for achieving strategic objectives [2.1b(1)] as a basis for defining and monitoring expected progress closely [1.1b(1)].

C   Leaders [(1.1a(1)] ensure that plans are clearly communicated and understood (deployed) at all levels throughout the organization and used to align work [2.2a(1)]. Leaders [1.1a] also approve the overall goals set forth in the plan based, in part, on information about the expected levels of competitor performance [2.2b].

D   Leaders [1.1a(1)] use information from students and stakeholders about requirements and preferences [3.1a] and satisfaction/dissatisfaction [3.2] to set direction and create opportunity for the organization. Leaders [1.1] also have a responsibility for personally building relationships with key students and stakeholders [3.2a] (creating a bi-directional relationship).

E   Leaders [1.1b(1)] use analyses of data [4.1b(1 and 3)] to monitor organizational performance and understand relationships among performance; faculty and staff satisfaction; and student, stakeholder, markets, and financial success. These analyses are also used for decision making at all levels to set priorities for action and allocate resources for maximum advantage [1.1b(2)]. They are also responsible for using comparative data [from 4.1a(3)] to set meaningful goals to achieve organizational success.

F   Leaders [1.1a(2)] create an environment for faculty and staff empowerment, innovation, and learning throughout the entire organization through the design of work and jobs [5.1a(1)]. They ensure that the compensation and recognition system [5.1a(3)] encourages faculty and staff at all levels to achieve performance excellence in areas most critical to the organization. Leaders [1.1a(2)] are also responsible for supporting appropriate skill development of all faculty and staff through training and development systems and reinforcing learning on the job [5.2a], as well as creating effective systems to enhance faculty and staff satisfaction, well-being, and motivation [5.3].

G   Leaders [1.1] are responsible for creating an environment that supports high performance, including monitoring processes for design and delivery [6.1], student services [6.2], and support services [6.3] processes. Leaders must ensure that design, delivery, support, and supplier performance processes are aligned and consistently evaluated and refined.

H   Senior leaders [1.1b] use performance results data [from Category 7] for many activities, including monitoring organizational performance [1.1b(1)]; deploying review findings to focus work and ensure alignment [1.1b(2)]; strategic planning [2.1a]; setting goals and priorities [2.1b(1)]; reinforcing or rewarding faculty and staff performance [5.1a(3)]; and for improving their effectiveness and the effectiveness of leaders at all levels [1.1b(3)].

1.1 Organizational Leadership
Sample Effective Practices for Senior Leaders

There are several effective practices that focused on organizational performance review (1.1b) and leadership development with the aim of improving student learning. One such program, the principal's executive program, is operating at the Center for Leadership Development in North Carolina. This program is modeled after Harvard University's leadership program for business executives. (For information contact Ken Jenkins, Principal's Executive Program, Center for Leadership Development, University of North Carolina, CB 3335, D-3 Carr Mill, Chapel Hill, NC 27599 or at www.ga.unc.edu/pep.)

Another program focused on assessing organizational success for school-level leaders has been organized by the Council of Chief State School Officers in partnership with the National Policy Board for Educational Administration, ISLLC. They have developed standards for school leaders, and their goal is to raise the bar for school leaders through model standards and assessments. (For more information contact Amy Mast, Interstate School Leaders Licensure Consortium, Council of State Chief School Officers, One Massachusetts Avenue, N.W. Suite 700, Washington, D.C. 20001-1431 or at amym@ccsso.org, www.ccsso.org.) Following are sample effective practices:

*   The CEO of a major university and his direct reports take new faculty on a bus tour of the state in the summer preceding their first year of appointment. This allows senior leaders to communicate core values to new faculty. At the same time, it communicates the university's interest in state students and stakeholders.
*   All senior leaders are personally involved in performance improvement.
*   Senior leaders spend a significant portion of their time on performance improvement activities.
*   Senior leaders carry out many visible activities, such as goal setting, planning, and recognition and reward of performance and education process improvement.
*   Senior leaders regularly communicate values to leaders and administrators and ensure that they demonstrate those values in their work.
*   Senior leaders participate on performance improvement teams and use tools and practices to enhance performance.
*   Senior leaders spend time with students and stakeholders, seeking input about strengths and opportunities for improvement.
*   Senior leaders mentor faculty and staff and ensure that promotion criteria reflect organizational values.
*   Senior leaders study and learn about the improvement practices of other organizations.
*   Senior leaders clearly and consistently articulate values, such as student and stakeholder focus, student and stakeholder satisfaction, role model leadership, continuous improvement, faculty and staff involvement, and performance optimization throughout the organization.
*   Senior leaders base their decisions on reliable data and facts pertaining to students and stakeholders, teaching and learning processes, and faculty and staff performance and satisfaction.
*   Senior leaders ensure that organizational values are used to provide direction to all students, faculty, and staff in the organization to help achieve the mission, vision, and performance goals.

- Senior leaders hold regular meetings to review performance data and use two-way communication for problems, successes, and effective approaches to improve work.
- Senior leaders use effective and innovative approaches to reach out to all faculty and staff to spread the organization's values and align its work to support organizational goals.
- Senior leaders effectively surface problems and encourage faculty and staff creativity.
- Senior leaders conduct monthly reviews of organizational performance. This requires that organization leaders and department chairs conduct biweekly reviews and that faculty and staff and teams provide daily performance updates. Corrective actions are developed to improve performance that deviates from planned performance.
- Roles and responsibilities of leaders are clearly defined, understood by them, and used to judge their performance.
- Leaders and administrators "walk the walk," serving as role models in leading systematic performance improvement.
- Job definitions with performance indices are clearly delineated for each level of the organization, objectively measured, and presented in a logical and organized structure.
- Many different communication strategies are used to reinforce high-performance values.
- Leader behavior (not merely words) clearly communicates what is expected of the organization and its faculty and staff.
- Systems and procedures are deployed that encourage cooperation and a cross-functional approach to administration, team activities, and problem solving.
- Leaders monitor faculty and staff acceptance and adoption of vision and values using annual surveys, focus groups, and e-mail questions.
- Reviews against measurable performance standards are held frequently.
- Actions are taken to assist units that are not meeting goals or performing to plan.
- A systematic process is in place for evaluating and improving the integration or alignment of Performance Excellence values throughout the organization.
- Senior leaders systematically and routinely check the effectiveness of their leadership activities (for example, seeking annual feedback from faculty, staff, students, and peers in an upward evaluation, and taking steps to improve).
- Leaders at all levels determine how well they carried out their activities (what went right or wrong and what could be done better).
- There is evidence of changes made to improve leader effectiveness.
- Priorities for organizational improvement are driven by student performance, faculty, and staff results; stakeholder and student satisfaction; and other results key to the organization's mission.

1.1 Organizational Leadership
Sample Effective Practices for Teaching Faculty:
Leaders of the Classroom Learning System

- Teachers involve students in creating mission, vision statements, and values for classes, and these are posted prominently. This involves and engages students in their studies and contributes to a feeling of ownership to their school.
- Teachers role model fact-based decision making using data and performance tools.
- The management of classrooms is based on the Baldrige values.
- Continuous improvement is encouraged by seeking routine feedback from students about teaching strengths and opportunities for improvement. On a daily basis, students develop a list of strengths and opportunities for improvement to be acted upon and to drive classroom (or team) process improvements. These are frequently called +/delta comments.

- There are clear behavioral metrics (rubrics) and nearly immediate feedback to enable all students to monitor their own academic, social, and personal performance.

- Teachers provide students with endless examples of continuous improvement in classroom management and teaching. They use tests as tools to provide feedback, to sharpen instruction, and to enhance learning—not to limit progress, rank performance, or punish.

- Progress toward goals is tied to the organization's overall goals. These are displayed and communicated to students and parents through parent visitation days, assemblies, newsletters, posters, and so on.

1.2 Public Responsibility and Citizenship (40 Points)
Approach/Deployment Scoring

Describe how your organization addresses its responsibilities to the public and practices good citizenship.

Within your response, include answers to the following questions:

a. Responsibilities to the Public

(1) How do you address the impacts on society of your operations? Include your key processes, measures, and targets for safety, regulatory, accreditation, and legal requirements and for addressing risks associated with your operations.

(2) How do you anticipate public concerns with current and future services and operations? How do you prepare for these concerns in a proactive manner?

(3) How do you accomplish ethical practices in all transactions and interactions with students and stakeholders?

b. Support of Key Communities

How do your organization, your senior leaders, your faculty and staff, and students actively support and strengthen your key communities? Include how you identify key communities and determine areas of emphasis for organizational involvement and support. Include how community involvement reflects your organization's mission and/or values.

Notes:

N1. Public responsibilities in areas critical to your organization also should be addressed in Strategy Development (Item 2.1) and/or in Process Management (Category 6). Key results, such as results of regulatory, legal, and accreditation compliance, should be reported as Organizational Effectiveness Results (Item 7.5).

N2. Areas of community support appropriate for inclusion in 1.2b might include your efforts to strengthen local community services, community education, the environment, and practices of professional associations.

N3. Health and safety of faculty and staff are not addressed in Item 1.2; you should address these factors in Item 5.3.

This Item looks at how the organization fulfills its public responsibilities and encourages, supports, and practices good citizenship.

The first part of this Item [1.2a] looks at how the organization addresses current and future impacts on society in a proactive manner and how it ensures ethical business practices in all student and stakeholder interactions. The practices are expected to cover all relevant and important areas—educational organizations, services, and operations:

- An integral part of performance management and improvement is proactively addressing legal, accreditation, and regulatory requirements and risk factors. Addressing these areas requires establishing appropriate measures and/or indicators that senior leaders track in their overall performance review. The organization should be sensitive to issues of public concern, whether or not these issues are currently embodied in law. The failure to address these areas can expose the organization to future problems when it least expects them. Problems can range from a sudden decline in public confidence to extensive and costly litigation. In this regard, it is important to anticipate potential problems the public may have with both current and future educational services. Sometimes a well-intended program or service could create adverse public consequences.

- Good public responsibility implies going beyond minimum compliance with laws and regulations. Top-performing organizations frequently serve as role models of responsibility and provide leadership in areas key to academic success. For example, a university office might develop an innovative and award-winning educational program to teach protection of the environment and pollution reduction.

- Ensuring ethical practices are followed by all faculty and staff lessens the organization's risk of adverse public reaction, as well as prosecution. Programs to ensure ethical practices typically seek to prevent activities that might be perceived as negligent. Examples of unethical practices might include falsifying expense reports or research, or seeking gains from assigning grades.

The second part of this Item [1.2b] looks at how the organization, its senior leaders, and its faculty and staff identify, support, and strengthen key communities as part of good citizenship practices:

- Good citizenship practices typically vary according to the size, complexity, and location of the organization. Larger organizations are generally expected to have a more comprehensive approach to citizenship than small organizations.

- Examples of organizational community involvement include partnering with businesses and health care providers to improve health education in the local community by providing education and volunteer services to address public health issues; and partnering to influence community and business associations to engage in beneficial, cooperative activities, such as sharing best practices to improve overall U.S. global competitiveness and the environment.

- In addition to activities directly carried out by the organization, opportunities to practice good citizenship include faculty and staff community service that is encouraged and supported by the organization. Frequently, the organization's leaders actively participate on community boards and actively support their work.

1.2 Public Responsibility and Citizenship

How the organization addresses public responsibilities and practices good citizenship.

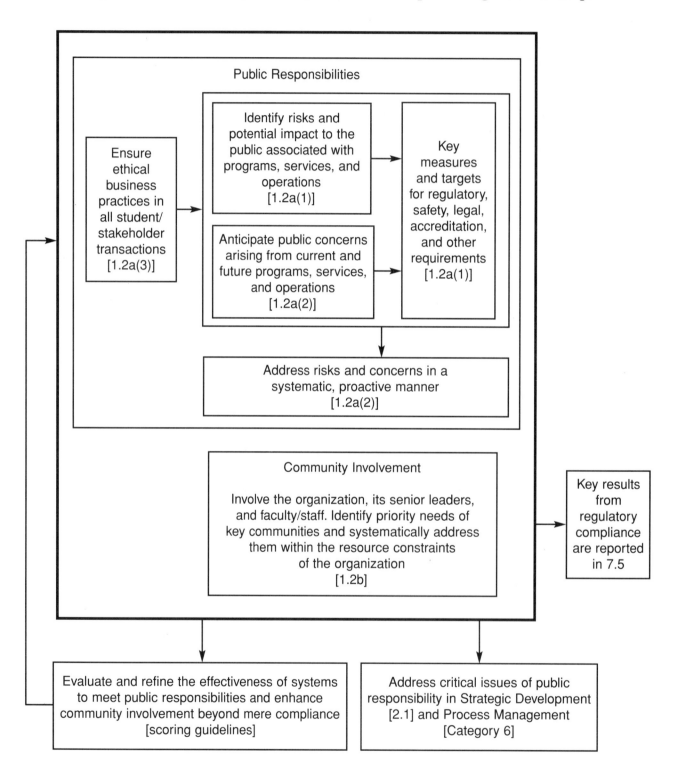

1.2 Public Responsibility and Citizenship Item Linkages

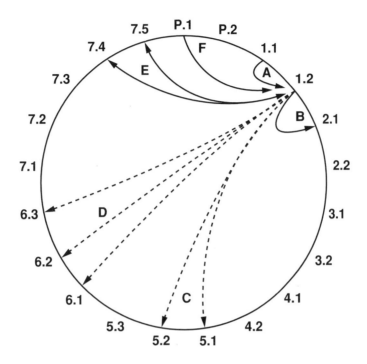

Nature of Relationship

A   Leaders, in support of organizational values [1.1a], have a responsibility for setting policies and ensuring that practices and products of the organization and its faculty and staff do not adversely impact society or violate ethical standards, regulations, or law [1.2a]. They are also responsible to be personally involved and to ensure that the organization and its faculty and staff strengthen key communities in areas such as local community services, education, the environment, and professional associations [1.2b].

B   Safety, regulatory, accreditation, and legal concerns [1.2a] are important factors to consider in strategy development [2.1a(2)].

C   Training [5.2] is provided to ensure all faculty and staff understand organization ethical practices [1.2a(3)] as well as the importance of strengthening key communities [1.2b]. In addition, recruitment and hiring and the design of work systems should capitalize on the ideas, culture, and thinking of key communities and their impact on the organization [5.1a(5)].

D   Leaders at all levels have responsibility for ensuring that practices of the organization [6.1, 6.2, 6.3] are consistent with the organization's standards of ethics and public responsibility [1.2].

E   Key results, such as results of regulatory compliance, environmental improvements, and support to key communities, are reported in Organizational Effectiveness Results [7.5b]. In addition, these results are monitored to determine if process changes are needed. (Compliance results in areas of faculty and staff safety are reported in 7.4, based on processes described in Item 5.3. Employee Well-Being and Satisfaction, and are not a part of the requirements in 1.2.)

F   The legal/regulatory environment described in P.1a(5) sets the context for the review of the management systems for public responsibility citizenship [1.2a (1)].

1.2 Public Responsibility and Citizenship
Sample Effective Practices

Several school districts have successfully and creatively addressed the requirement for public accountability. Beaverton School District #48 in Oregon publishes and updates a District Profile that describes progress on the district's key indicators of school system performance. The district maintains public accountability through "user-friendly" charts, graphs, and tables that report data such as percentages of students meeting standards on state tests, percentages of secondary students with a 2.0 or above grade point average, SAT scores for Beaverton schools and the nation's schools, percentages of students in postsecondary education one year after graduating, dropout rates, parent and student ratings of their schools, supervisor ratings of staff quality, staff job satisfaction ratings, and safety-related incidents. (For information contact *www.beaverton.k12.or.us/District_Info/District_ profile.htm*)

Another way for schools to communicate with its public is through report cards, which display indicators and performance similar to a wide-spread business practice. Research conducted by education week and A-Plus Communications in 1999 gathered input from stakeholders (including parents and taxpayers) on data and information they value about their schools and the best ways for schools to communicate this information. (For information contact A-Plus Communications. Reporting Results: What the public Wants to Know. Arlington, VA: or contact *www.ksagroup.com/ aplu/index.html*).

A. Responsibilities to the Public

- The organization's principal business activities include systems to analyze, anticipate, and minimize public hazards or risk.
- Indicators for risk areas are identified and monitored.
- Continuous improvement strategies are used consistently, and progress is reviewed regularly.
- The organization considers the impact its operations, programs, and services might have on society and considers those impacts in planning.
- The effectiveness of systems to meet or exceed accreditation, regulatory, or legal requirements is systematically evaluated and improved.

B. Support of Key Communities

- Faculty and staff at various levels in the organization are encouraged to be involved in professional organizations, committees, task forces, or other community activities.
- Organizational resources are allocated to support involvement in community activities outside the organization.
- Faculty and staff participate in local, state, or national performance award programs and receive recognition from the organization.
- Faculty and staff participate in a variety of professional, educational, and leadership improvement associations.
- The effectiveness of processes to support and strengthen key communities is systematically evaluated and improved.

1.2 Public Responsibility and Citizenship
Sample Effective Practices for Teaching Faculty:
Leaders of the Classroom Learning System

- Students are encouraged to be involved in community activities, committees, and task forces.
- Students can earn extra credit and recognition for involvement in community and civic improvement/ volunteerism relevant to their course content.
- Teachers partner with parents and community groups to improve the classroom, the organization, and the community.
- Teachers are involved in their community in a variety of ways and communicate this to students.
- Teachers actively encourage student participation in the community.

2 Strategic Planning—85 Points

The Strategic Planning Category examines how your organization develops strategic objectives and action plans. Also examined are how your chosen strategic objectives and action plans are deployed and how progress is measured.

The Strategic Planning Category looks at the organization's process for strategic and action planning, and deployment of plans to make sure everyone is working to achieve those plans. Student and operational Performance Excellence are key strategic issues that need to be integral parts of the organization's overall planning:

- Student- and stakeholder-driven quality is a strategic view of quality. The focus is on the drivers of student and stakeholder satisfaction, student retention, market needs, and expectations—key factors in educational programs and student success.

- Operational performance improvement contributes to short-term and longer-term capabilities growth and cost/price competitiveness. Building operational capability—including speed, responsiveness, and flexibility—represents an investment in strengthening your competitive position now and into the future.

Over the years, much debate and discussion has taken place around planning. Universities and businesses spend a great deal of time trying to differentiate strategic planning, long- and short-term planning, tactical planning, operational planning, quality planning, business planning, and faculty and staff resource planning, to name a few. However, a much simpler view might serve us better. For our purposes, the following captures the essence of planning:

- *Strategic planning is simply an effort to identify the things we must do to be successful in the future.*

- Once we have determined what we must do to be successful (the plan), we must take steps to execute that plan (the actions).

Accordingly, the key role of strategic planning is to provide a basis for aligning the organization's work processes with its strategic directions, thereby ensuring people and processes in different parts of the organization are not working at cross purposes. To the extent that alignment does not occur, the organization's effectiveness and competitiveness is reduced.

The Strategic Planning Category looks at how the organization:

- Understands the key student and stakeholder, market, and operational requirements as input to setting strategic directions. This helps to ensure that ongoing process improvements are aligned with the organization's strategic directions.

- Optimizes the use of resources and ensures bridging between short- and longer-term requirements that may entail capital expenditures, partner development, new faculty and staff resource recruitment strategies, and other factors affecting educational success.

- Ensures that deployment will be effective—that there are mechanisms to transmit requirements and achieve alignment on three basic levels: (1) the organization/executive level; (2) the key process level; and (3) the work-unit/individual-job level.

The requirements for the Strategic Planning Category are intended to encourage strategic thinking and acting to develop a basis for achieving and maintaining a competitive position. These requirements do not demand formalized plans, planning systems, departments, or specific planning cycles. They do, however, require plans and the alignment of actions to those plans at all levels of the organization. An effective system to improve performance and competitive advantage requires fact-based strategic guidance, particularly when improvement alternatives compete for limited resources. In most cases, priority setting depends heavily upon a cost rationale. However, an organization might also have to deal with critical requirements, such as public responsibilities, that are not driven by cost considerations alone.

Strategic planning consists of the planning process, the identification of goals and actions necessary to achieve success, and the deployment of those actions to align the work of the organization.

Strategy Development

- Current and future student/stakeholder and market requirements and new educational service and student development opportunities using short- and longer-term planning time horizons;
- Competitive environment: capabilities and new technology;
- Budgetary and societal risks;
- Faculty and staff resource capabilities and needs;
- Operational capabilities and needs, including resource availability and capability to assess student learning and development;
- Partner capabilities and needs; and
- Clear strategic objectives with timetables.

Strategy Deployment

- Translate strategy into action plans and related faculty and staff resource plans;
- Align and deploy action plan requirements, performance measures, and resources throughout the organization; and
- Project expected performance results, including assumptions of competitor performance increases and approaches to addressing your future, as well as ensuring that strategic objectives address all other key organizational challenges.

2.1 Strategy Development (40 points)
Approach/Deployment Scoring

Describe how your organization establishes its strategic objectives, including addressing key student and stakeholder needs; enhancing its performance relative to competitors, comparable schools, and/or appropriately selected organizations; and enhancing its overall performance.

Within your response, include answers to the following questions:

a. Strategy Development Process

(1) What is your overall strategic planning process? Include key steps, key participants, and your short- and longer-term planning time horizons.

(2) How do you ensure that planning addresses the following key factors? Briefly outline how relevant data and information are gathered and analyzed to address these factors:

- current and future student/stakeholder and market needs, expectations, and opportunities, including student achievement;
- key external factors, requirements, and opportunities, including your suppliers' and/or partners' strengths and weaknesses; your competitive environment; and your capabilities relative to competitors, comparable schools, and/or appropriately selected organizations;
- technological and other key changes that might affect your services and/or how you operate;
- your strengths and weaknesses, including faculty, staff, and other resources;
- your capability to assess student learning and development; and
- ethical, societal, budgetary, and other potential risks.

b. Strategic Objectives

(1) What are your key short- and longer-term strategic objectives and your timetable for accomplishing them? Include key goals/targets, as appropriate.

(2) How do your strategic objectives address the challenges identified in response to P.2 in your Organizational Profile? How do you ensure that your strategic objectives balance the needs of students and stakeholders?

Notes:

N1. *Strategy development* refers to your organization's approach (formal or informal) to preparing for the future. Strategy development might utilize various types of forecasts, projections, options, scenarios, and/or other approaches to envisioning the future for purposes of decision making and resource allocation.

N2. *Strategy* should be interpreted broadly. Strategy might be built around or lead to any or all of the following: addition or termination of services and programs, modifications in instructional design, use of technology, changes in testing and/or adoption of standards, services to new/changing student populations, research priorities, and new partnerships and alliances.

N3. Challenges (2.1b[2]) addressed in your strategy might include rapid response, customization of educational offerings, understanding a changing education market, rapid innovation, Web-based stakeholder/partner/supplier relationship management, and information management. Responses to Item 2.1 should focus on your specific challenges—those most important to your students' success and to strengthening your organization's overall performance.

N4. Item 2.1 addresses your overall organizational strategy, which might include changes in educational services and programs. However, the Item does not address educational service and program design; you should address these factors in Item 6.1.

This Item looks at how the organization sets strategic directions and develops strategic objectives, with the aim of strengthening overall performance and competitiveness.

The first part of this Item [2.1a(1)] asks the organization to describe its strategic planning process and identify the key participants, key steps, and planning time horizons. This helps examiners and others understand the steps and data used in the planning process. It is usually a good idea to provide a flowchart of the planning process. This helps examiners and others understand how the planning process works without wasting valuable space in the application.

Organizations need to consider the key factors that affect its future success. These factors cover external and internal influences on the organization. Each factor must be addressed and outlined to show how relevant data and information are gathered and analyzed. Although the organization is not limited to the number of factors it considers important in planning, the six factors identified in Item 2.1a(2) must be addressed unless a valid rationale can be offered as to why the factor is not appropriate. Together, these six factors will cover the most important variables for any organization's future success:

- The planning process should examine all the key influences, risks, challenges, and other requirements that might affect the organization's future opportunities and directions—taking as long-term a view as possible. This approach is intended to provide a thorough and realistic context for the development of a student/stakeholder- and market-focused strategy to guide ongoing decision making, resource allocation, and overall management.

- This planning process is intended to cover all types of future scenarios, competitive situations, and strategic issues. The Item does not require formalized planning, planning departments, planning cycles, or a specified way of visualizing the future.

- This Item focuses on identifying the factors and actions the organization takes to achieve a leadership position in a changing and competitive educational market. This usually requires ongoing revenue growth and improvements in operational effectiveness. Achieving and sustaining a leadership position in a competitive and changing educational market requires a view of the future that includes not only the markets or segments in which the organization competes, but also how it competes. How it competes presents many options and requires an understanding of the organization's and competitors' strengths and weaknesses. No specific time horizon for planning is required by the criteria; but short and longer time horizons need to be considered.

- In order to maintain competitive leadership, an important part of strategic planning requires processes to project the competitive environment accurately. Such projections help to detect and reduce competitive threats, shorten reaction time, and identify opportunities. Depending on the size and type of organization, pace of change, and competitive parameters (such as price or innovation rate), organizations might use a variety of modeling, scenario, or other techniques and judgments to project the competitive environment.

The second part of this Item [2.1b] asks for a summary of the organization's key strategic objectives and the timetable for accomplishing them [2.1b(1)], as well as how the objectives address the organizational challenges outlined in the Organizational Profile and balance the needs of students and stakeholders [2.1b(2)]:

- The purpose of the timetable is to provide a basis for projecting the path that improvement is likely to take. This allows the organizations' leaders to monitor progress more accurately. Consider Figure 10. The performance goal four years into the future is to achieve a level of performance of 100. Currently, the organization is at 20. At the end of year 1, the organization achieved a performance level of 40, represented by the circle symbol. It appears that that level of performance is on track toward the goal of 100. However, the path from the current state to the future state is rarely a straight line. Unless the expected trajectory is known (or at least estimated), it is not possible to evaluate the progress accurately.

- The focus on challenges needs to be on those most important to student success and overall educational performance.

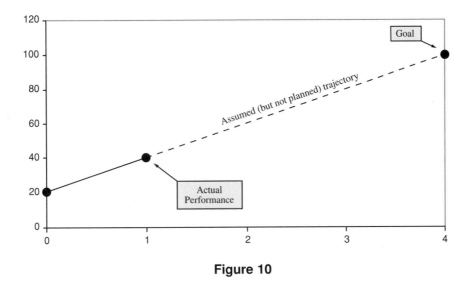

Figure 10

In Figure 11, the planned trajectory is represented by the triangle symbols. When compared with the current level of performance (the circle symbol), it is clear that there is a performance shortfall of approximately 30.

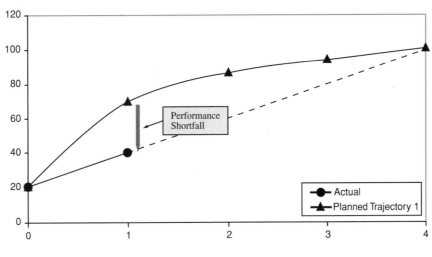

Figure 11

In Figure 12, the planned trajectory is represented by square symbols. When compared with the current level of performance (circle symbol), it is clear that performance is ahead of schedule. There are several possible decisions that leaders could make based on this information. It might mean that the original goals were low and should be reset. It might also mean that the process did not need all of the resources it had available. These resources may be better used in areas where performance is not ahead of schedule.

In any case, without knowing the expected path toward a goal, it requires leaders to guess whether the level of progress is appropriate or not.

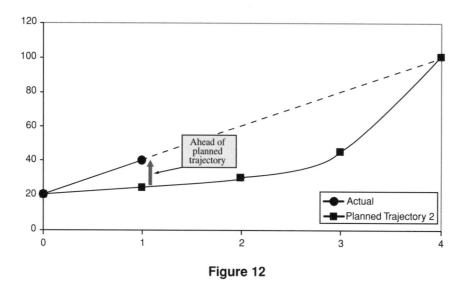

Figure 12

Finally, the last part of this Item requires the organization to evaluate the options it considered in the strategic planning process to ensure it responded fully to the six factors identified in Item 2.1a(2) that were most important to business success. This last step helps the organization "close the loop" to make sure that the factors influencing organization success were adequately analyzed and support key strategic objectives.

2.1 Strategy Development

How the organization sets strategic directions to define and strengthen competitive position.

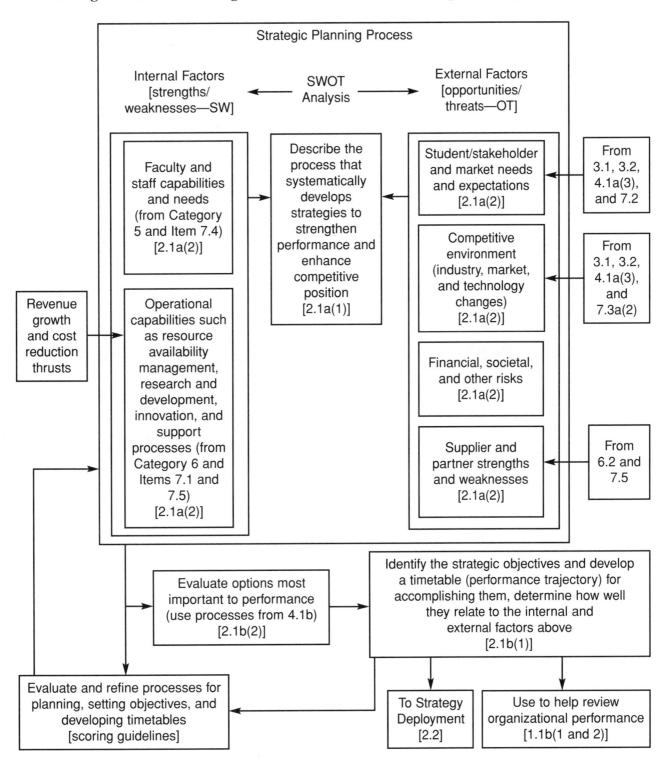

2.1 Strategy Development Item Linkages

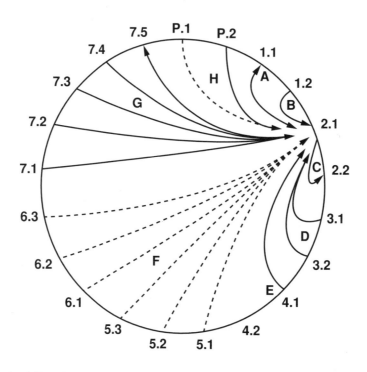

Nature of Relationship

A   The planning process [2.1] includes seniors as part of their responsibilities for setting direction and expectations, ensuring a strong focus on student learning; and student/stakeholder and faculty/staff empowerment [1.1a]. In addition, the timelines or performance trajectory [2.1b(1)] provide a basis for leaders monitoring progress [1.1b(1)]. Without timelines it is difficult to determine if the organization is on track.

B   Safety, regulatory, accreditation, legal, and related concerns [1.2a] are considered, as appropriate, in the strategy development process [2.1a(2)].

C   The planning process [2.1a] produces a set of strategic objectives [2.1b(1)] that must be converted into action plans that are deployed to faculty and staff [2.2a].

D   The planning process [2.1] includes information on current and potential student requirements and the projected competitive environment [3.1], as well as intelligence obtained from student/stakeholder-contact people (complaints and comments) [3.2a] and student/stakeholder satisfaction data [3.2b].

E   Key organizational and competitive comparison data [4.1a(3)] and analytical data including various forecasts and projections [4.1b] are used for planning [2.1a(2)].

F   Information on faculty and staff capabilities [Category 5] and work process capabilities [Category 6] is considered in the strategic planning process as part of the determination of internal strengths and weaknesses. To avoid cluttering diagrams 5.1–6.3, these arrows will not be repeated there.

G   Student learning, student- and stakeholder-focused, budgetary, financial, and market results [7.1, 7.2, and 7.3], faculty/staff, and organization effectiveness results [7.4 and 7.5] are used in the planning process [2.1a(2)] to set strategic objectives [2.1b(1)]. In addition, results in 7.5a(2) must specifically report on progress toward achieving the strategic objectives.

H   Faculty and staff educational levels, diversity, and other characteristics [P.1a(3)] may affect the determination of human resource strengths and weaknesses as a part of the strategic planning process [2.1a(2)]. The competitive environment defined in P.2a should also be examined as part of the strategy development process [2.1a(2)].

NOTE: The many inputs to strategy development will not all be repeated on other linkage diagrams to avoid clutter.

2.1 Strategy Development
Sample Effective Practices

- Goals, strategies, and issues are addressed and reported in measurable terms. Goals consider future requirements needed to achieve organizational leadership after considering the performance levels other organizations are likely to achieve.
- The planning and goal-setting process encourages input (but not necessarily decision making) from a variety of people at all levels throughout the organization.
- Data on stakeholder and student requirements, key communities, benchmarks, faculty and staff, and organizational capabilities are used to develop strategic plans.
- Plans are evaluated each cycle for accuracy and completeness—more often if needed to keep pace with changing requirements.
- Areas for improvement in the planning process are identified systematically and carried out each planning cycle.
- Refinements in the process of planning, deploying plans, and receiving input from work units have been made. Improvements in plan cycle time, plan resources, and planning accuracy are documented.

2.1 Strategy Development
Sample Effective Practices for Teaching Faculty:
Leaders of the Classroom Learning System

- Teachers survey parents and students prior to the course to gain a better understanding of requirements and expectations.
- The course and curriculum planning process encourages input (but not necessarily decision making) from students and stakeholders.
- Students are involved in educational planning appropriate for their age and educational level (intensely in higher education, as much as possible in elementary school) to identify and meet their needs.
- Students have developed a learning strategy based on learning style and interests, of which teachers are aware.

2.2 Strategy Deployment (45 points)
Approach/Deployment Scoring

Describe how your organization converts its strategic objectives into action plans. Summarize your organization's action plans and related key performance measures/indicators. Project your organization's future performance on these key performance measures/indicators.

Within your response, include answers to the following questions:

a. Action Plan Development and Deployment

(1) How do you develop and deploy action plans to achieve your key strategic objectives? Include how you allocate resources to ensure accomplishment of your action plans.

(2) What are your key short- and longer-term action plans? Include key changes, if any, in your services/programs, in your anticipated or planned student and stakeholder markets, and in how you operate.

(3) What are your key human resource plans that derive from your short- and longer-term strategic objectives and action plans?

(4) What are your key performance measures/indicators for tracking progress relative to your action plans? How do you ensure that your overall action plan measurement system achieves organizational alignment and covers all key deployment areas, students, and stakeholders?

b. Performance Projection

What are your performance projections for your key measures/indicators for both your short- and longer-term planning time horizons? How does your projected performance compare with the performance of competitors, comparable schools, and appropriately selected organizations; key benchmarks; goals; and past performance, as appropriate?

Notes:

N1. Action plan development and deployment are closely linked to other Items in the criteria. Examples of key linkages follow:

- Item 1.1 for how your senior leaders set and communicate directions;

- Category 3 for gathering knowledge of students, stakeholders, and markets as input to your strategy and action plans and for deploying action plans;

- Category 4 for information and analysis to support your key information needs, to support your development of strategy, to provide an effective basis for your performance measurements, and to track progress relative to your strategic objectives and action plans;

- Category 5 for your work system needs; faculty and staff education, training, and development needs; and related human resource factors resulting from action plans;

- Category 6 for process requirements resulting from your action plans; and

- Item 7.5 for specific accomplishments relative to your organizational strategy.

N2. Human resource plans might include faculty, academic staff members, nonacademic staff members, contract employees, and volunteers.

N3. Measures/indicators of projected performance (2.2b) might include changes resulting from innovations in education delivery and/or use of technology, redirection of resources, effectiveness of research and services, improved performance of administrative and other support functions, and improvement in safety.

The first part of this Item looks at how the organization translates its strategic objectives into action plans to accomplish the objectives and to enable assessment of progress relative to your action plans. The aim is to ensure that your strategies are deployed for goal achievement.

The first part of this Item [2.2a] calls for information on how action plans are developed and deployed. This includes spelling out key performance requirements and measures, as well as aligning work throughout the organization. Leaders must develop action plans that address the key strategic objectives (which were developed using the processes and Item 2.1). Organizations must summarize key short- and longer-term action plans. Particular attention is given to services and programs, students and stakeholders markets, faculty and staff resource requirements, and resource allocations.

Of central importance in this area is how alignment and consistency are achieved—for example, via key processes and key measurements. Alignment and consistency are intended also to provide a basis for setting and communicating priorities for ongoing improvement activities—part of the daily work of all departments. You also are asked to specify key measures and/or indicators used in tracking progress relative to the action plans and how you communicate and align strategic objectives, action plans, and performance.

Without effective alignment, routine work and acts of improvement can be random and serve to suboptimize organizational performance. In Figure 13, the arrows represent the well-intended work carried out by faculty and staff of organizations who lack a clear set of expectations and direction. Each person, each leader and supervisor, and each department works diligently to achieve goals they believe are important. Each is pulling hard—but not necessarily in the direction that ensures Performance Excellence. This encourages the creation of "feifdoms" within organization. For example, in education, various disciplines can compete within a high school or college for students and resources.

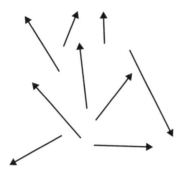

Figure 13 Nonaligned Work

With a clear, well-communicated strategic plan, it is easier to know when daily work is out of alignment. The large arrow in Figure 14 represents the strategic plan defining the direction the organization must take to be successful and achieve its mission and vision. The strategic plan and accompanying measures make it possible to know when work is not aligned and help faculty and staff, including administrators, to know when adjustments are required.

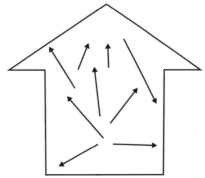

Figure 14 Strategic Direction

A well-deployed and understood strategic plan helps everyone in the organization distinguish between random acts of improvement and aligned improvement. Random acts of improvement give a false sense of accomplishment and rarely benefit the organization. For example, a decision to improve an educational process that is not aligned with the strategic plan (as the small bold arrow in Figure 15 represents) usually results in a wasteful expenditure of time, money, and faculty and staff resources—improvement without benefiting students and stakeholders or enhancing operating effectiveness.

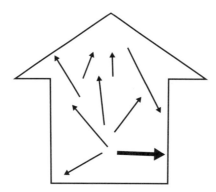

Figure 15 Random Improvement

On the other hand, by working systematically to strengthen processes that are aligned with the strategic plan, the organization moves closer to achieving success, as Figure 16 indicates. Ultimately, all processes and procedures of an organization should be aligned to maximize the achievement of strategic plans, as Figure 17 demonstrates.

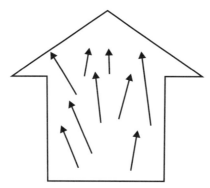

Figure 16 Moving Toward Alignment

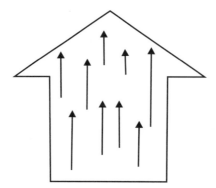

Figure 17 Systematic Alignment

Critical action plan resource requirements include faculty and staff resource plans that support your overall strategy. Examples of possible faculty and staff resource plan elements follow:

- Redesign of your work organization and/or jobs to increase faculty and staff empowerment and decision making;
- Initiatives to promote greater faculty/staff-management cooperation, such as union partnerships;
- Initiatives to foster knowledge sharing and organizational learning;
- Modification of your compensation and recognition systems to recognize team, organizational, market, or other performance attributes; and
- Education and training initiatives, such as developmental programs for future leaders, partnerships to help ensure the availability of future faculty and staff, and/or establishment of technology-based training capabilities.

Finally, the second part of this Item [2.2b] asks the organization to provide a short- to longer-term projection of key performance measures and/or indicators, including key performance targets and/or goals. This projected performance is the basis for comparing past performance and performance relative to competitors and benchmarks, as appropriate:

- Projections and comparisons in this area are intended to help the organization's leaders improve their ability to understand and track dynamic, competitive performance factors. Through this tracking process, they should be better prepared to take into account its rate of improvement and change relative to competitors and relative to their own targets or stretch goals. Such tracking serves as a key diagnostic management tool.
- In addition to improvement relative to past performance and to competitors, projected performance also might include changes resulting from new business ventures, entry into new markets, product/service innovations, or other strategic thrusts. Without this comparison information, it is possible to set goals that, even if attained, may not result in competitive advantage. More than one high-performing organization has been surprised by a competitor that set and achieved more aggressive goals. Reference the global competition learning at a faster rate than our students. Consider the following example illustrated in Figure 18. Imagine that you are ahead of your competition and committed to a 10 percent increase in student achievement over your base year. After eight years, your achievement is twice as high. To your surprise, you find that your competitor has increased 20 percent each year. You have achieved your goal, but your competitor has beaten you. After 10 years, the competitor has a significant lead. It is not enough to make your goals; your goals should place you in a leadership position.

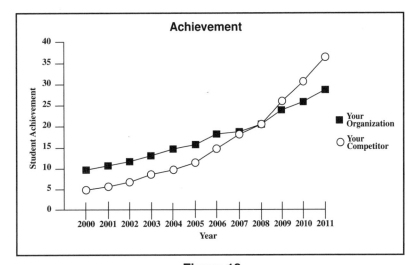

Figure 18

2.2 Strategy Deployment

Summary of strategy, action plans, and performance projections; how they are developed, communicated, and deployed.

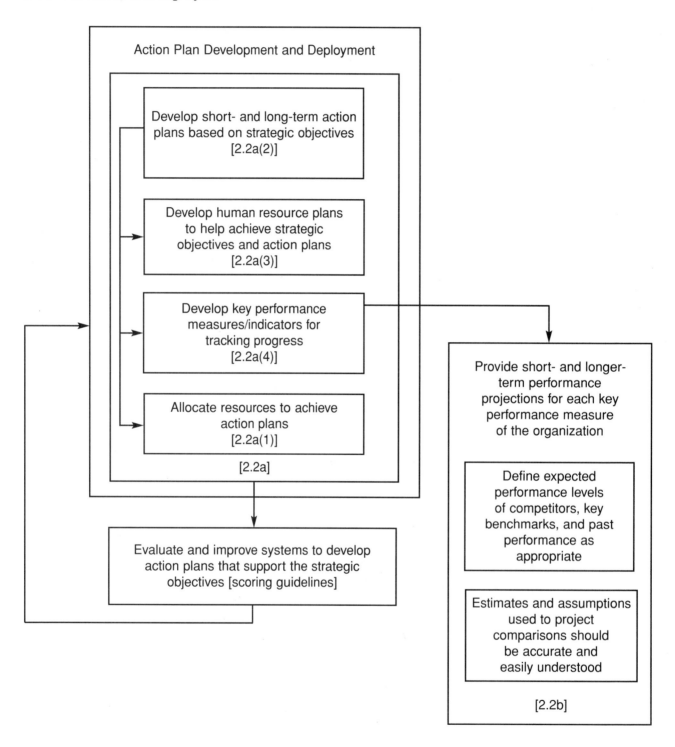

2.2 Strategy Deployment Item Linkages

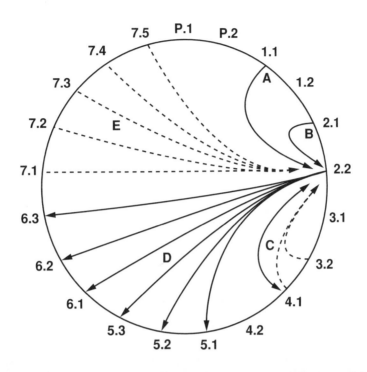

A   The leadership team [1.1a(1)] ensures that action plans are aligned throughout the organization with strategic objectives and that resources are allocated to ensure the actions are accomplished [2.2a(1)].

B   The planning process [2.1] develops the strategic objectives that are converted into action plans to support these objectives [2.2a(1)].

C   The action plans [2.2a(1)] and related performance measures [2.2a(4)]; define part of the data that need to be collected to monitor alignment [4.1a]; analyze to support decision making [4.1b]; and help define requirements for data availability [4.2a], hardware and software reliability [4.2b], student and stakeholder relations management [3.2a], and student and stakeholder satisfaction determination [3.2b]. Benchmarking comparison data [4.1a(3)] and analytical processes [4.1b] are used to set organizational measures and objectives [2.2].

D   Measures, objectives, action plans, and human resource plans [2.2a], are used to drive and align actions to achieve improved performance [Category 6] and develop faculty and staff [Category 5]. It is particularly important that action plans and measures [2.2a], are aligned with and supported by faculty and staff feedback, recognition, and reward [5.1a(3)].

E   Results data [Category 7] are used to help determine performance projections for short- and longer-term planning and goal setting [2.2b]. In addition, specific accomplishments related to organizational strategy and actions must be reported in Item 7.5a(2). (To avoid clutter and make the diagrams more readable, these relationships will not be repeated on the Category 7 linkage diagrams.)

2.2 Strategy Deployment
Sample Effective Practices

A. Action Plan Development and Deployment

- Student and stakeholder surveys focus on critical faculty and staff development needs for meeting requirements.

- Plans are in place to optimize operational performance and improve student and stakeholder focus, using such tools as streamlining and reducing cycle time.

- Strategies to retain or establish leadership positions exist for major educational programs and services for key student and stakeholder groups.

- Strategies to achieve key organizational results are defined.

- Performance levels are defined in measurable terms for key features of educational programs and services.

- Planned actions are challenging, realistic, achievable, and understood by faculty and staff and, in some instances, students, throughout the organization. Each understands his or her role in achieving strategic and operational goals and objectives.

- Resources are available and committed to achieve the plans (no unfunded mandates).

- Plans are realistic and used to guide performance improvements.

- Incremental (short-term) strategies to achieve long-term plans are defined in measurable terms.

- Strategic plans, short- and long-term goals, and performance measures are understood and used to drive actions throughout the organization.

- Each individual in the organization (including students as possible), understands how his or her work contributes to achieving organizational goals and plans.

- Plans are followed to ensure that resources are deployed and redeployed as needed to support goals.

- Capital projects are funded according to business improvement plans.

- Faculty and staff plans support strategic plans and goals. Plans show how the workforce will be developed to enable the organization to achieve its strategic goals.

- Key issues of training and development, hiring, retention, faculty and staff participation, involvement, empowerment, and recognition and reward are addressed as a part of the faculty and staff plan.

- Innovative strategies may involve one or more of the following:

- Redesign of work to increase faculty/staff responsibility.

  - Improved labor-management relations (that is, prior to contract negotiations, both sides are trained in effective negotiation skills so that people focus on the merits of issues, not on positions. The goal is to improve relations and shorten negotiation time by 50 percent).

  - Forming partnerships to develop faculty and staff and ensure a supply of well-prepared future faculty/staff.

  - Broadening faculty/staff responsibilities; creating self-directed or high-performance work teams.

  - Key performance measures (for example, faculty/staff satisfaction or work climate surveys) have been identified to gather data to manage progress. (Note: Improvement results associated with these measures should be reported in Item 7.4.)

  - The effectiveness of faculty and staff planning and alignment with strategic plans is evaluated systematically.

  - Data are used to evaluate and improve performance and participation for all types of faculty and staff (for example, absenteeism, turnover, grievances, accidents, recognition and reward, and training participation).

  - Routine, two-way communication about performance of faculty/staff occurs.

B. Performance Projection

- Projections of short- to longer-term changes in performance levels are developed and used to track progress.
- Data from competitors and/or key benchmarks form a valid basis for comparison.
- The organization has strategies and goals in place to exceed the planned levels of performance for these competitors and benchmarks.
- Plans include expected future levels of competitor or comparison performance and are used to set and validate the organization's own plans.

2.2 Strategy Deployment
Sample Effective Practices for Teaching Faculty:
Leaders of the Classroom Learning System

- Routine, two-way communication about performance of students occurs.
- Data are used to evaluate and improve performance and participation for all types of students (for example, tardiness, suspensions, absenteeism, and participation in class).
- Key performance measures have been identified for classes.
- Teachers make sure that each student understands the classroom mission, vision, and the things each student must do to be successful.
- Teachers reference and use identified learning strategies for students based on learning style and interests.

3 Student, Stakeholder, and Market Focus—85 Points

The Student, Stakeholder, and Market Focus Category examines how your organization determines requirements, expectations, and preferences of students, stakeholders, and markets. Also examined is how your organization builds relationships with students and stakeholders and determines the key factors that attract students and partners and lead to student and stakeholder satisfaction and persistence and to excellence in educational services/programs.

This category identifies the systems for gathering intelligence about student, stakeholder, and market requirements and levels of student/stakeholder satisfaction that leaders use to plan, set direction, and set goals. In addition, information about student and stakeholder satisfaction and dissatisfaction, including complaints, are used to identify systems and processes needing improvement. Information from complaints helps organizations identify and prevent future problems.

Student, stakeholder, and market focus contains two Items that focus on understanding student, stakeholder, and market requirements, and determining student/stakeholder satisfaction.

Knowledge of Student, Stakeholder, and Market Needs and Expectations

- Determine student and market segments.
- Determine student and market information validity.
- Determine important educational program or service features.
- Use information and data from potential, current, and former students and stakeholders.
- Determine future educational service needs.
- Ensure methods to listen and learn are kept current.

Student and Stakeholder Relationships and Satisfaction

- Make student and stakeholder contact and feedback easy and useful.
- Handle complaints effectively and responsively.
- Ensure complaint data are used to eliminate causes of complaints.
- Build stakeholder relationships and loyalty.
- Systematically determine stakeholder satisfaction and the satisfaction of similar organization's stakeholders.

3.1 Knowledge of Student, Stakeholder, and Market Needs and Expectations (40 points)
Approach/Deployment Scoring

Describe how your organization determines requirements, expectations, and preferences of current and future students, stakeholders, and markets to ensure the continuing relevance of your educational programs and support services, to develop new opportunities, and to create an overall climate conducive to learning and development for all students.

Within your response, include answers to the following questions:

a. Knowledge of Student and Market Needs and Expectations

(1) How do you determine which student segments and/or markets your educational programs will address? How do you include student segments currently served by other education providers and other potential segments and/or markets in this determination?

(2) How do you listen and learn to determine students' general and special needs and expectations and their relative importance/value to students' and stakeholders' decision making for purposes of educational program and support service planning, marketing, improvements, and other service development? In this determination, how do you use relevant information from current, former, and future students, student segments, and stakeholders? Include information on utilization of offerings, facilities, and services; complaints; demographic data and trends that may bear upon enrollments and needs; changing requirements and expectations your graduates will face; changing requirements and expectations resulting from national, state, or local requirements; and education alternatives available to your pool of future students. If determination methods vary for different student segments or stakeholder groups, describe the key differences in your determination methods.

(3) How do you keep your listening and learning methods current with educational service needs and directions?

b. Knowledge of Stakeholder Needs and Expectations

(1) How do you use relevant information from current, former, and future stakeholders to determine and anticipate changing stakeholder needs and expectations? Include complaints; demographic data and trends that may bear upon stakeholder needs; changing requirements and expectations that stakeholders will face; changing requirements and expectations resulting from national, state, or local requirements; and alternatives available to your pool of stakeholders. If determination methods vary for different stakeholder groups, describe the key differences in your determination methods.

(2) How do you keep your listening and learning methods current with stakeholder needs and directions?

Notes:

N1. Student segments (3.1a[1]) refers to groups of students with similar needs. The basis for the groupings might reflect their career interests, learning styles, service delivery (classroom and/or Web-based), living status (residential versus commuter), family income, or other factors.

N2. Student needs might take into account information from your students and key stakeholders, such as families, employers, and other schools. Needs include educational, developmental, and other requirements, such as safety and social and ethical development.

N3. Information on "trends" (3.1a[2]) refers to information your organization collects that shows year-to-year changes. Such changes might reflect specific and/or local factors important to your organization. In some cases, such local factors could be different from national trends.

N4. Keeping your listening and learning methods current with educational service needs and directions (3.1a[3]) might include use of current and new technology, such as Web-based data gathering.

This Item looks at the organization's key processes for gaining knowledge about its current and future students, markets, and stakeholders, in order to offer relevant educational programs and services; understand emerging student, market, and stakeholder requirements and expectations; and keep pace with changing educational service needs. This information is intended to support educational program and services development and planning. In a rapidly changing, competitive environment, many factors may affect student and stakeholder preference and loyalty, making it necessary to listen and learn on a continuous basis. To be effective, such listening and learning strategies need to have a close connection with the organization's overall strategy. For example, if the organization customizes its educational programs and services, the listening and learning strategy needs to be backed by a capable information system—one that rapidly accumulates information about students, markets, and stakeholders and makes this information available where needed throughout the organization or elsewhere within the overall value chain.

The organization needs to have a process for determining or segmenting key market and student groups. To ensure a complete and accurate picture of student requirements and concerns is obtained, organizations need to consider the requirements of current, potential, and future students, markets and stakeholders, including competitors. In addition, the effective organization will tailor its listening and learning techniques to different student, market, and stakeholder groups. A relationship or listening strategy might work with some students and stakeholders, but not with others:

- Information sought should be sensitive to specific educational program and service requirements and their relative importance or value to the different student and stakeholder groups. This determination should be supported by use of information and data, such as complaints and gains and losses of students and markets.

- In addition to defining student, market, and stakeholder requirements, organizations must determine key requirements and drivers of attendance/loyalty decisions and key educational program/service features. In other words, the organization must be able to prioritize key student and stakeholder requirements and drivers of their decisions. These priorities are likely to be different for different groups and segments. Knowledge of student groups and segments allows the organization to tailor listening and learning strategies and program offerings, to support marketing strategies, and to develop new educational services.

- In a rapidly changing competitive environment, many factors may affect student and stakeholder preference and loyalty. This makes it necessary to listen and learn on a continuous basis. To be effective as an organization, listening and learning need to be closely linked with the overall educational organization strategy and strategy planning process.

- Electronic commerce is changing the competitive arena rapidly. This may significantly affect the relationships with students, markets, and stakeholders and the effectiveness of listening and learning strategies. It may also force the organization to redefine student, market, and stakeholder groups and segments.

- A variety of listening and learning strategies are commonly used. The selection of a particular strategy depends upon the type and size of the organization and other factors. Some examples of listening and learning strategies include the following:
  - Close integration with students and stakeholders;
  - Rapid innovation and trials of educational programs and services to better link research and design to the classroom;
  - Close tracking of technological, competitive, and other factors that may bear upon student, market, and stakeholder requirements, expectations, preferences, or alternatives;
  - Defining the students' and stakeholders' value chains and how they are likely to change;
  - Focus groups with students and stakeholders;
  - Use of critical incidents, such as complaints, to understand key service attributes from the point of view of stakeholders and student- and stakeholder-contact faculty and staff;
  - Interviewing exiting students to determine strengths and opportunities to improve relationships; and
  - Won/lost analysis relative to competitors.

Finally, the effective organization has a system in place to improve its student and stakeholder listening and learning strategies to keep current with changing educational service needs and directions. If the organization competes in a rapidly changing environment, such as computer science or microelectronics, it may need to evaluate and improve its student and stakeholder listening and learning strategies more frequently. The organization is able to demonstrate that it has made appropriate improvements to ensure its techniques for understanding requirements and priorities keeps pace with changing educational service needs.

3.1 Knowledge of Student, Stakeholder, and Market Needs and Expectations

How the organization determines longer-term requirements, expectations, and preferences of current and future students, stakeholders, and markets to anticipate their needs and to develop new opportunities.

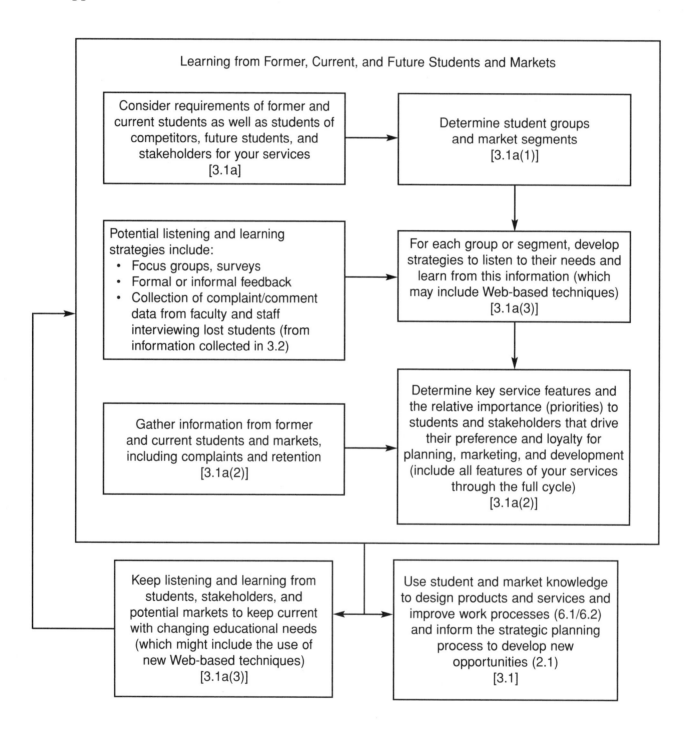

3.1 Knowledge of Student, Stakeholder, and Market Needs and Expectations Item Linkages

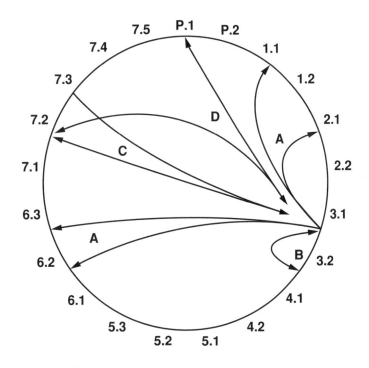

Nature of Relationship

A   Information about current and future student and market requirements [3.1] is used for strategic planning [2.1a(1)]; to design educational [6.1a(2)] and student services [6.2]; to revise design, delivery [6.1(3)], and student service processes [6.2a(2 and 3)]; and to help leaders set directions for the organization [1.1a(1)].

B   Student and stakeholder complaints [3.2a(3)] are used to help assess current student and stakeholder expectations and refine requirements [3.1a(2)]. Information about student requirement priorities [3.1a(2)] is used to build instruments and better questions to assess student and stakeholder satisfaction [3.2b(1)].

C   Student learning outcomes [7.1], student and stakeholder satisfaction data and complaint trends [7.2a], and market growth data [7.3a(2)] are used to help validate expectations and refine requirements [3.1]. In addition, processes to gather intelligence about student and stakeholder requirements [3.1] are used to define and produce student and stakeholder satisfaction results [7.2].

D   The student, stakeholder, and market groups reported in P.1b(1) were determined using the processes described in 3.1a(1 and 2). The information in P.1b(1) helps examiners identify the kind of results, broken out by student and stakeholder or market segment, which should be reported in Item 7.2.

3.1 Knowledge of Student, Stakeholder, and Market Needs and Expectations Sample Effective Practices

- Various systematic methods are used to gather data and identify current requirements and expectations of students and stakeholders (for example, surveys and focus groups).
- Key offerings, facilities, and feature services are defined. Educational service features refer to all-important characteristics and performance of offerings that students and stakeholders experience or perceive throughout their use. The focus is primarily on factors that bear on preference, such as learning styles and loyalty—for example, those features that enhance or differentiate educational programs and services from competing offerings.
- Student/stakeholder and market segments are identified or grouped by requirements. For example, an industry that needs specific technical skills may be a market for a college. New online, computer certification programs may be a market for a high school or college.
- Various systematic methods are used to identify the future requirements and expectations of students and stakeholders.
- Students of competitors are considered and processes are in place to gather expectation data from potential students.
- Effective listening and learning strategies include the following:
  - Close monitoring of technological, competitive, societal, environmental, economic, and demographic factors that may bear on student, stakeholder, and market requirements, expectations, preferences, or alternatives;
  - Focus groups with demanding or leading-edge students and stakeholders; and
  - Analysis of major factors affecting key students and stakeholders.

3.1 Knowledge of Student, Stakeholder, and Market Needs and Expectations Sample Effective Practices for Teaching Faculty: Leaders of the Classroom Learning System

- Various methods are used to identify requirements and expectations of students, parents, and other stakeholders.
- The classroom focuses on the learning style and preferences of the students.
- Meaningful relationships are built, starting at the earliest possible contact date, with parents, students, and other key stakeholders. For example, curriculum and a cover note sent during the summer recess to parents and students is an advance contact and relationship builder.
- Several different methods are used to identify student issues and concerns affecting the course, such as surveys, focus groups, and suggestion boxes. These methods are used regularly and frequently.

3.2 Student and Stakeholder Relationships and Satisfaction (45 points)
Approach/Deployment Scoring

Describe how your organization builds relationships to attract and retain students, to enhance student learning and the organization's overall ability to deliver its services, to satisfy students and stakeholders, and to develop new opportunities. Describe also how your organization determines student and stakeholder satisfaction.

Within your response, include answers to the following questions:

a. Student and Stakeholder Relationships

(1) How do you build relationships to attract and retain students, to enhance student performance and the organization's overall ability to deliver its services, to satisfy students and stakeholders, and to foster new and continuing interactions and positive referrals?

(2) How do you determine key student and stakeholder contact requirements and maintain effective stakeholder relationships, including partnerships with key stakeholders, to pursue common purposes? How do you ensure that these requirements are deployed to all people involved in maintaining these relationships? What key measures/indicators do you use to monitor the effectiveness and progress of the organization's key relationships? Include a summary of your key access mechanisms for stakeholders to seek information, to pursue common purposes, and to make complaints.

(3) What is your complaint management process? Include how you ensure that complaints are resolved effectively and promptly and that all complaints are aggregated and analyzed for use in improvement throughout your organization and by your partners, as appropriate.

(4) How do you keep your approaches to relationship building and student and stakeholder access current with educational service needs and directions?

b. Student and Stakeholder Satisfaction Determination

(1) How do you determine student and stakeholder satisfaction and dissatisfaction and use this information for improvement? Include how you ensure that your measurements capture actionable information that reflects your organization's learning and developmental climate and predicts students' and stakeholders' future interactions with your organization and/or potential for positive referral. Describe significant differences in determination methods for different student and stakeholder groups.

(2) How do you follow up on your interactions with students and key stakeholders to receive prompt and actionable feedback?

(3) How do you obtain and use information on the satisfaction of students and stakeholders relative to benchmarks or to the satisfaction of these groups with your competitors or other organizations delivering similar educational services, as appropriate?

(4) How do you keep your approaches to determining satisfaction current with educational service needs and directions?

Notes:

N1. Student and stakeholder relationships (3.2a) might include the development of partnerships or alliances.

N2. *Partnerships* (3.2a[2]) refers to cooperative relationships with other schools, places of work, and parents, as appropriate, for purposes of ensuring effective transitions for students. Partners might include schools for which "feeder" relationships exist, into or out of your school, whether this relationship is formal or informal. Partnering organizations also might include social service organizations that are involved in helping students make effective transitions.

continued on next page

N3.   Determining student and stakeholder satisfaction and dissatisfaction (3.2b) might include use of any or all of the following: surveys, formal and informal feedback, dropout rates, absenteeism, student conflict data, and complaints. Information might be gathered on the Internet, through personal contact or a third party, or by mail.

N4.   Student and stakeholder satisfaction measurements might include both a numerical rating scale and descriptors for each unit in the scale. Actionable student and stakeholder satisfaction measurements provide useful information about specific educational program/service features, delivery, interactions, and transactions that bear upon student development and learning and the students' and stakeholders' future actions (e.g., transfer and/or positive referral). Measures might include trends and levels in performance of student/stakeholder services or the effectiveness of handling student/stakeholder complaints (e.g., complaint response time, effective resolution of complaints, and the percentage of complaints resolved on first contact).

N5.   Your student and stakeholder satisfaction and dissatisfaction results should be reported in Item 7.2.

This Item looks at the organization's processes for determining student and stakeholder relationships and satisfaction, with the aim of loyalty, retaining existing students, and developing new opportunities. Relationships provide an important means for organizations to understand and manage student and stakeholder expectations and to develop new educational opportunities. Faculty and staff in contact with students may provide vital information to build partnerships with students and stakeholders and other longer-term relationships.

Overall, Item 3.2 emphasizes the importance of obtaining actionable information, such as feedback and complaints from students and stakeholders. To be actionable, the information gathered should meet two conditions:

1. Responses should be tied directly to key educational or operational processes, so that opportunities for improvement are clear; and

2. Responses should be translated into cost implications to support the setting of improvement priorities.

This Item also addresses how the organization determines student and stakeholder satisfaction and satisfaction relative to competitors and similar organizations. Satisfaction relative to competitors and the factors that lead to preference are of critical importance to managing in a competitive environment.

The first part of this Item [3.2a(1)] looks at the organization's processes for providing easy access for students, stakeholders, and potential students to receive information or assistance and/or to comment and complain:

- Student and stakeholder access makes it easy to get timely information from students and stakeholders about issues that are of real concern to them. Timely information, in turn, is transmitted to the appropriate place in the organization to drive improvements or new levels of educational programs and service.

- Information from students and stakeholders needs to be used to improve key educational processes, and to determine cost implications for improvement priority setting.

Organizations must also determine student and stakeholder contact requirements and make sure all faculty and staff who interact with students and stakeholders understand these requirements:

- Student and stakeholder contact requirements essentially refer to expectations for service after contact with the organization has been made. Typically, the organization translates student and stakeholder contact requirements into service standards. Student and stakeholder contact requirements should be set in measurable terms to permit effective monitoring and performance review.

- A good example of a measurable student and stakeholder contact requirement might be the expectation that a malfunctioning computer would be back online within 24 hours of the request for service. Another example might be the requirement that a knowledgeable and polite human being is available within five minutes to resolve a problem with school bus transportation. In both cases, a clear requirement and a measurable standard were identified.

- An example of a poor service standard might be "we get back to the parents as soon as we can." With this example, no standard of performance is defined. Some faculty and staff might get back to parents within a matter of minutes. Others might take hours or days. The failure to define precisely the contact requirement makes it difficult to allocate appropriate resources to meet that requirement consistently.

- These student and stakeholder service standards must be deployed to all faculty and staff. Such deployment needs to take account of all key points in the response chain—all departments or individuals in the organization that make effective interactions possible. These standards then become one source of information to evaluate the organization's performance in meeting student and stakeholder contact requirements.

Organizations should capture, aggregate, analyze, and learn from the complaint information and comments it receives. Prompt and effective responses and solutions to student and stakeholder needs and expectations are a source of satisfaction and loyalty:

- The principal issue in complaint management is prompt and effective resolution of complaints, including recovery of student and stakeholder confidence. This is enhanced by resolution made by the first person the student or stakeholder contacts. This helps ensure higher levels of loyalty. Even if the organization ultimately resolves a problem, the likelihood of maintaining a loyal student/stakeholder is nearly cut in half each time that student/stakeholder is referred to another place in the organization.

- The organization must also have a mechanism for learning from complaints and ensuring faculty and staff receive information needed to eliminate the causes of complaints. Effective elimination of the causes of complaints involves aggregation of complaint information from all sources for evaluation and use in overall organizational improvement—both educational program design and delivery stages (see Items 6.1 and 6.2).

- Complaint aggregation, analysis, and root cause determination should lead to effective elimination of the causes of complaints and to priority setting for educational process and service improvements. Successful outcomes require effective deployment of information throughout the organization.

For long-term success, organizations should build strong relationships with its students and stakeholders, since program development and service innovation increasingly depend on maintaining close relationships with students and stakeholders:

- Organizations should keep approaches to all aspects of relationships current with changing educational service needs and directions, since approaches to and bases for relationships may change quickly.

- Organizations should also develop an effective process to determine the levels of satisfaction and dissatisfaction for the different student and stakeholder groups. Satisfied students and stakeholders are a requirement for loyalty, retention, and positive referrals.

Finally, organizations should systematically follow up with students and stakeholders regarding service and recent transactions. Determine student and stakeholder satisfaction relative to competitors so that you may improve future performance:

- A key aspect of student and stakeholder satisfaction determination is satisfaction relative to competitors and competing or alternative offerings. Such information might be derived from your own comparative studies or from independent studies. The factors that lead to student and stakeholder preference are of critical importance in understanding factors that drive markets and potentially affect longer-term competitiveness. This is particularly true today in the higher education arena.

The second part of this Item [3.2b] looks at how the organization determines student and stakeholder satisfaction and dissatisfaction. Four types of requirements are considered:

1. The organization must gather information on satisfaction and dissatisfaction, including any important differences in approaches for different groups or segments. This highlights the importance of the measurement scale in determining those factors that best reflect students' and stakeholders' behaviors—retention, future services, and positive referral.

2. The organization should follow up with students and stakeholders regarding educational programs, services, and recent transactions to determine satisfaction and to resolve problems quickly.

3. The organization should determine the levels of student and stakeholder satisfaction relative to competitors. Such information might be derived from organization-based comparative studies or independent studies. The purpose of this comparison is to develop information that can be used for improving performance relative to competitors and to better understand the factors that drive attendance, retention, and positive referrals.

4. The organization keeps their approaches to determining student and stakeholder satisfaction current with changing educational service needs and directions.

3.2 *Student and Stakeholder Relationships and Satisfaction*

How student and stakeholder satisfaction is determined, relationships strengthened, and current services enhanced to improve student- and market-related planning.

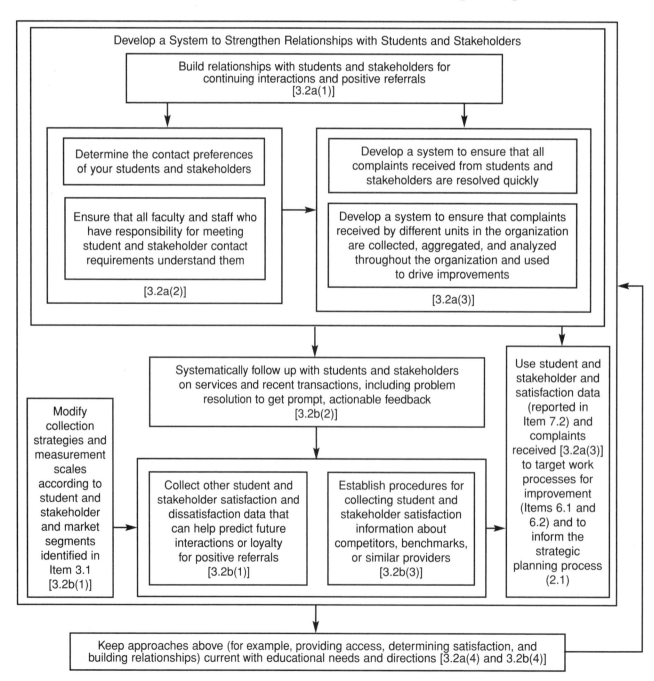

Develop a System to Strengthen Relationships with Students and Stakeholders

Build relationships with students and stakeholders for continuing interactions and positive referrals
[3.2a(1)]

Determine the contact preferences of your students and stakeholders

Ensure that all faculty and staff who have responsibility for meeting student and stakeholder contact requirements understand them

[3.2a(2)]

Develop a system to ensure that all complaints received from students and stakeholders are resolved quickly

Develop a system to ensure that complaints received by different units in the organization are collected, aggregated, and analyzed throughout the organization and used to drive improvements

[3.2a(3)]

Systematically follow up with students and stakeholders on services and recent transactions, including problem resolution to get prompt, actionable feedback
[3.2b(2)]

Modify collection strategies and measurement scales according to student and stakeholder and market segments identified in Item 3.1
[3.2b(1)]

Collect other student and stakeholder satisfaction and dissatisfaction data that can help predict future interactions or loyalty for positive referrals
[3.2b(1)]

Establish procedures for collecting student and stakeholder satisfaction information about competitors, benchmarks, or similar providers
[3.2b(3)]

Use student and stakeholder and satisfaction data (reported in Item 7.2) and complaints received [3.2a(3)] to target work processes for improvement (Items 6.1 and 6.2) and to inform the strategic planning process (2.1)

Keep approaches above (for example, providing access, determining satisfaction, and building relationships) current with educational needs and directions [3.2a(4) and 3.2b(4)]

3.2 Student and Stakeholder Relationships and Satisfaction Item Linkages

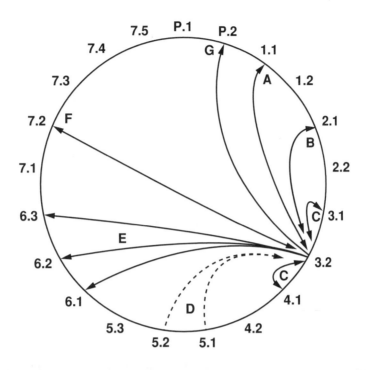

Nature of Relationship

A   Priorities and student and stakeholder contact requirements (service standards) for faculty and staff [3.2a(1)] are driven by top leadership [1.1a(1)]. Leaders [1.1a(1)] personally interact with and build better relationships with students and stakeholders [3.2a(1)]. They receive useful information from those students and stakeholders to improve management of decision making.

B   Information about student and stakeholder satisfaction [3.2b(1)] and complaints [3.2a(3)] collected by faculty and staff is used in the planning process [2.1a(2)]. In addition, strategic objectives [2.1b(1)] influence student and stakeholder relationship management [3.2a] and student and stakeholder satisfaction determination processes [3.2b] by identifying key focus areas.

C   Information concerning student and stakeholder requirements, expectations [3.1a], and benchmark data [4.1a(3)] are used to help identify, set, and deploy student and stakeholder contact requirements (service standards) [3.2a(2)]. Complaint data [3.2a] are used to help assess student and stakeholder requirements and expectations [3.1]. Student and stakeholder relations and satisfaction data [3.2b(1)] are analyzed [4.1b] and used to set priorities for action.

D   Training [5.2] and improved flexibility and self-direction [5.1a(1)] should enhance the ability of faculty and staff [3.2a(2)] to understand requirements and develop the skills to satisfy students and stakeholders [3.2a(3)].

E   Information collected through faculty and staff [3.2a(2)] is used to enhance design of products and services and to improve operational, student service, and support processes [6.1, 6.2, and 6.3].

F   Information from student and stakeholder relations processes [3.2a(3)] can help in the design of student and stakeholder satisfaction measures [3.2b(1)] and produce student and stakeholder satisfaction results data. Results [7.2a(1)] are used to set student and stakeholder contact requirements (service standards) [3.2a]. Efforts of improved accessibility and responsiveness in complaint management [3.2a] should result in improved complaint response time, effective complaint resolution, and a higher percentage of complaints resolved on first contact. These results should be reported in 7.2.

G   Information about the satisfaction of competitors' students and stakeholders, which is needed to create the description for P.2a, use processes discussed in Item 3.1a(1) and 3.2b(3).

3.2 Student and Stakeholder Relationships and Satisfaction
Sample Effective Practices

A. Student and Stakeholder Relationships

- Requirements for building relationships are identified and may include such factors as faculty and staff responsiveness and various stakeholder contact methods.

- Problem resolution priority setting is based on the potential impact of stakeholder decisions to buy, or recommend to others, the offering or service. For example, a business that sponsored and then employed many students would have a direct impact on the organization.

- Feedback is sought on the effectiveness of service.

- A systematic approach exists to evaluate and improve stakeholder relationships. For example, organizations may want to allow their buildings to be used for community events, even at a certain cost, to open and strengthen relationships of stakeholders who pay school taxes but do not directly use its services.

- Feedback from stakeholders, including faculty and staff, is systematically used in the improvement process.

- Several methods are used to ensure ease of student and stakeholder contact, 24 hours a day if necessary (for example, homework hotlines, school calendars with emergency and other numbers listed prominently, Web sites, toll-free numbers, pagers for contact personnel, surveys, interviews, focus groups, and electronic bulletin boards).

- The process of developing relationships with all key stakeholders is regularly evaluated and improved. Several improvement cycles are evident.

- Procedures are in place and evaluated to ensure that student/stakeholder contact is initiated to follow up on recent transactions to build relationships.

- Training and development plans and replacement procedures exist for first-contact employees (office staff, bus drivers, and cafeteria workers).

B. Student and Stakeholder Satisfaction Determination

- Faculty and staff are empowered to make decisions to address student and stakeholder concerns. For example, parents are asked to talk with instructors before contacting department chairs or principals, and faculty/staff are motivated and have the responsibility to solve problems at that level whenever possible.

- Adequate staff are available for, and their schedules permit, maintaining effective student and stakeholder contact.

- Performance expectations are set for faculty and staff whose jobs bring them in regular contact with students and stakeholders.

- The process of collecting complete, timely, and accurate stakeholder satisfaction and dissatisfaction data is regularly evaluated and improved. Several improvement cycles are evident.

- The performance of faculty and staff against these expectations is measured and tracked. For example, bus drivers are held responsible for transportation being safe, orderly, and on time.

- A system exists to ensure that student and stakeholder complaints are resolved promptly and effectively.

- Complaints and student/stakeholder concerns are resolved at first contact. This often means training faculty and staff who are first contacts and giving them authority to resolve a broad range of problems.

- Complaint data are tracked and used to initiate prompt corrective action to prevent the problem from recurring.

- An actionable student and stakeholder satisfaction measurement system exists that provides the organization with reliable information about ratings of specific offerings and service features and the relationship between these ratings and the student/stakeholder likely future market behavior (loyalty).

- Several satisfaction indicators are used (for example, repeat enrollment within families and schools, praise letters, and direct measures using survey questions and interviews).

- Comprehensive satisfaction and dissatisfaction data are collected and segmented or grouped to enable the organization to predict student and stakeholder behavior (likelihood of remaining a student, positive referrals).

- Several means of collecting satisfaction data are used (for example, surveys, interviews, and focus groups).
- Student/stakeholder dissatisfaction indicators are evaluated, including complaints; refunds; repeat services; such as examinations or course content, litigation, performance rating downgrades, and warranty work (if the college guarantees its graduates on-the-job performance or the learning center guarantees a grade level increase); and warranty costs.
- Satisfaction data are collected from former students and stakeholders.
- Competitors' student/stakeholders satisfaction is determined using various means, such as external or internal studies.
- Methods are in place to ensure objectivity of these data.
- Organization-based or independent organization comparative studies take into account one or more indicators of student/stakeholder dissatisfaction, as well as satisfaction. The extent and types of such studies depend on industry and organization size.

3.2 Student and Stakeholder Relationships and Satisfaction
Sample Effective Practices for Teaching Faculty:
Leaders of the Classroom Learning System

- Student and stakeholder requirements are included when developing classroom improvement goals.
- Instructional faculty and staff take into account the requirements of the next grade, content level, or course as a basis for curriculum and instructional goals.
- Methods are in place to build, maintain, and track positive relationships with students and stakeholders. (For example, data is kept on return calls or e-mails, number of contacts, tutoring after class, feedback, and so on.)
- The level of student and stakeholder satisfaction/dissatisfaction is routinely assessed, and this information drives improvement in the classroom system.

4 Information and Analysis—90 Points

The Information and Analysis Category examines your organization's information management and performance measurement systems and how your organization analyzes performance data and information.

Information and analysis is the main point within the criteria for all key information to effectively measure performance and manage the organization, and to drive improvement of performance and competitiveness. In the simplest terms, Category 4 is the "brain center" for the alignment of the organization's operations and its strategic directions. However, since information and analysis might themselves be primary sources of competitive advantage and performance improvement, the category also includes such strategic considerations.

Information and Analysis evaluates the selection, management, and effectiveness of use of information and data to support processes, action plans, and the performance management system. The analysis and review of data are evaluated. Information and Analysis is also concerned with how quality and availability of data and information are managed so faculty/staff, students and stakeholders, and suppliers/partners have access to needed data.

Measurement and Analysis of Organizational Performance

- This Item looks at the mechanical processes associated with data collection, information, and measures (including comparative data) for planning, decision making, improving performance, and supporting action plans and operations. This Item also looks at the analytical processes used to make sense out of the data, and how these analyses are deployed throughout the organization and used to support organization-level review, decision making, and planning.

Information Management

- This Item looks at data availability and how these mechanisms are kept current with educational service needs and directions. Data and information integrity, reliability, accuracy, timeliness, security, and confidentiality are also examined. The Item looks at hardware and software quality as part of information management.

4.1 Measurement and Analysis of Organizational Performance (50 points)
Approach/Deployment Scoring

Describe how your organization provides effective performance measurement systems for understanding, aligning, and improving organizational performance at all levels and in all parts of your organization.

Within your response, include answers to the following questions:

a. Performance Measurement

(1) How do you gather and integrate data and information from all sources to support daily operations and organizational decision making as an education organization?

(2) How do you select and align measures/indicators for tracking your daily operations, overall organizational performance, and education climate?

(3) How do you select and ensure the effective use of key comparative data and information from within and outside the academic community?

(4) How do you keep your performance measurement system current with educational service needs and directions?

b. Performance Analysis

(1) What analyses do you perform to support your senior leaders' organizational performance review and your organization's strategic planning?

(2) How do you communicate the results of organizational-level analysis to faculty and staff and/or educational programs to enable effective support for decision making?

(3) How do you align the results of organizational-level analysis with your key education results, strategic objectives, and action plans? How do these results provide the basis for projections of continuous and breakthrough improvements in performance?

Notes:

N1. Performance measurement is used in fact-based decision making for setting and aligning organizational direction and resource use at the classroom, departmental, key process, school/college, and whole organization levels.

N2. Comparative data and information sources (4.1a[3]) include benchmarking and competitive comparisons. *Benchmarking* refers to identifying processes and results that represent best practices and performance for similar activities, inside or outside the academic community. Competitive comparisons relate your organization's performance to that of comparable organizations and/or student populations and competing organizations, as appropriate.

N3. Analysis includes examining trends; organizational, academic community, and technology projections; and comparisons, cause-effect relationships, and correlations intended to support your performance reviews, help determine root causes, and help set priorities for resource use. Accordingly, analysis draws upon all types of data: student, student group, school program, stakeholder, market, operational, budgetary, and comparative data.

N4. The results of organizational performance analysis should contribute to your senior leaders' organizational performance review in 1.1b and organizational strategic planning in Category 2.

N5. Your organizational performance results should be reported in Items 7.1, 7.2, 7.3, 7.4, and 7.5.

The first area of this Item is performance measurement. The effective organization selects and uses measures for tracking daily operations and integrates these measures for monitoring overall organizational performance:

- Alignment and integration are key concepts for successful implementation of your performance measurement system. They are viewed in terms of extent and effectiveness of use to meet your performance assessment needs. Alignment and integration include how measures are aligned throughout the organization, how they are integrated to yield organizationwide measures, and how performance measurement requirements are deployed by your senior leaders to track workgroup and process-level performance on key measures targeted for organizationwide significance and/or improvement.

- Performance data and information are especially important in education networks, alliances, and supply chains. Your responses to this Item should take into account this strategic use of data and information, and should recognize the need for rapid data validation and reliability assurance given the increasing use of electronic data transfer.

- Organizations need to ensure data and information reliability, since reliability is critical to good decision making, successful monitoring of operations, and successful data integration for assessing overall performance.

You are asked how you select and use competitive comparisons and benchmarking information to help drive performance improvement:

- The use of competitive and comparative information is important to all organizations. The major premises for using competitive and comparative information are: (1) the organization needs to know where it stands relative to competitors and to best practices; (2) comparative and benchmarking information often provides the impetus for significant ("breakthrough") improvement or change; and (3) preparation for comparing performance information frequently leads to a better understanding of your processes and their performance. Benchmarking information also may support organizational analysis and decisions relating to core competencies, alliances, and outsourcing.

- Your effective selection and use of competitive comparisons and benchmarking information require: (1) determination of needs and priorities; (2) criteria for seeking appropriate sources for comparisons—from within and outside the organization's industry and markets; and (3) use of data and information to set stretch targets and to promote major, nonincremental improvements in areas most critical to the organization's competitive strategy.

Finally, you are asked how you keep the organization's performance measurement system current with changing educational service needs. This involves ongoing evaluation and demonstrated refinement.

The second measurement area in this Item is performance analysis. Individual facts and data do not usually provide an effective basis for organizational priority setting. This Item emphasizes that close alignment is needed between your analysis and the organizational performance review, and between your analysis and organizational planning. This ensures that analysis is relevant to decision making and that decision making is based on relevant facts.

Action depends upon understanding cause-effect connections among and between processes and organizational performance results. Process improvement actions and their results may have many resource implications. Organizations have a critical need to provide an effective analytical basis for decisions, because resources for improvement are limited and cause-effect connections are often unclear.

Analyses that the organization conducts to gain an understanding of performance and needed actions may vary widely, depending upon your type of organization, size, competitive environment, and other factors. Examples of possible analyses include:

- How educational service improvement correlates with key student performance indicators, such as satisfaction, student retention, and enrollment;
- Cost/revenue implications of student/stakeholder-related problems and problem resolution effectiveness;
- Interpretation of market share changes in terms of gains, losses, and changes in student and stakeholder satisfaction;
- Improvement trends in key operational performance indicators, such as productivity, cycle time, waste reduction, new educational program introduction, and failures;
- Relationships between faculty and staff/organizational learning and value added per faculty and staff;
- Financial benefits derived from improvements in faculty and staff safety, absenteeism, and turnover;
- Benefits and costs associated with education and training, improved organizational knowledge management, and sharing;
- The ability to identify and meet faculty and staff requirements, and its correlation with retention, motivation, and productivity;
- Individual or aggregate measures of productivity and quality relative to competitors;
- Cost trends relative to competitors;
- Relationships between educational service quality, operational performance indicators, and overall financial and budgetary performance trends as reflected in indicators, such as operating costs, revenues, asset utilization, and value added per faculty and staff;
- Allocation of resources among alternative improvement projects based on cost/revenue implications and improvement potential;
- Student retention derived from quality/operational/faculty and staff resource performance improvements;
- Comparisons among departments showing how quality and operational performance improvement affect financial and budgetary performance;
- Contributions of improvement activities to student performance;
- Budgetary impacts of student retention;
- Cost/revenue implications of new market entry, including global market entry or expansion;
- Cost/revenue, student/stakeholder, and productivity implications of engaging in and/or expanding electronic commerce; and
- Trends in economic, market, and stakeholder indicators of value.

4.1 Measurement and Analysis of Organizational Performance

How the organization selects, manages, analyzes, and uses information and data to support decision making for key processes and to improve performance at all levels and parts of the organization.

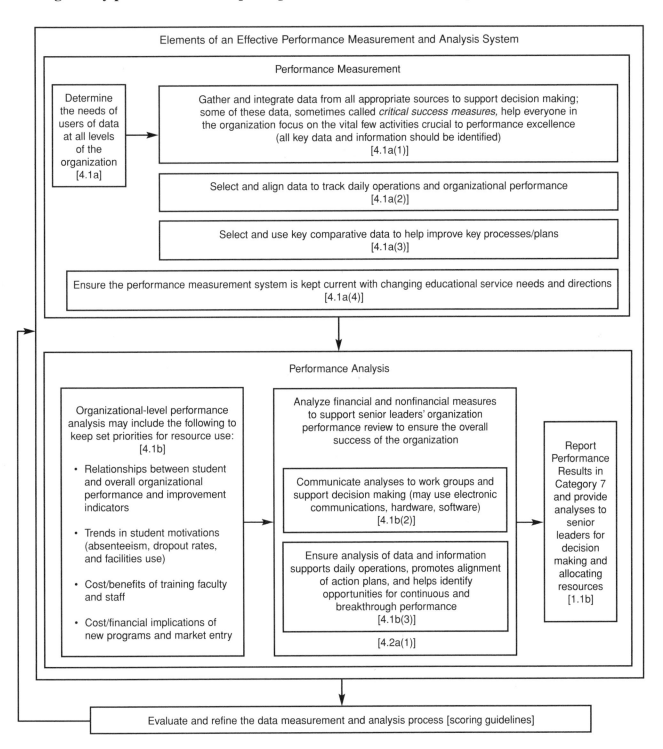

4.1 Measurement and Analysis of Organizational Performance Item Linkages

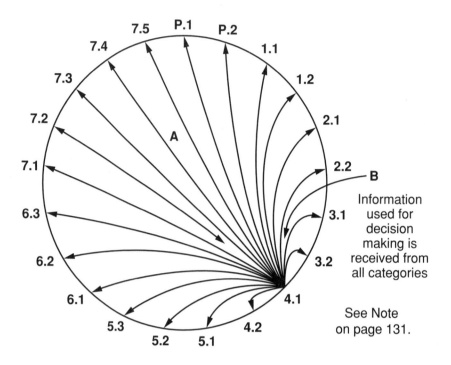

Nature of Relationship

A   Data and information are collected and analyzed [4.1] and made available [4.2] for developing the Organizational Profile [P.1 and P.2], planning [2.1a(2)], setting strategic objectives [2.1b(1)], benchmarking priority setting [4.1], day-to-day leadership decisions [1.1], setting public responsibility standards (accreditation, regulatory, legal, ethical) for community involvement [1.2], reporting performance results [7.1, 7.2, 7.3, 7.4, and 7.5], improving work processes [6.1, 6.2, 6.3] and faculty/staff systems [5.1, 5.2, 5.3], determining student and stakeholder requirements [3.1], managing complaints and building student and stakeholder relations [3.2a], and determining student and stakeholder satisfaction [3.2b].

B   Data and information used to support analysis, decision making, and continuous improvement [4.1] are received from all processes. Information from student and stakeholder satisfaction data [7.2] are analyzed [4.1b] and used to help determine ways to assess student and stakeholder requirements [3.1a(2)], to determine standards or required levels of service and relationship development [3.2a(2)], and to design instruments to assess satisfaction [3.2b(1)]. Data and information are received from the following areas and analyzed to support decision making: human resources capabilities, including work system efficiency, initiative, and self-direction [5.1a(1)]; training and development needs [5.2a(2)] and effectiveness [5.2a(4)]; safety; retention; absenteeism; organizational effectiveness; and well-being and satisfaction [5.3]. Data are aggregated and analyzed [4.1] to improve work processes [6.1, 6.2, 6.3] that will reduce cycle time, waste, and defect levels. Performance data from all parts of the organization are integrated and analyzed [4.1] to assess performance in key areas, such as student learning [7.1]; student and stakeholder-related performance [7.2]; operational performance [7.5]; financial, budgetary, and market performance [7.3]; and faculty and staff performance [7.4], relative to competitive performance in all areas.

NOTE: Because the information collected and used for decision making links with all other Items, the linkage arrows will not all be repeated on the other Item maps. The more relevant connections will be identified.

4.1 Measurement and Analysis of Organizational Performance
Sample Effective Practices

- Data collected at the individual faculty and staff level are consistent across the organization to permit consolidation and organizationwide performance monitoring.
- Every person has access to the data they need to make decisions about their work, from top leaders to individuals, work teams, and departments.
- Performance and operational data are collected and routinely used for management decisions.
- Internal and external data are used to describe student and stakeholder satisfaction, and product and service performance.
- The cost of poor quality and other financial concerns are measured for internal operations and processes.
- Data are maintained on faculty- and staff-related issues of satisfaction, morale, safety, education and training, use of teams, and recognition and reward.
- The data collection and analysis system is systematically evaluated and refined.
- Improvements are made to reduce cycle time for data collection and to increase data access and use.
- Formal processes are in place to ensure data reliability, objectivity, and confidentiality.
- Faculty, staff, and stakeholders are involved in validating data.
- A systematic process exists for data review and improvement, standardization, and easy faculty and staff access to data. Training on the use of data systems is provided as needed.
- Data used for management decisions' focus on critical success factors are integrated with work processes for the planning, design, and delivery of educational programs and services.
- Users of data help determine what data systems are developed and how data are accessed.
- A systematic process is in place for identifying and prioritizing comparative information and benchmark targets.
- Research has been conducted to identify best-in-class organizations, which may be competitors or noncompetitors.
- Key processes or functions are the subject of benchmarking. Activities such as those that support the organization's goals and objectives, action plans, and opportunities for improvement and innovation are the subject of benchmarking.
- Benchmarking covers key offerings, services, student/stakeholder satisfiers, faculty, and support operations.
- The organization reaches beyond its own education facilities to conduct comparative studies.
- Benchmark or comparison data are used to improve the understanding of work processes and to discover the best levels of performance that have been achieved. Based on this knowledge, the organization sets goals or targets to stretch performance, as well as drive innovations.
- A systematic approach is used to evaluate and improve processes for selecting, gathering, and using comparative information.
- Benchmarking processes are fully documented.
- Systematic actions have been taken to evaluate and improve the quality and use of comparative information and benchmark data.

4.1 Measurement and Analysis of Organizational Performance
Sample Effective Practices for Teaching Faculty:
Leaders of the Classroom Learning System

- Tests are analyzed to determine student mastery as well as teaching areas that need to be strengthened.
- Knowledge about educational trends and priorities are used to develop and track goals of the classroom or course.
- Information systems are used to track and report results.
- Students have access to their performance data and comparative data for other students and the class (not personally identifiable data).
- Information systems are used to support academic and operational improvement for the course or class. (For example, a kindergarten class used a control chart to track the amount of time they spent on cleanup so they could spend more time on instructional activities like stories.)
- Comparative data are used to track, report, and improve the rate and extent of course and classroom performance improvement.
- When appropriate, students and parents are given data to improve their performance, for example, charts with overall course/class performance, rubrics, flowcharts, and timelines.
- Processes are in place for analyzing student- and stakeholder-related data and results (including complaint data) and setting priorities for action.
- Facts, rather than intuition, are used to support decision making at all levels, based on the analyses conducted to make sense out of the data collected.
- The analysis process itself is analyzed to make the results more timely and useful for decision making for quality improvement at all levels.
- Analysis processes and tools, and the value of analyses to decision making, are systematically evaluated and improved.

4.2 Information Management (40 points)
Approach/Deployment Scoring

Describe how your organization ensures the quality and availability of needed data and information for faculty and staff, students and stakeholders, and suppliers/partners.

Within your response, include answers to the following questions:

a. Data Availability

(1) How do you make needed data and information available? How do you make them accessible to faculty and staff, students and stakeholders, and suppliers/partners, as appropriate?

(2) How do you ensure data and information integrity, reliability, accuracy, timeliness, security, and confidentiality?

(3) How do you keep your data and information availability mechanisms current with educational service needs and directions?

b. Hardware and Software Quality

(1) How do you ensure that hardware and software are reliable and user-friendly?

(2) How do you keep your software and hardware systems current with educational service needs and directions?

Notes:

N1. Data availability (4.2a) is of growing importance as the Internet and school Web sites are used increasingly for student-school and stakeholder-school interactions and intranets become more important as a major source of organizationwide communications.

N2. Data and information access (4.2a [1]) might be via electronic and other means.

This Item examines how the organization ensures the availability of high-quality, timely data and information for all key users—faculty and staff, students and stakeholders, and suppliers/partners.

The organization is asked how data and information is made available and accessible to user communities; how it ensures that the data and information have all the characteristics the users expect: integrity, reliability, accuracy, timeliness, and appropriate levels of security and confidentiality; how it ensures that hardware and software systems are reliable and user-friendly so that access is facilitated and encouraged; and how data availability mechanisms, software, and hardware are kept current with changing educational service needs and directions.

Managing information can require a significant commitment of resources as the sources of data and information grow dramatically. Organizational abilities to ensure reliability and availability in a user-friendly format are challenged by the expanding use of electronic information within organizations' operations; as part of organizational knowledge networks; from the Internet, intranet, and school Web sites; and in communications between students and their school, as well as between stakeholders and the school.

Data and information are especially important in grade-to-grade, school-to-school, and school-to-work transitions and in partnerships with business, social services, and the community. Responses to this Item should take into account this use of data and information and should recognize the need for rapid data validation and reliability assurance, given the increasing use of electronic data transfer.

4.2 Information Management

How the organization ensures the quality and availability of data for faculty and staff, students and stakeholders, and partners

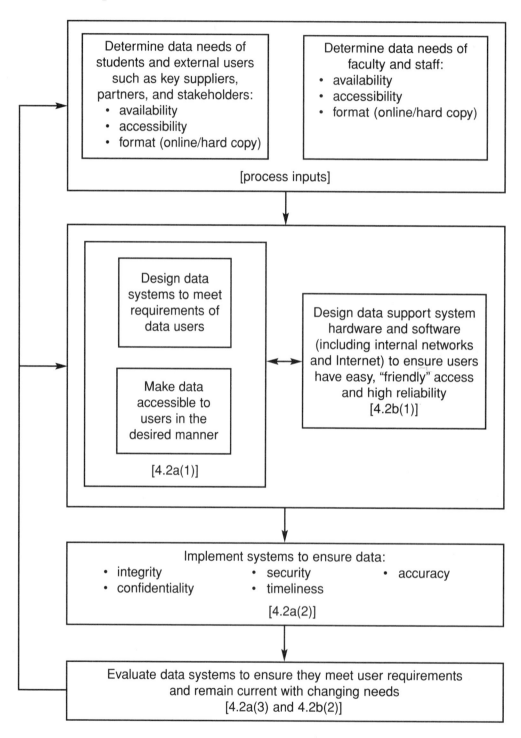

4.2 Information Management Item Linkages

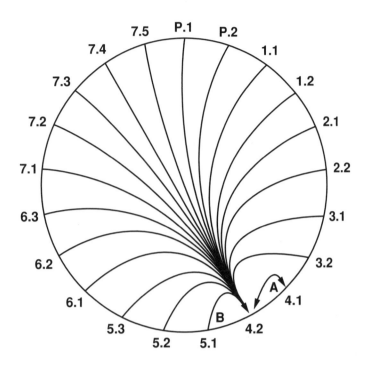

Nature of Relationship

A   This Item, Information Management, enables the data flow within the organization and indirectly interacts with all other Items (similar to the relationships identified and reported in the Item 4.1 diagram). The simplest way to show these relationships is to tie this Item [4.2] with the Measurement and Analysis of Organizational Performance Item [4.1].

B   In order to ensure that hardware and software systems are reliable and user-friendly [4.2b], information from the following types of system users is gathered: leaders [Category 1], planners [Category 2], student and stakeholder relations and contact staff [Category 3], information specialists [Category 4], human resource staff, faculty and staff [Category 5], student and support process people [Category 6], and people who monitor and interpret results [Category 7] for use in decision making.

4.2 Information Management Sample Effective Practices

- Knowledge networks from internet, intranet, and school Web sites are reliable and available.
- Students and parents can understand information and data because it is in a user-friendly format.
- Information and data is available and shared easily when students go to another school, or a before- or after-school program.
- Data can be quickly validated and reliability is checked for electronic transfer of information.
- Appropriate levels of security and confidentiality are built in as part of data and information planning processes.
- Safety and security concerns are reported on a dedicated hotline with no questions asked when students, parents, or faculty/staff need to report a serious or potentially serious problem.

4.2 Information Management Sample Effective Practices for Teaching Faculty: Leaders of the Classroom Learning System

- Students and teachers are electronically connected so they can exchange information or teachers can respond to homework questions while they are working.

- A homework hotline is operational after school hours, with faculty and staff rotating coverage in different subjects.

- Faculty publish online course curriculums, due dates for assignments, test dates, and quick results with codes to protect confidentiality.

- Writing and mathematics assistance is available online after school hours.

- Faculty and staff use e-mail to communicate in real time with parents, students, and other stakeholders so they are not playing "telephone tag" and wasting time trying to return or respond to messages.

5 Faculty and Staff Focus—85 Points

The Faculty and Staff Focus Category examines how your organization motivates and enables faculty and staff to develop and utilize their full potential in alignment with your organization's overall objectives and action plans. Also examined are your organization's efforts to build and maintain a work environment and faculty and staff support climate conducive to performance excellence and to personal and organizational growth.

Faculty and staff focus addresses key human resource practices—those directed toward creating a high-performance workplace and developing faculty and staff to enable them and the organization to adapt to change. The category covers faculty and staff resource development and management requirements in an integrated way, that is, aligned with the organization's strategic directions. Included in the focus on faculty and staff resources is a focus on the work environment and the faculty and staff support climate.

To ensure the basic alignment of faculty and staff resource management with overall strategy, the criteria also include faculty and staff planning as part of organizational planning in the Strategic Planning Category. Faculty and staff focus evaluates how the organization enables faculty and staff to develop and use their full potential.

Work Systems

- Design, organize, and manage work and jobs to optimize faculty and staff performance and potential.
- Recognition and reward practices support objectives for student and stakeholder satisfaction, performance improvement, and faculty and staff organization learning goals.
- Identify skills needed by potential faculty and staff, recruit, and hire.
- Ensure communication cooperation and knowledge/skill sharing across the organization.

Faculty and Staff Education, Training, and Development

- Deliver, evaluate, and reinforce appropriate training to achieve action plans and address organization needs, including building knowledge, skills, and abilities to improve faculty and staff development and performance.

Faculty and Staff Well-Being and Satisfaction

- Improve faculty and staff safety, well-being, development, and satisfaction and maintain a work environment conducive to high performance.
- Leaders at all levels encourage and motivate faculty and staff to reach full potential.
- Systematically evaluate faculty and staff well-being, satisfaction, and motivation and identify improvement priorities that promote key organizations results.

5.1 Work Systems (35 Points)
Approach/Deployment Scoring

Describe how your organization's work and jobs, compensation, career progression, and related workforce practices motivate and enable faculty and staff and the organization to achieve high performance.

Within your response, include answers to the following questions:

a. Work Systems

(1) How do you organize and manage work and jobs to promote cooperation, initiative/innovation, your organizational culture, and the flexibility to keep current with educational service needs? How do you achieve effective communication and knowledge/skill sharing across departments, jobs, and locations, as appropriate?

(2) How do you motivate faculty and staff to develop and utilize their full potential? Include formal and/or informal mechanisms you use to help faculty and staff attain job- and career-related development/learning objectives and the role of administrators, faculty leaders, and supervisors in helping faculty and staff attain these objectives.

(3) How does your faculty and staff performance management system, including feedback to faculty and staff, support high performance and a student and stakeholder focus? How do your compensation, recognition, and related reward/incentive practices reinforce these objectives, including your overall objectives for student learning and development?

(4) How do you accomplish effective succession planning for senior leadership and career progression throughout the organization?

(5) How do you identify characteristics and skills needed by potential faculty and staff? How do you recruit, hire, and retain new faculty and staff? How do your work systems capitalize on the diverse ideas, cultures, and thinking of the communities with which you interact (your hiring and student and stakeholder communities)?

Notes:

N1. *Faculty and staff* refers to your organization's permanent, temporary, and part-time personnel, as well as any contract employees supervised by your organization. Faculty and staff include team leaders, supervisors, faculty leaders, and administrators at all levels. Contract staff supervised by a contractor should be addressed in student services, educational processes, or support processes in Category 6.

N2. *Your organization's work* refers to how your faculty and staff are organized and/or organize themselves in formal and informal, temporary, or longer-term units. This might include work teams, curriculum design teams, problem-solving teams, centers of excellence, research teams, cross-functional teams, and departments that are self-managed or managed by supervisors.

Jobs refers to responsibilities, authorities, and tasks of individuals. In some work systems, jobs might be shared by a team.

N3. Compensation and recognition (5.1a[3]) include promotions and bonuses that might be based upon performance, skills acquired, and other factors. Recognition includes monetary and nonmonetary, formal and informal, and individual and group mechanisms. Recognition systems for volunteers who contribute to the work of your organization should be included, as appropriate.

This Item looks at the organization's systems for work and job design, compensation, faculty and staff performance management, motivation, recognition, communication, and hiring, with the aim of enabling and encouraging all faculty and staff to contribute effectively and to the best of their ability. These systems are intended to foster high performance, to result in individual and organizational learning, and to enable adaptation to change.

Work and jobs should be designed in such a way as to allow faculty and staff to exercise discretion and decision making, resulting in high performance:

- High-performance work is enhanced by systems that promote faculty and staff flexibility, innovation, and knowledge and skill sharing. Work should support organizational objectives, student and stakeholder focus, and rapid response to changing educational service needs and requirements of the marketplace. To achieve high levels of organizational performance, it is essential to develop fully the capabilities of the workforce. In addition to the enabled faculty and staff and proper work system design, high-performance work requires ongoing education and training, and information systems that ensure proper information flow. To help faculty and staff realize their full potential, many organizations use individual development plans prepared with the input of each faculty and staff and designed to address career and learning objectives.

- The ability to respond quickly to changing student/stakeholder and workplace requirements demands a workforce characterized by initiative and self-direction. Hierarchical, command-and-control management styles work directly against fast response and high-performance capability. After all, the opposite of individual initiative is an environment where administrators demand review and approval of decisions that are typically better made by the faculty and staff doing the work.

- Factors to consider in work and job design include simplification of job classifications, cross-training, job rotation, use of teams (including self-directed teams), and changes in work layout and location.

- Effective communication across functions and departments is also important to ensure a focus on student and stakeholder requirements and to ensure an environment of trust, knowledge sharing, and mutual respect.

Leaders and administrators throughout the organization should consistently encourage and motivate faculty and staff to achieve Performance Excellence objectives. Faculty and staff compensation, recognition, and rewards should be lined up to support educational service and program objectives. In addition, to make sure all faculty and staff understand their responsibilities, systems should exist to promote effective communication and cooperation at all levels of the organization:

- Once the organization determines its key strategic objectives, it should review compensation, reward, and recognition systems to ensure they support those objectives. The organization needs to create an environment where faculty and staff are focused on the same set of activities the organization has determined are necessary for success.

- Compensation and recognition might be tied to demonstrated skills and/or to peer evaluations. Compensation and recognition approaches also might include team or unit performance and linkage to student and stakeholder satisfaction and loyalty measures.

Finally, organizations must profile, recruit, and hire faculty and staff who will meet skill requirements. Obviously, the workforce is a key driver of high performance:

- As the pool of skilled talent continues to shrink, it becomes more important than ever for organizations to specifically define the skills needed by potential faculty and staff and create a work environment to attract them. Accordingly, it is critical to take into account characteristics of diverse and special populations to make sure appropriate support systems exist that make it possible to attract skilled faculty and staff.

5.1 Work Systems

How the organization's work and job design, compensation and recognition approaches, career progression, and recruitment enable and encourage all faculty and staff to contribute effectively to achieving high performance.

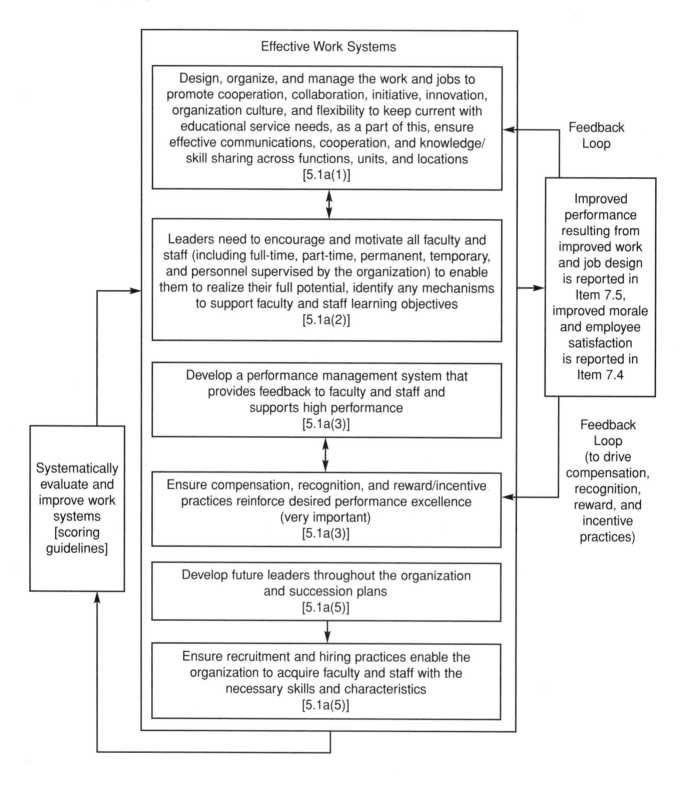

5.1 Work Systems Item Linkages

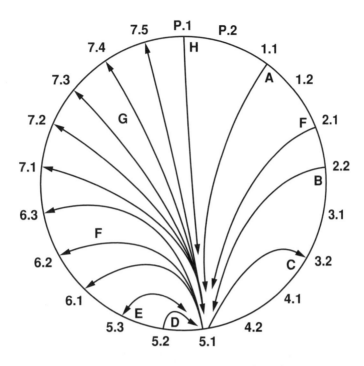

Nature of Relationship

A Top leaders (and subsequently leaders at all levels) [1.1a(2)] set the policies and role model actions essential to improving work and job design to enhance faculty and staff empowerment, initiative, self-direction, and flexibility [5.1a(1)].

B Human resource development plans and goals [2.2a(3)] address ways to improve faculty and staff performance and involvement [5.1].

C Flexibility, initiative, and communication and knowledge sharing [5.1a(1)] are essential to enhance the effectiveness and ability of student- and stakeholder-contact faculty and staff to resolve student concerns promptly [3.2a(3)].

D Effective training [5.2] is critical to enable faculty and staff at all levels to improve skills and improve their ability to manage, organize, and design better work processes [5.1].

E A safe, secure work climate [5.3] enhances faculty and staff participation, self-direction, and initiative [5.1], and vice versa.

F Effective performance feedback, compensation, and recognition [5.1a(3)] are essential to improving educational, student, and support processes [6.1, 6.2, and 6.3] and ensuring alignment to overall strategic objectives [2.1b(1)].

G Compensation, incentives, recognition, and rewards [5.1a(3)] are based in part on performance results [Category 7]. Improvements in work and job design, flexibility, innovation, empowerment, sharing, communication [5.1a(1)], and developing faculty and staff potential [5.1a(2)] result in improved performance and learning results [Category 7]. Processes to improve initiative and flexibility [5.1] can enhance all performance results [Category 7].

H Faculty and staff characteristics such as educational levels, workforce and job diversity, the existence of bargaining units, and other special requirements help set the context for determining the requirements for knowledge and skill sharing across work units, jobs, and locations [5.1a(1)].

5.1 Work Systems Sample Effective Practices

- Fully using the talents of all faculty and staff is a basic organizational value.

- Organization leaders at all levels use cross-functional work teams to break down barriers, improve effectiveness, and meet goals. For example, this could be a team of teachers in the same discipline across several grade levels or cross-disciplinary teams.

- Teams have access to data and are authorized to take responsibility for decisions affecting their work.

- Faculty and staff opinion is sought regarding work design and work processes.

- Prompt and regular feedback is provided to teams regarding their performance. Feedback covers both results and team process.

- Using teams and self-directed faculty and staff to improve performance is the way regular work is done.

- Self-directed or self-managed work teams are used throughout the organization to improve performance and address issues and concerns. They have appropriate authority over matters such as curriculum, instruction, and team membership and roles.

- A systematic process is used to evaluate and improve the effectiveness and extent of faculty and staff involvement.

- Many indicators of faculty and staff involvement effectiveness exist, such as the improvements in time or cost reduction produced by teams.

- Initiatives are undertaken to promote labor-management cooperation, such as partnerships with unions and faculty associations.

- Prioritization of faculty/staff problems is based on their potential impact on productivity.

- Recognition and rewards are provided for generating successful improvement ideas. Also, a system exists to encourage and provide rapid reinforcement for submitting improvement ideas.

- Recognition and rewards are provided for results, such as for reductions in cycle time for course introduction or services offered at less than projected cost.

- Faculty and staff, as well as administrators, participate in creating the recognition and rewards system and help monitor its implementation and systematic improvement.

- The organization evaluates and improves its approaches to faculty and staff performance and compensation, recognition, and rewards to determine the extent to which faculty and staff are satisfied with them, the extent of their participation, and the impact of the system on improved performance.

- Evaluations are used to make improvements. Top-scoring organizations have several improvement cycles. (Many improvement cycles can occur in one year.)

- Performance measures exist, and goals are expressed in measurable terms. These measurable goals form the basis for performance recognition.

- Recognition, reward, and compensation are influenced by student and stakeholder satisfaction ratings, as well as other performance measures.

5.2 Faculty and Staff Education, Training, and Development (25 points)
Approach/Deployment Scoring

Describe how your organization's faculty and staff education and training support the achievement of your overall objectives, including building faculty and staff knowledge, skills, and capabilities and contributing to high performance.

Within your response, include answers to the following questions:

a. Faculty and Staff Education, Training, and Development

(1) How do faculty and staff education and training contribute to the achievement of your action plans? How does your education and training approach balance short- and longer-term organizational objectives and faculty and staff needs, including certification, licensure, development, learning, and career progression?

(2) How do you seek and use input from faculty, staff, and their senior leaders, and supervisors/administrators on education and training needs and delivery options?

(3) How do you address in your faculty and staff education, training, and development your key organizational needs associated with technological change, leadership/supervisor development, new faculty and staff orientation, safety, performance measurement/improvement, and diversity?

(4) How do you deliver faculty and staff education and training? Include formal and informal delivery, including mentoring and other approaches, as appropriate. How do you evaluate the effectiveness of faculty and staff education and training, taking into account individual and organizational performance?

(5) How do you reinforce the use of knowledge and skills on the job?

Notes:

N1. Technological change (5.2a[3]) might include computer and Internet literacy.

N2. Education and training delivery (5.2a[4]) might occur inside or outside your organization and involve on-the-job, classroom, computer-based, distance learning, and/or other types of delivery (formal or informal).

This Item looks at the organization's system for workforce education, training, and on-the-job reinforcement of knowledge and skills, with the aim of meeting ongoing needs of faculty and staff and a high-performance workplace.

To help the organization achieve its high-performance objectives, education and training must be effectively designed, delivered, reinforced on the job, and evaluated. To optimize organization effectiveness, the education and training system should place special emphasis on meeting individual career progression and organizational needs:

- Education and training needs might vary greatly depending on the level and nature of the organization's work, faculty and staff responsibility, and stage of organizational and personal development. These needs might include certification, licensure, knowledge-sharing skills, communications, teamwork, problem solving, interpreting and using data, meeting student and stakeholder requirements, process analysis and simplification, waste and cycle time reduction, and priority setting based on strategic alignment or cost/benefit analysis.

Organizations are wise to consider job and organizational performance in education and training design and evaluation in support of a fact-based management system. Faculty, staff, and their administrators will help determine training needs and contribute to the design and evaluation of education and training, because these individuals frequently are best able to identify critical needs and evaluate success:

- Education and training delivery might occur inside or outside the organization and could involve on-the-job, classroom, computer-based, distance learning, or other types of delivery. Training also might occur through developmental assignments within or outside the organization.

- When you evaluate education and training, seek effectiveness measures as a critical component of evaluation. Such measures might address impact on individual, unit, and organizational performance, impact on student-related performance, and cost/benefit analysis of the training.

- Although this Item does not require specific training for student- and stakeholder-contact faculty and staff, the Item does require that education and training "keep current with educational service and individual needs" and "address Performance Excellence." If an objective of the organization is to enhance student and stakeholder satisfaction and loyalty, it may be critical to identify job requirements for student- and stakeholder-contact faculty and staff. Such training is increasingly important and common among high-performing organizations. It frequently includes acquiring critical knowledge and skills with respect to services, students, and stakeholders; skills on how to listen to students and stakeholders; recovery from problems or failures; and learning how to manage expectations effectively.

The organization needs to address Performance Excellence in its education and training programs:

- Faculty, staff, and administrators need to use performance measures and standards to ensure excellence in education and training.

- Performance Excellence education and training may include the use of performance measures, skill standards, quality control methods, benchmarking, problem-solving processes, and performance improvement techniques.

- Finally, the organization needs to address key developmental and training needs, including high-priority needs, such as management and leadership development, diversity training, and safety. Leadership development at all levels is becoming more critical, as organizations find it more difficult to recruit and retain skilled workers and leaders.

5.2 Faculty and Staff Education, Training, and Development

How the organization's education and training addresses overall objectives, building faculty and staff knowledge, skills, and capabilities, and contributes to improving faculty and staff performance.

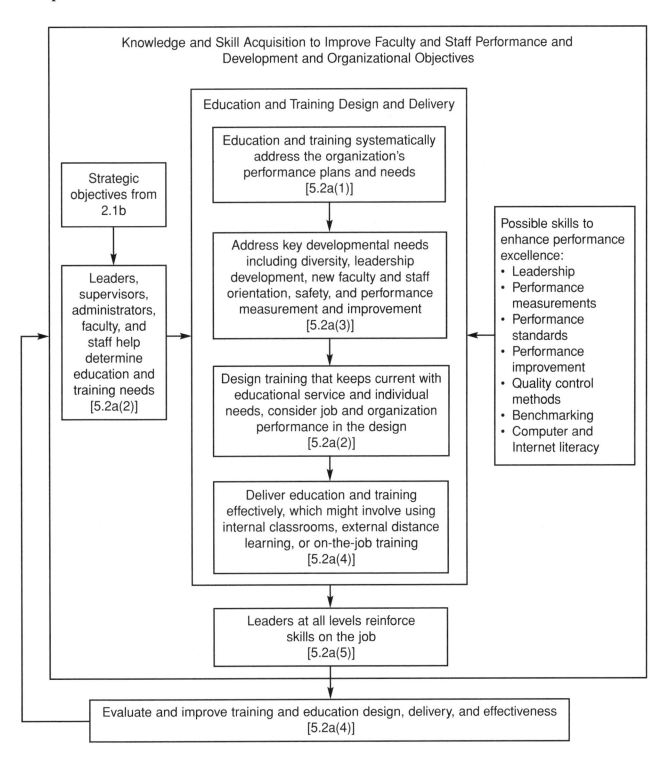

Knowledge and Skill Acquisition to Improve Faculty and Staff Performance and Development and Organizational Objectives

Education and Training Design and Delivery

Education and training systematically address the organization's performance plans and needs
[5.2a(1)]

Strategic objectives from 2.1b

Leaders, supervisors, administrators, faculty, and staff help determine education and training needs
[5.2a(2)]

Address key developmental needs including diversity, leadership development, new faculty and staff orientation, safety, and performance measurement and improvement
[5.2a(3)]

Possible skills to enhance performance excellence:
• Leadership
• Performance measurements
• Performance standards
• Performance improvement
• Quality control methods
• Benchmarking
• Computer and Internet literacy

Design training that keeps current with educational service and individual needs, consider job and organization performance in the design
[5.2a(2)]

Deliver education and training effectively, which might involve using internal classrooms, external distance learning, or on-the-job training
[5.2a(4)]

Leaders at all levels reinforce skills on the job
[5.2a(5)]

Evaluate and improve training and education design, delivery, and effectiveness
[5.2a(4)]

5.2 Faculty and Staff Education, Training, and Development Item Linkages

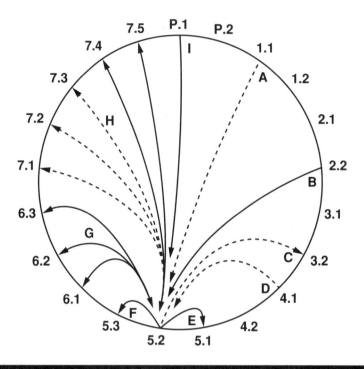

Nature of Relationship

A Leaders [1.1a(2)] are responsible for supporting appropriate skill development of all faculty and staff through training and development systems and reinforcing learning on the job [5.2a].

B Human resource development plans [2.2a(3)] (which were developed to support strategic objectives in [2.1b(1)]) are used to help align training [5.2a(1)] to ensure faculty, staff, and leaders possess appropriate knowledge, skills, and ability.

C Training [5.2] can enhance capabilities of student- and stakeholder-contact employees and strengthen student and stakeholder relationships [3.2a(2 and 3)].

D Key measures and benchmarking data [4.1] are used to improve training [5.2]. Information regarding training effectiveness [5.2] is analyzed [4.1].

E Effective training [5.2a(3)] enables leaders and administrators at all levels to improve their ability to design, organize, and manage better work processes that promote empowerment, innovation, creativity, and sharing [5.1a(1)]; develop faculty and staff potential [5.1a(2)]; make performance feedback and recognition and reward more relevant [5.1a(3)]; enhance succession planning [5.1a(4)]; and recruit and retain the best faculty and staff [5.1a(5)].

F Effective training [5.2a(3)] is critical to maintaining and improving a safe, healthful work environment [5.3a] and improved faculty and staff motivation and well-being [5.3b].

G Training [5.2a(3)] is essential to managing technological change and improving work-in-process effectiveness and innovation [6.1, 6.2, and 6.3]. In addition, training requirements [5.2] are defined in part by process requirements [6.1, 6.2, and 6.3].

H Results of improved training and development [5.2] are reported in 7.4. In addition, results pertaining to student learning [7.1]; student and stakeholder satisfaction [7.2]; financial, budgetary, and market performance [7.3]; and operational performance [7.5] reflect, in part, training effectiveness [5.2a(4)].

I Faculty and staff characteristics such as educational levels, workforce and job diversity, the existence of bargaining units, and other special requirements help set the context for determining appropriate training needs by faculty and staff segment [5.2a(1)].

5.2 Faculty and Staff Education, Training, and Development
Sample Effective Practices

- Hiring criteria and/or standards are developed to produce a workforce with necessary skills.
- Opportunities are created for faculty and staff to learn and use skills that go beyond current job assignments through redesign of processes or organizations.
- Education and training initiatives, including those that involve developmental assignments, are implemented.
- Partnerships with educational institutions are formed to develop faculty and staff or to help ensure the future supply of well-prepared faculty and staff.
- Partnerships are established with other organizations and/or networks to share training and/or spread job opportunities.
- Distance learning or other technology-based learning approaches are introduced.
- Systematic needs analyses are conducted to ensure that skills required to perform work are routinely assessed, monitored, and maintained.
- Clear linkages exist between strategic plans and the education and training provided. Skills are developed based on work demands and faculty and staff needs. For example, one might expect extensive technology training to be a major budget training item for most organizations at all levels.
- Faculty and staff input is considered when developing training plans.
- Faculty and staff career and personal development options, including development for leadership at all levels of the organization, are enhanced through formal education and training and through on-the-job training, such as rotational assignments or job exchange programs.
- The organization uses various methods to deliver training to ensure that it is suitable for faculty and staff knowledge and skill levels.
- Training is linked to work requirements, which are reinforced on the job. Just-in-time training is preferred (rather than just-in-case training) to help ensure that the skills will be used immediately after training.
- Faculty and staff feedback on the appropriateness of the training is collected and used to improve course delivery and content.
- The organization systematically evaluates training effectiveness on the job. Performance data are collected on individuals and groups at all levels to assess the impact of training.
- Faculty and staff satisfaction with courses is tracked.
- Training is systematically refined and improved based on evaluations.

5.2 Faculty and Staff Education, Training, and Development
Sample Effective Practices for Teaching Faculty:
Leaders of the Classroom Learning System

- Practices that develop and improve the performance of faculty and staff are used to improve student performance. These may include faculty/student cooperation initiatives; creation of assignments for students that go beyond current academic assignments through redesign of processes; developmental assignments, such as tutoring or community service; partnerships with other educational providers, such as community colleges or distance learning; systematic needs analyses; and tracking student satisfaction.

5.3 Faculty and Staff Well-Being and Satisfaction (25 points)
Approach/Deployment Scoring

Describe how your organization maintains a work environment and faculty and staff support climate that contribute to the well-being, satisfaction, and motivation of all faculty and staff.

Within your response, include answers to the following questions:

a. Work Environment

How do you improve workplace health, safety, and ergonomics? How do faculty and staff take part in improving them? Include performance measures and/or targets for each key environmental factor. Also include significant differences, if any, based on varying work environments for faculty and staff groups and/or work units.

b. Faculty and Staff Support and Satisfaction

(1) How do you determine the key factors that affect faculty and staff well-being, satisfaction, and motivation? How are these factors segmented for a diverse workforce and for varying categories and types of faculty and staff, as appropriate?

(2) How do you support your faculty and staff via services, benefits, and policies? How are these tailored to the needs of a diverse workforce and varying categories and types of faculty and staff, as appropriate?

(3) What formal and/or informal evaluation methods and measures do you use to determine faculty and staff well-being, satisfaction, and motivation? How do you tailor these methods and measures to a diverse workforce and to different categories and types of faculty and staff, as appropriate? How do you use other indicators, such as faculty and staff retention, absenteeism, grievances, safety, and productivity, to assess and improve faculty and staff well-being, satisfaction, and motivation?

(4) How do you relate evaluation findings to key organizational performance results to identify priorities for improving the work environment and faculty and staff support climate?

Notes:

N1. Specific factors that might affect your faculty and staff well-being, satisfaction, and motivation (5.3b[1]) include effective faculty and staff problem or grievance resolution; safety factors; faculty and staff views of administrators, faculty leadership, and/or supervisors; faculty and staff training, development, and career opportunities; faculty and staff preparation for changes in technology or the work organization; the work environment and other work conditions; empowerment of faculty and staff by administrators, faculty leadership, and/or supervisors; information sharing by administrators, faculty leadership, and/or supervisors; workload; cooperation and teamwork; recognition; services and benefits; communications; job security; compensation; and equal opportunity.

N2. Approaches for faculty and staff support (5.3b[2]) might include providing counseling, career development and employability services, recreational or cultural activities, nonwork-related education, day care, job rotation or sharing, special leave for family responsibilities or for community service, home safety training, flexible work hours and location, outplacement, and retirement benefits (including extended health care).

N3. Measures/indicators of well-being, satisfaction, and motivation (5.3b[3]) might include data on safety and absenteeism, the overall faculty and staff turnover rate segmented by employee type, faculty and staff charitable contributions, grievances, strikes, other job actions, insurance costs, worker's compensation claims, and results of surveys. Survey indicators of satisfaction might include faculty and staff knowledge of job roles, faculty and staff knowledge of organizational direction, and faculty and staff perception of empowerment and information sharing. Your results relative to such measures/indicators should be reported in Item 7.4.

N4. Setting priorities (5.3b[4]) might draw upon your faculty and staff results presented in Item 7.4 and might involve addressing faculty and staff problems based on their impact on your organizational performance.

This Item looks at the organization's work environment, your faculty and staff support climate, and how you determine faculty and staff satisfaction, with the aim of fostering the well-being, satisfaction, and motivation of all faculty and staff, recognizing their diverse needs.

The first part of this Item [5.3a] looks at how the organization provides a safe and healthful work environment for all faculty and staff, taking into account their differing work environments and associated requirements. Faculty and staff should help identify and improve factors important to workplace safety:

- The organization should be able to show how it includes such factors in its planning and improvement activities. Important factors in this area include establishing appropriate measures and targets for faculty and staff safety and health. Organizations should also recognize that faculty and staff groups might experience very different environments and need different services to ensure workplace safety.

- Organizations should also identify appropriate measures and targets for key environmental factors so that status and progress can be tracked.

The second part of this Item [5.3b] looks at the organization's approach to enhance faculty and staff well-being, satisfaction, and motivation based upon a holistic view of faculty and staff as key stakeholders. Organizations need to consider a variety of services, facilities, activities, and opportunities to address the needs of different faculty and staff groups and to tailor these to their well-being, satisfaction, and motivation. Increasingly, the needs of a diverse workforce have to be addressed in order to reduce attrition and increased motivation.

You are asked how you enhance faculty and staff well-being, satisfaction, and motivation based upon a holistic view of this key stakeholder group. Special emphasis is placed on the variety of approaches you use to satisfy a diverse workforce with differing needs and expectations:

- Examples of services, facilities, activities, and other opportunities are personal and career counseling; career development and employability services; recreational or cultural activities; formal and informal recognition; nonwork-related education; day care; special leave for family responsibilities and/or for community service; home safety training; flexible work hours; outplacement; and retiree benefits, including extended health care. Also, these services might include career enhancement activities, such as skills assessments, helping faculty and staff develop learning objectives and plans, and conducting employability assessments.

The last part of this Item [5.3c] looks at how the organization determines faculty and staff well-being, satisfaction, and motivation. Many factors might affect faculty and staff morale, well-being, and satisfaction. Although satisfaction with pay and promotion potential is important, these factors might not be adequate to understand the factors that contribute to the overall climate for motivation and high performance. For this reason, the high-performing organizations usually consider a variety of factors that might affect well-being, satisfaction, and motivation, such as effective faculty and staff problem or grievance resolution; safety; faculty and staff views of leadership and management; development and career opportunities; preparation for changes in technology or work organization; work environment; workload; cooperation and teamwork; recognition; benefits; communications; job security; compensation; diversity; and capability to provide required services to students and stakeholders:

- In addition to direct measurement of faculty and staff satisfaction and well-being through formal or informal surveys, some other indicators of satisfaction and well-being include absenteeism, turnover, grievances, strikes, and worker's compensation claims.

- Information and data on the well-being, satisfaction, and motivation of faculty and staff are actually used in identifying improvement priorities. Priority setting might draw upon faculty and staff resource results presented in Item 7.4 and might involve addressing faculty and staff problems, based on impact on organizational performance. Factors inhibiting motivation need to be prioritized and addressed. Failure to address these factors are likely to result in even more problem symptoms and adversely affect the results (Item 7.4).

5.3 Faculty and Staff Well-Being and Satisfaction

How the organization maintains a work environment and faculty and staff support climate that supports their well-being, satisfaction, and motivation.

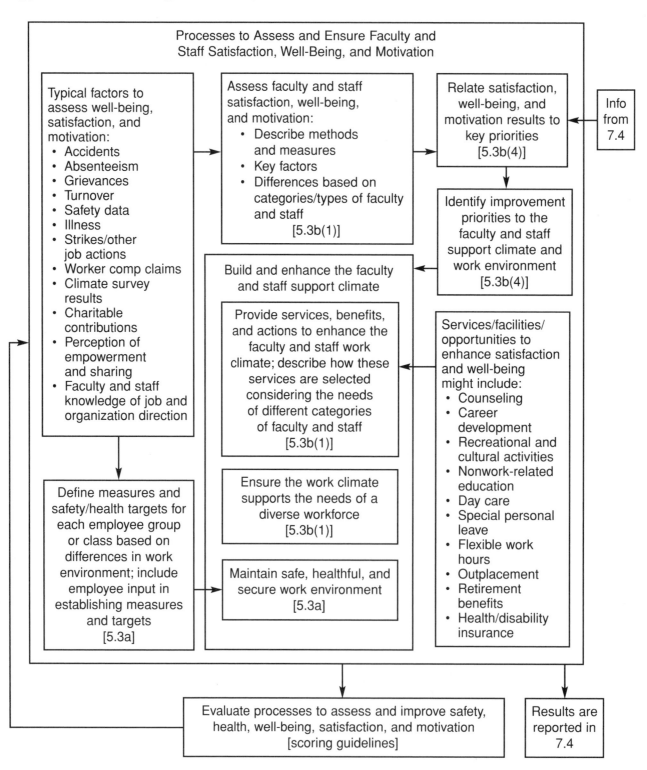

Processes to Assess and Ensure Faculty and Staff Satisfaction, Well-Being, and Motivation

Typical factors to assess well-being, satisfaction, and motivation:
- Accidents
- Absenteeism
- Grievances
- Turnover
- Safety data
- Illness
- Strikes/other job actions
- Worker comp claims
- Climate survey results
- Charitable contributions
- Perception of empowerment and sharing
- Faculty and staff knowledge of job and organization direction

Assess faculty and staff satisfaction, well-being, and motivation:
- Describe methods and measures
- Key factors
- Differences based on categories/types of faculty and staff
[5.3b(1)]

Relate satisfaction, well-being, and motivation results to key priorities [5.3b(4)]

Info from 7.4

Identify improvement priorities to the faculty and staff support climate and work environment [5.3b(4)]

Build and enhance the faculty and staff support climate

Provide services, benefits, and actions to enhance the faculty and staff work climate; describe how these services are selected considering the needs of different categories of faculty and staff [5.3b(1)]

Services/facilities/opportunities to enhance satisfaction and well-being might include:
- Counseling
- Career development
- Recreational and cultural activities
- Nonwork-related education
- Day care
- Special personal leave
- Flexible work hours
- Outplacement
- Retirement benefits
- Health/disability insurance

Ensure the work climate supports the needs of a diverse workforce [5.3b(1)]

Define measures and safety/health targets for each employee group or class based on differences in work environment; include employee input in establishing measures and targets [5.3a]

Maintain safe, healthful, and secure work environment [5.3a]

Evaluate processes to assess and improve safety, health, well-being, satisfaction, and motivation [scoring guidelines]

Results are reported in 7.4

5.3 Faculty and Staff Well-Being and Satisfaction Item Linkages

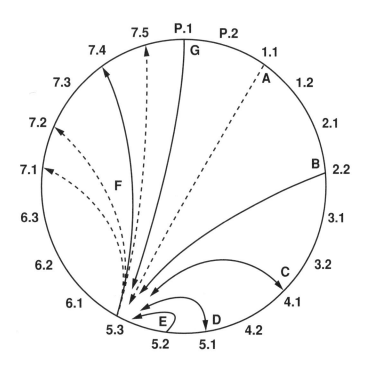

Nature of Relationship

A   Leaders [1.1a(2)] are responsible for creating effective systems to enhance faculty and staff satisfaction, well-being, and motivation [5.3].

B   Human resource development plans [2.2a(3)] typically address or set the context for safety, motivation, satisfaction, and well-being systems [5.3].

C   Key benchmarking data [4.1a(3)] are used to design processes to enhance faculty and staff motivation and well-being [5.3b]. Information regarding faculty and staff well-being and motivation [5.3b(3)] is used to gain a better understanding of problems and performance capabilities [4.1].

D   High motivation [5.3] enhances faculty and staff participation, self-direction, and initiative [5.1], and vice versa.

E   Effective training [5.2a(3)] is critical to maintaining and improving a safe, healthful work environment [5.3a] and improved faculty and staff motivation, satisfaction, and well-being [5.3b].

F   Systems that enhance faculty and staff motivation, satisfaction, and well-being [5.3] can boost performance [7.1 and 7.5] and student and stakeholder satisfaction [7.2]. Specific results of faculty and staff well-being and satisfaction systems are reported in 7.4.

G   Characteristics such as educational levels, workforce and job diversity, the existence of bargaining units, and other special requirements help set the context for tailoring benefits, services, and satisfaction assessment methods for faculty and staff according to various types and categories [5.3b(1,2,3)].

5.3 Faculty and Staff Well-Being and Satisfaction
Sample Effective Practices

A. Work Environment

- Performance management will consider issues relating to faculty and staff health, safety, and workplace environment. Plans exist to optimize these conditions and eliminate adverse conditions.
- Root causes for health and safety problems are systematically identified and eliminated. Corrective actions are communicated widely to help prevent the problem in other parts of the organization.

B. Faculty and Staff Support Climate

- Special activities and services are available for faculty and staff. These can be quite varied, depending on such needs as the following:
  - Flexible benefits plan, including health care; on-site day care; dental; portable retirement; education (both work and nonwork-related); maternity, paternity, and family illness leave;
  - Group purchasing power program, where the number of participating merchants is increasing steadily; and
  - Special facilities, such as teacher centers, for faculty and staff to discuss their concerns.
- Senior leaders motivate faculty and staff by building a work climate that addresses the well-being of all.

C. Faculty and Staff Satisfaction

- Key faculty and staff satisfaction opinion indicators are gathered periodically, based on the stability of the organization (organizations in the midst of rapid change conduct assessments more frequently).
- Satisfaction data are derived from focus groups, e-mail data, satisfaction survey results, turnover, absenteeism, stress-related disorders, and other data that reflect faculty and staff satisfaction. (A key satisfaction indicator is one that reflects conditions affecting morale and motivation.)
- On-demand electronic surveys are available for quick response and tabulations any time administrators seek faculty and staff satisfaction feedback.
- Administrators use the results of these surveys to focus improvements on work systems and enhance satisfaction.
- Faculty and staff satisfaction indicators are correlated with drivers of performance to help identify where resources should be placed to provide maximum organization benefit.
- Creation or redesign of faculty/staff surveys to assess the factors in the work climate that contribute to or inhibit high performance.

5.3 Faculty and Staff Well-Being and Satisfaction
Sample Effective Practices for Teaching Faculty:
Leaders of the Classroom Learning System

- Students are viewed as co-producers of knowledge.
- Cooperative approaches and teams of students use learning and decision making.
- Systems are in place that recognize and reward students when they contribute to organization and classroom goals.
- Students are motivated and involved in planning and operating the learning system as appropriate for their level. For example, in middle school, students may develop flowcharts and rubrics for tasks; in graduate school they may participate on committees that write the exam.
- Focus on the level of student involvement by monitoring, assessment, and improvements.
- Focus on the classroom work climate through assessing and improving well-being and student morale.
- Recognize and focus on specific factors that affect student well-being and satisfaction, such as problem resolution procedures; student view of the faculty; work environment; safety factors; workload; cooperation and teamwork; and equal opportunity.

6 Process Management—85 Points

The Process Management Category examines the key aspects of your organization's process management, including learning-focused education design and delivery, key student services, and support processes. This Category encompasses all key processes and all work units.

The Process Management Category examines the key aspects of your organization's process management, including learning-focused education design and delivery, student services and support services involving all work units. Process management is the focal point within the criteria for all key work processes. Built into the category are the central requirements for efficient and effective process management—effective design and delivery; a prevention orientation; student services linkage to partners; operational performance; cycle time; and evaluation, continuous improvement, and organizational learning.

Flexibility, cost reduction, and cycle time reduction are increasingly important in all aspects of process management and design. In simplest terms, flexibility refers to your ability to adapt quickly and effectively to changing requirements. Depending on the nature of the organization's strategy, flexibility might mean rapid development of curriculum or assessment approach, rapid response to changing demands, or the ability to produce a wide range of customized services. Flexibility might demand special strategies, such as implementing several program designs and sharing knowledge. Flexibility also increasingly involves controlling and outsourcing decisions and novel partnering arrangements.

Cost and cycle time reduction often involve many of the same process management strategies as achieving flexibility. Thus, it is crucial to utilize key measures for these requirements in your overall process management.

Process management contains three Items that evaluate the management of learning-focused design and delivery processes, student services, and support processes.

Education Design and Delivery Processes

- Design, develop, and introduce educational programs to meet student educational needs and performance requirements;
- Ensure programmed offerings focus on active learning and address student differences;
- Measure/assess formatively and summatively;
- Prepare faculty and staff to implement programs; and
- Improve design and delivery and share improvements across the organization.

Student Services

- Design, develop, and introduce student services with input from all key stakeholders and to meet student and operational performance requirements; and
- Manage and continuously improve student services and share improvements across the organization.

Support Processes

- Design, develop, and introduce support programs to meet student and stakeholder requirements and operational performance requirements; and
- Manage and continuously improve support processes and share improvements across the organization.

6.1 Education Design and Delivery Processes (50 points)
Approach/Deployment Scoring

Describe how your organization manages key processes for design and delivery of your educational programs and offerings.

Within your response, include answers to the following questions:

a. Education Design Processes

(1) What are your design processes for educational programs and offerings and their related delivery systems and processes?

(2) How do you ensure that all programs and offerings address student educational, developmental, and well-being needs; meet high standards; and focus on active learning?

(3) How do you anticipate and prepare for individual differences in student learning rates and styles?

(4) How is information on student segments and/or individual students developed and used for purposes of engaging all students in active learning? How do you incorporate changing student, stakeholder, and market requirements into the design of educational programs and offerings and their related delivery systems and processes?

(5) How do you incorporate new technology, including e-technology, into educational programs and offerings and their related delivery systems and processes, as appropriate?

(6) How do your design processes address sequencing, linkages among educational offerings, transfer of learning from past design projects and other parts of the organization, new design technology, cycle time, and other efficiency/effectiveness factors?

(7) How do you incorporate a measurement plan that makes effective use of formative and summative assessment?

(8) How do you ensure that faculty and staff are properly prepared to implement your educational programs and offerings?

b. Education Delivery Processes

(1) What are your key educational programs, offerings, and delivery processes and their key performance requirements?

(2) How do you ensure that ongoing educational programs and offerings meet key design and delivery requirements?

(3) What key observations and measures/indicators are used to monitor and improve the delivery of your key educational programs and offerings? Include how key formative and summative assessments of students; in-process measures of programs and offerings; and real-time student, faculty, staff, and stakeholder input are used in managing your educational programs and offerings to help students and faculty achieve learning objectives, as appropriate.

(4) How do you evaluate programs and offerings to minimize redesign efforts and their costs?

(5) How do you improve your educational programs and offerings to achieve better student learning and improvements to services, as appropriate? Include use of research on learning, assessment, and instructional methods and new learning technology, as appropriate. How are improvements shared with other organizational units and programs, students, faculty, staff, and stakeholders, as appropriate?

continued on next page

Notes:

N1. *Education* should be interpreted broadly. Educational programs and offerings may include courses, research, outreach, cooperative projects, and overseas studies.

N2. Responses to Item 6.1 should include how your stakeholders and key partners are involved in your design processes, as appropriate.

N3. Education design and delivery might take into account computer-assisted, distance, and Web-based learning and making offerings available at different locations and times to meet student needs.

N4. Sequencing and linkages among educational offerings (6.1a[6]) include not only relationships within a single discipline but also relationships among related disciplines. Linkages also may address your organization's mission-specific activities, such as basic and applied research and outreach.

N5. A measurement plan (6.1a[7]) should be holistic and define what is to be assessed and measured, how and when assessments and measurements are to be made, and how the results will be used.

N6. Proper preparation of your faculty (6.1a[8]) might address subject matter expertise and an understanding of the cognitive, social-emotional, and ethical development of students. It also might address training/experience in teaching strategies, facilitation skills, and learning assessment, as well as how to recognize and use learning research theory and how to report information and data on student progress. Preparation of faculty is linked to Item 5.2, which asks for information on how your training is tied to your organizational objectives.

N7. Education delivery refers to instructional approaches—modes of teaching and organizing activities and experiences so that learning takes place.

N8. For educational programs and offerings, measurements and observations (6.1b[3]) should include key learning and developmental dimensions, e.g., factors that enable early intervention when learning is not progressing adequately. Observations and measures/ indicators also should reveal whether the programs or offerings require corrective action. The focus of 6.1b(5) is ongoing improvement to achieve better performance. Periodically, programs and offerings might need to be changed or redesigned.

N9. The results of improvements in the design and delivery processes for your educational programs and offerings should be reported in Item 7.5. Results of improvements in student performance should be reported in Item 7.1.

This Item looks at the organization's key educational program and related service design and delivery processes, with the aim of improving your educational programs and operational performance. This includes curriculum and instructional design and delivery.

The first part of this Item looks at key design processes for educational programs and offerings and their related delivery processes. Organizations need to have a process to address key requirements, such as changing student and stakeholder requirements and new technology:

- Your design approaches could differ appreciably, depending upon the nature of your organization—whether the programs and offerings are entirely new, variants, or involve major or minor process changes. Factors that might need to be considered in design include student educational development and well-being needs, high standards, focus on active learning, and individual differences in student learning rates and styles. Effective design also must consider cycle time and delivery processes. This might involve redesigning those processes to achieve efficiency, as well as to meet changing/different student requirements.

- Frequently, this process includes capturing information from student/stakeholder complaint data that are collected using the processes described in Item 3.2a. Immediate access to complaint data allows the organization to make design changes quickly to prevent problems from recurring.

- Many organizations need to consider requirements for the next level or partners at the design stage. For example, as students transition into high school, middle school course design needs to take into account the next level of skill. Overall, effective design must take into account all stakeholders in the value chain.

- To ensure the design process is efficient, all related activities should be coordinated within the organization. Coordination of educational program design and delivery processes involves all work units and/or individuals who will take part in delivery and whose performance materially affects overall process outcome. This might include such groups as research, marketing, and curriculum development and discipline experts.

- Design processes should cover all key operational performance requirements and appropriate coordination and testing to ensure effective product/service launch.

The last part of this Item [6.1b] looks at how the organization ensures that its educational programs meet design and delivery process key performance requirements consistently:

- As part of the assessment, organizations must identify key educational programs and monitor related delivery processes, their key performance requirements, and key performance measures. These requirements and measures are the basis for maintaining and improving your educational programs and related delivery processes. Organizations should describe the key processes, their specific requirements, and how performance relative to these requirements is determined and maintained.

- Organizations should also identify research or learning assessments, instructional methods, and new technology to improve educational programs. The organization needs to use measures, observations, and indicators to achieve learning objectives. These activities should occur at the earliest points possible in processes to minimize problems and costs that may result from deviations from expected performance. Expected performance frequently requires setting performance levels or standards to guide decision making. When deviations occur, corrective action is required to restore the performance of the process to its intent. Depending on the nature of the process, the corrective action could involve technical and/or human considerations. Proper corrective action involves changes at the source (root cause) of the deviation. Such corrective action should minimize the likelihood of this type of variation occurring again or anywhere else in the organization. When student interactions are involved, differences among students must be considered in evaluating how well the process is performing.

- Finally, the organization must have a system in place to evaluate and improve educational programs to achieve better student learning and achievements. Better performance means better academic, financial, and operational performance—such as productivity—from the organization's perspective. A variety of process improvement approaches are commonly used. These approaches include the following:
  - Sharing successful strategies across the organization
  - Process analysis and research (for example, process mapping)
  - Research and development results
  - Benchmarking
  - Using alternative and new technology
  - Using information from users of the processes—within and outside of the organization

Process improvement approaches might utilize financial and budgetary data to evaluate alternatives and set priorities. Together, these approaches offer a wide range of possibilities, including complete redesign of processes.

6.1 Education Design and Delivery Processes

How key design and delivery processes are designed, managed, and improved for educational programs and offerings.

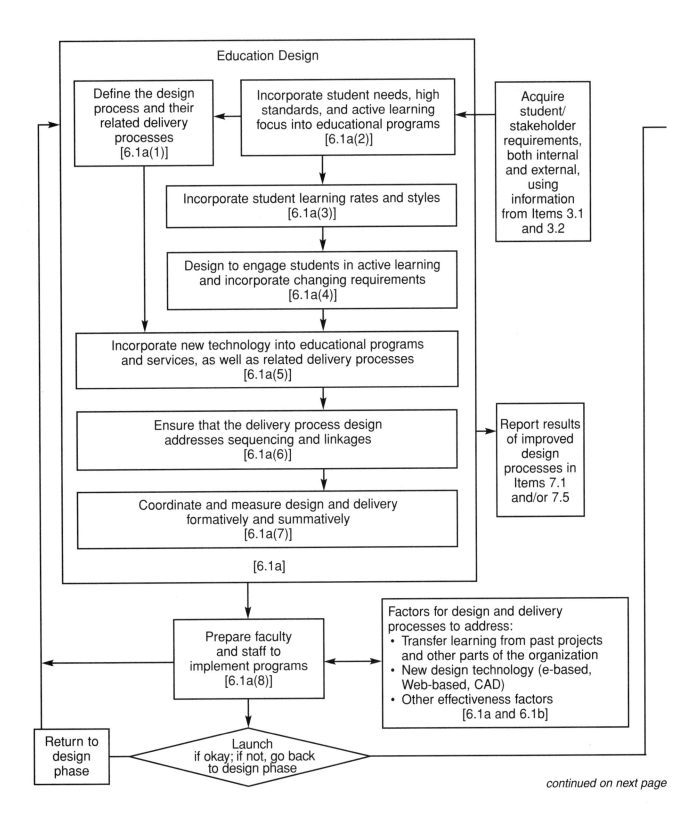

continued on next page

continued from previous page

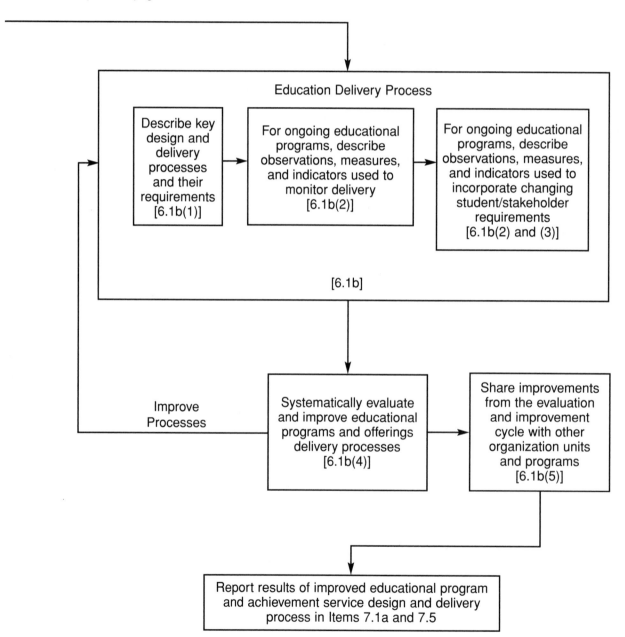

6.1 Education Design and Delivery Processes Item Linkages

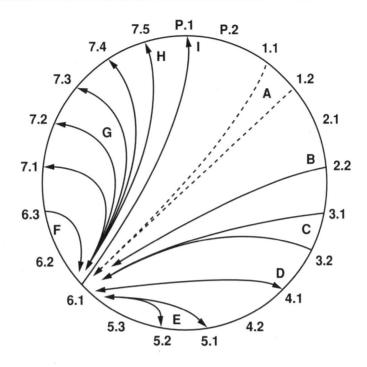

Nature of Relationship

A   Leaders at all levels [1.1] have a responsibility for ensuring that work processes are designed [6.1a] consistent with organizational objectives, including those relating to public responsibility and corporate citizenship [1.2].

B   Goals, deployed to the workforce [2.2], are used to drive and align actions to achieve improved performance [6.1].

C   Information about student needs [3.1] and complaints or comments from students and stakeholders through faculty and staff [3.2a] are used to design or modify educational programs to meet requirements better.

D   Key educational design and delivery processes [6.1] are used to help identify and prioritize benchmarking or comparison targets [4.1]. Benchmarking and comparison data [4.1] are used to improve educational design and delivery [6.1]. Priorities for educational design and delivery improvements [6.1] are set based on performance data analysis [4.1].

E   The design and delivery of new or modified programs [6.1] often defines skills to be acquired [5.2] and more flexible work systems [5.1] to implement them. In addition, high performance, flexible work systems [5.1], and training [5.1] are essential to improving educational design and delivery [6.1].

F   Effective management of student services [6.3] can result in improved educational programs [6.1] by improving student satisfaction.

G   Information about student achievement [7.1]; student and stakeholder satisfaction [7.2]; budgetary, market, and financial results [7.3]; faculty and staff satisfaction [7.4], and organization effectiveness [7.5] is used to target areas needing improvement in educational program design and delivery [6.1]. Educational programs [6.1a] and related delivery services [6.1b], affect performance results [Category 7].

H   In addition, information about student services performance [7.5] is essential to the design and implementation of new, modified, or customized educational programs [6.1a].

I   The information in P.1a(1) derives from the delivery processes described in 6.1b and helps set the context for the examiner review of those processes [6.1b(1)].

6.1 Education Design and Delivery Processes
Sample Effective Practices

A. Education Design

- A systematic process is used to maintain a focus on students and convert student requirements into the design and delivery of educational programs and offerings.
- The work of various functions is coordinated to bring the program or offering through the design-to-delivery phases. Functional barriers between disciplines, departments, and work units have been eliminated organizationwide.
- All design activities are closely coordinated through effective communication and teamwork.
- Internal process capacity and capability are reviewed and considered before educational programs and offerings are finalized.
- Design, service, and delivery reviews occur at defined intervals or as needed.
- Steps are taken (such as curriculum design testing or prototyping) to ensure that the delivery process will work as designed and will meet student or stakeholder requirements.
- Design processes are evaluated and improvements made so that future designs are developed faster (shorter cycle time), at lower cost, and with higher quality, relative to key program or offering characteristics that predict student satisfaction.
- The results of improved design process performance are reported in Item 7.5.

B. Education Delivery

- Performance requirements (from Item 6.1a, Design Processes and Requirements) are set using facts and data and are monitored using statistical process control techniques.
- Education delivery processes are measured and tracked. Measures (quantitative and qualitative) should reflect or assess the extent to which requirements are met, as well as consistency.
- For processes that produce errors, root causes are systematically identified and corrective action is taken to prevent their recurrence.
- Corrections are monitored and verified. The process used and results obtained should be systematic and integrated throughout the organization.
- Processes are systematically reviewed to improve productivity and reduce cycle time and rework.
- Tools, such as flowcharting and work redesign, are used throughout the organization to improve work processes.
- Benchmarking, competitive comparison data, or information from users of the process (in or out of the organization) are used to gain insight to improve processes.

6.1 Education Design and Delivery Processes
Sample Effective Practices for Teaching Faculty:
Leaders of the Classroom Learning System

- Feedback from students is used on an ongoing basis to improve course design.
- Course delivery takes into account different learning modalities, such as auditory or visual learners.
- Assessments are analyzed to improve course designs and instructors.

6.2 Student Services (20 points)
Approach/Deployment Scoring

Describe how your organization manages its key student services.

Within your response, include answers to the following questions:

a. Student Services

(1) What are your key student services?

(2) How do you determine key student service requirements, incorporating input from students, faculty, staff, other stakeholders, and suppliers/partners, as appropriate? What are the key requirements for these services?

(3) How do you design and deliver these services to meet all the key requirements?

(4) What are your key performance measures/indicators used for the control and improvement of these services? Include how in-process measures and feedback from students, faculty, staff members, stakeholders, and suppliers are used in managing your student services, as appropriate.

(5) How do you improve your student services to keep them current with educational service needs and directions, to achieve better performance, and to control overall costs? How are improvements shared with other organizational units and processes, as appropriate?

Notes:

N1. Your key student services are those considered most important to student matriculation and success. These might include services related to counseling, advising, and tutoring students; libraries and information technology; and student recruitment, enrollment, registration, placement, financial aid, and housing. They also might include food services, security, health services, transportation, and bookstores. The key services to be included in Item 6.2 are distinctive to your organization and how you operate.

N2. Key student service requirements may include timeliness, confidentiality, accuracy, due process, and safety.

N3. To provide as complete and concise a response as possible for your key student services, you might want to use a tabular format identifying the key services and the attributes of each as called for in questions 6.2a(1)–6.2a(4).

N4. Key student service performance results should be reported in Item 7.5.

The organization needs to identify key student services and requirements for these services. This area looks at how the organization designs and delivers its student services to meet requirements of students, with input from faculty, staff, stakeholders, and suppliers, as needed.

It is important to understand how to measure performance so the organization can control and improve these services, including in-process measures and ongoing feedback from all stakeholders and students.

Finally, you are asked how you improve student services to achieve better performance, to control overall costs and to improve key services current with changing educational needs.

6.2 Student Services

How student services closely associated with student matriculation and student success are designed, managed, and improved.

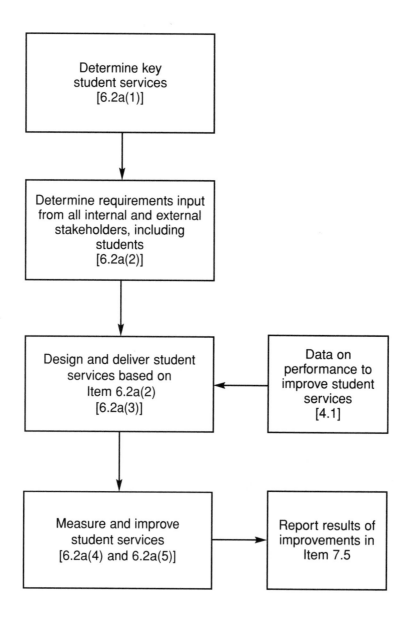

6.2 Student Services Item Linkages

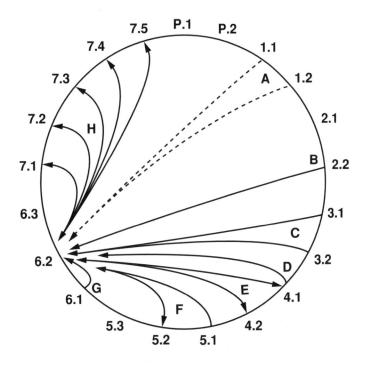

Nature of Relationship

A   Leaders at all levels [1.1 and 1.2] ensure that student services [6.2] are aligned with organization priorities, including matriculation, student success, and organizational program performance [7.1 and 7.5].

B   Goals deployed to the workforce [2.2] are used to drive and align actions to achieve improved student services [6.2].

C   Information about student requirements [3.1] and from student/stakeholder-contact personnel [3.2a] is used to identify improvement opportunities in services processes [6.2].

D   Priorities for student services improvement [6.2] are set based on performance data and analysis [4.1].

E   Key student services [6.2] are used to help identify and prioritize benchmarking targets [4.1]. Benchmarking data [4.1] are used and made available [4.2] to improve student services [6.2].

F   High performance, flexible work systems, and effective recognition [5.1] and training [5.2] are essential to improving student services [6.2]. In addition, design and delivery of new or modified student services [6.2] can help define new, flexible work systems [5.1] and skills that need to be acquired [5.2].

G   New or modified design or delivery processes for ongoing educational programs [6.1] can help define requirements and set priorities for student services [6.2].

H   Information about performance results [Category 7] is used to target improvement efforts in student services [6.2]. Improved student services [6.2] produce better performance results [Category 7].

6.2 Student Services Sample Effective Practices

- Counseling, tutoring, and advisement services effectiveness is monitored and improved including hours, assignments, and matching student needs to capabilities.
- Libraries and information services are available in a wide variety of formats and hours, such as online, 24 hours, and via television, and are assessed to see if needs are being met.
- Student recruitment, enrollment, and academic support services are closely integrated with student satisfaction data so students, once enrolled, are retained.
- Food service is tasty, nutritious, cost effective, and improved based on user comments on an ongoing basis.
- Security services are monitored and data on student and faculty/staff security are monitored and improved without turning schools into prisons.
- Bookstores offer a wide variety of services, job opportunities for students, and products that support academic success and enrichment.
- Student housing is a planned phenomena whether to balance diverse interests or create a nurturing atmosphere for common interests to grow. Students do not become racially or otherwise segregated as part of the process.
- Financial aid forms and scholarship applications are simple to complete and one form is used for all determinations. The same online application and information is used for many feeder schools and all those with which the school has articulation agreements.
- Health services communicate with other previous health care providers when necessary for student health. Costs are reasonable and shared with parents and students in an easy-to-understand way. Services are available quickly for students and usually do require a minimum of missed class time.
- Buses or other forms of transportation are reliable and scheduled according to user needs.

6.2 Student Services
Sample Effective Practices for Teaching Faculty:
Leaders of the Classroom Learning System

- Teaching faculty work closely with student service providers to enhance instruction (ex-counselors, tutors)
- Special student needs and learning preferences are communicated, as appropriate, to student services providers.

6.3 Support Processes (15 points)
Approach/Deployment Scoring

Describe how your organization manages its key processes that support your daily operations as an education organization and your faculty and staff in delivering services.

Within your response, include answers to the following questions:

a. Support Processes

(1) What are your key processes for supporting your daily operations and your faculty and staff in delivering educational programs, offerings, and student services?

(2) How do you determine key support process requirements, incorporating input from faculty and staff, as appropriate? What are the key operational requirements (such as productivity, timeliness, accuracy, and safety) for these processes?

(3) How do you design these processes to meet all the key requirements?

(4) How does your day-to-day operation of key support processes ensure meeting key performance requirements?

(5) What are your key performance measures/indicators used for the control and improvement of these processes? Include how in-process measures and faculty and staff feedback are used in managing your support processes, as appropriate.

(6) How do you minimize overall costs associated with inspections, tests, and process/performance audits of support processes?

(7) How do you improve your support processes to achieve better performance and to keep them current with organizational needs and directions? How are improvements shared with other organizational units and processes, as appropriate?

Notes:

N1. Your key support processes are those that are considered most important for support of your organization's design and delivery of educational programs, offerings, and student services. These might include processes for finance and accounting; plant and facilities management; legal, human resource, and marketing services; information services; public relations; central receiving; purchasing; management of supplier and/or partner processes; and secretarial and other administrative services.

N2. Key support process performance results should be reported in Item 7.5.

This Item looks at the organization's key educational support processes, with the aim of improving overall operational performance. The requirements of this Item are similar to the requirements in Item 6.1.

The organization must ensure its key educational support processes are designed to meet all operational and student/stakeholder, including faculty and staff, requirements. To do this, organizations must incorporate input from internal and external stakeholders, as appropriate:

- Educational support processes are those that support overall educational services. Support process design requirements usually depend significantly upon internal user requirements, and they must be coordinated and integrated to ensure efficient and effective linkage and performance.

- Support processes might include accounting, counseling, advising, placement, recruitment, enrollment, registration, public relations, information services, human resources, legal services, plant and facilities management, research and development, and secretarial and other administrative services.

As with core operating processes described in Item 6.1, the organization must ensure that the day-to-day operation of its key educational support processes consistently meet the key performance requirements. To do this, observations, indicators, and measures should be defined to permit rapid identification and correction of potential problems. Educational support processes should develop mechanisms to obtain and use student and stakeholder feedback to help identify problems and take corrective action.

Finally, organizations should systematically evaluate and improve its key support processes to achieve better performance and to keep them current with changing educational service needs and directions:

- This Item calls for information on how the organization evaluates and improves the performance of your key support processes. The following four approaches to evaluating and improving educational support processes are frequently used:
  - Process analysis and research
  - Benchmarking
  - Use of alternative technology
  - Use of information from users of the processes—within and outside the organization

Together, these approaches offer a wide range of possibilities, including complete redesign of processes.

6.3 Support Processes

How key support processes are designed, managed, and improved.

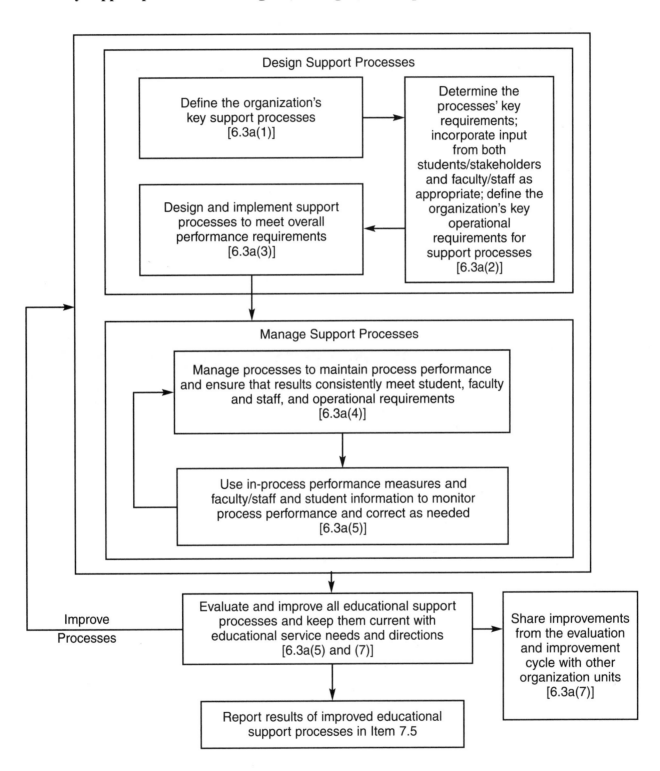

6.3 Support Processes Item Linkages

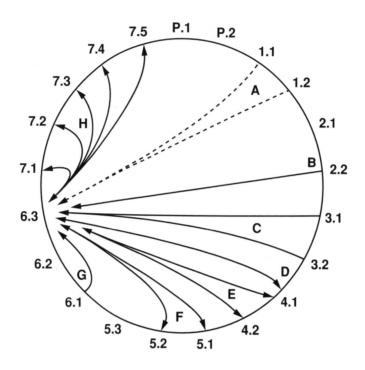

Nature of Relationship

A Leaders at all levels [1.1] ensure that support processes [6.3] are aligned with organization priorities, including regulatory, accreditational, and public responsibilities [1.2].

B Goals deployed to the workforce [2.2] are used to drive and align actions to achieve improved support performance [6.3].

C Information about student requirements [3.1] and from student/stakeholder-contact personnel [3.2a] is used to identify improvement opportunities in support work processes [6.3].

D Key support processes [6.3] are used to help identify and prioritize benchmarking targets [4.1]. Benchmarking data [4.1] are used to improve support processes [6.3].

E Priorities for support processes improvement [6.3] are set based on performance data and analysis [4.1 and 4.2].

F High performance, flexible work systems, and effective recognition [5.1] and training [5.2] are essential to improving support processes [6.3]. In addition, design and delivery of new or modified support services [6.3] can help define new, flexible work systems [5.1] and skills that need to be acquired [5.2].

G New or modified design or delivery processes for ongoing educational programs [6.1] can help define requirements and set priorities for support services [6.3].

H Information about performance results [Category 7] is used to target improvement efforts in support processes [6.3]. Improved support processes [6.3] produce better performance results [Category 7].

6.3 Support Processes Sample Effective Practices

- A formal process exists to understand internal user requirements, translate those requirements into efficient support processes, and measure their effectiveness.
- Specific improvements in support services are made with the same rigor and concern for the internal and external stakeholder as improvements in educational design and delivery processes. For example, food service must be operated in a manner that meets student and other stakeholder requirements.
- All support services are subject to continuous review and improvements in performance and user satisfaction.
- Systems to ensure process performance are maintained, and requirements are met.
- Root causes of problems are systematically identified and corrected for processes that produce defects.
- Corrections are monitored and verified. The process used and results obtained are systematic and integrated throughout the organization.
- Support processes are systematically reviewed to improve productivity, reduce cycle time and waste, and increase quality.
- Work process simplification or improvement tools are used with measurable sustained results.
- Stretch goals are used to drive higher levels of performance.
- Benchmarking, competitive comparison data, or information from users of the process (in or out of the organization) are used to gain insight to improve processes.

6.3 Support Processes
Sample Effective Practices for Teaching Faculty:
Leaders of the Classroom Learning System

- A systematic process is used to design, implement, and deliver teaching and learning products.
- The achievement of learning goals are supported by the physical classroom environment. For example, animals might be part of the science classroom but not if the noise interferes with normal classroom activity.
- Performance improvement tools are taught to students and used daily as part of the classroom. For example, teacher and students use rubrics, flowcharts, affinity diagrams, and control charts to plan, monitor, and assess learning and behavior.
- Classroom support processes are monitored and improved, for example, by e-mail, conferences, and discussion groups.
- Needed requirements for student success, such as materials, timelines, and learning content, are communicated to cosuppliers, such as parents or other teachers.

7 Organizational Performance Results—450 Points

The Organizational Performance Results Category examines student learning results; student- and stakeholder-focused results; budgetary, financial, and marketplace performance; faculty and staff results; and operational effectiveness. Also examined are performance levels relative to those of competitors, comparable schools, and/or appropriately selected organizations.

The Organizational Performance Results Category provides a results focus that encompasses student and stakeholders' evaluation of the organization's educational services; overall budget, financial, and market performance; and results of all key processes and process improvement activities. Through this focus, the criteria's dual purposes—superior value of offerings as viewed by students and stakeholders, and superior organizational performance reflected in operational and budgetary/financial/market indicators—are maintained. Category 7 thus provides "real-time" information (measures of progress) for evaluation and improvement of programs, processes, and services, aligned with overall organizational strategy:

- Item 4.1 calls for analysis of organizational results data and information to determine overall organizational performance.

Organizational results presents a balanced scorecard of organizational performance. Historically, organizations have been far too preoccupied with final test performance. Many performance reviews focused almost exclusively on achieving (or failing to achieve) expected levels of performance on tests. As such, the results were considered "unbalanced:"

- Final test results are considered lagging indicators of educational success. They are the net of all the good processes, bad processes, satisfied students and stakeholders, dissatisfied students and stakeholders, motivated faculty and staff, and disgruntled faculty and staff, to name a few. By the time year-end test indicators become available, students, faculty, and staff may already be discouraged and dissatisfied.

- On the other hand, leading indicators help organizations predict subsequent student and stakeholder satisfaction and financial/budgetary/market performance. Leading indicators include student engagement and satisfaction, operational effectiveness, and faculty and staff well-being and satisfaction.

Taken together, these measures represent a balance between leading and lagging indicators and enable decision makers to identify problems early and take corrective action.

Category 7 requires organizations to report current levels and improvement trends for the following:

- Student learning
- Student and stakeholder satisfaction and dissatisfaction
- Budgetary, financial, and market performance
- Faculty and staff performance
- Organizational effectiveness

For all of these areas, organizations must include appropriate comparative data to enable examiners to define what "good" means. Otherwise, even though performance may be improving, it is difficult to determine whether or not the level of performance is good or not.

7.1 Student Learning Results (200 points)
Results Scoring

Summarize your organization's key student learning results. Segment your results by student groups and market segments, as appropriate. Include appropriate comparative data relative to competitors, comparable organizations, and student populations.

Provide data and information to answer the following question:

a. Student Learning Results

What are your current levels and trends in key measures/indicators of student learning and improvement in student learning? Segment data by student groups and market segments, as appropriate, and include results normalized to comparable student populations.

Notes:

N1. Results reported in Item 7.1 might be based upon a variety of assessment methods that reflect the organization's overall mission and primary improvement objectives and that together represent holistic appraisals of student learning. For some recently implemented measures and/or assessment methods, data might not yet be sufficient to demonstrate meaningful trends. Such data should be reported, because they provide useful information regarding the organization's current performance levels. Results may include data indicating performance of recent graduates.

N2. Demonstrations of improvement in student learning should be normalized to comparable student populations. Methods for demonstrating improvement in student learning might involve longitudinal studies and cohort studies. Results covering three years or more are preferred.

N3. Comparisons should include a brief description of how the appropriateness of each comparison is ensured. Comparable organizations might include those of similar types/sizes, both domestic and international, as well as organizations serving similar populations of students.

This Item addresses the principal student learning results based upon mission-related factors and assessment methods. Critical to understanding the purposes of this Item are the following: (1) student learning should reflect holistic and mission-related results; (2) current levels and trends should be reported, the former to allow comparisons with other organizations and/or student populations, and the latter to demonstrate year-to-year improvement; (3) data should be segmented by student group(s) to permit trends and comparisons that demonstrate the organization's sensitivity to education improvement for all students. Overall, this Item is the most important one as it depends upon demonstrating improvement by the organization over time and higher achievement levels relative to comparable organizations or student populations.

Proper use of Item 7.1 depends upon appropriate normalization of data to compensate for initial differences in student populations. Although better admission criteria might contribute to improved education for all students, improved student learning based entirely upon changing students' entry-level qualifications should not be reported in Item 7.1. However, improvement trends in student admission qualifications are appropriate for inclusion in Organizational Effectiveness Results (Item 7.5). Improvement in student performance beyond that which could be attributed to entry-level qualifications is appropriate for inclusion in Item 7.1, along with other measures and/or indicators of improvement trends and comparisons.

In order to determine whether results, trends, and levels are good or not, comparative data need to be provided.

7.1 Student Learning Results

Summarize current levels and trends in key measures and/or indicators of student performance. Separately address different student groups and market segments, as appropriate. Include data showing how student performance and performance trends compare with comparable organizations and/or appropriately selected student populations.

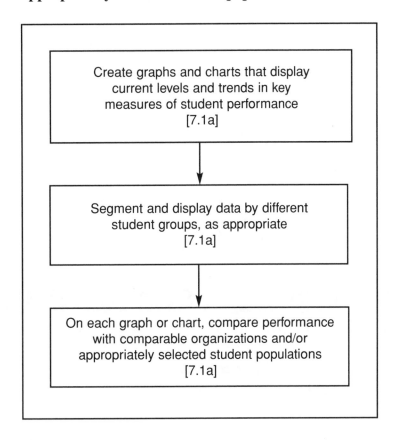

Create graphs and charts that display current levels and trends in key measures of student performance
[7.1a]

Segment and display data by different student groups, as appropriate
[7.1a]

On each graph or chart, compare performance with comparable organizations and/or appropriately selected student populations
[7.1a]

7.1 Student Learning Results Item Linkages

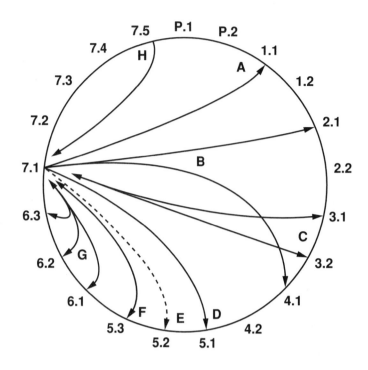

Nature of Relationship

A   Data on levels of student learning [7.1] are monitored by leaders at all levels [1.1] and used to set priorities for improvement.

B   Data on levels of student learning [7.1] are collected and analyzed [4.1] to set organization performance improvement priorities for strategic planning [2.1].

C   Processes used to gather information about current student needs and expectations [3.1], strengthen stakeholder relations [3.2a], and determine student and stakeholder satisfaction [3.2b] are used to produce student learning results data [7.1]. In addition, student learning results [7.1] are used to create bases for relationships with key stakeholders [3.2a] and help determine student needs [3.1].

D   Recognition and rewards [5.1a] must be based, in part, on learning results [7.1].

E   Student learning results data [7.1] are monitored, in part, to assess training effectiveness [5.2].

F   Systems to enhance faculty and staff satisfaction and well-being [5.3] can produce higher levels of student learning results [7.1] and, in turn, boost morale.

G   Data on student learning [7.1] are used to help design educational programs and services and to improve education [6.1] as well as student services [6.2] and support [6.3] processes.

H   Organizational effectiveness results [7.5] provide the operational basis and can be a predictor or leading indicator for student learning results [7.1].

7.1 Student Learning Results
Sample Effective Results

- Learning trends indicated on examinations, portfolios, and other assessments are positive and sustained over time.
- Key measures and indicators of student performance show steady improvement.
- All-important learning and performance data are presented.
- Comparative data include other schools and comparable organizations, and appropriate comparisons.

7.1 Student Learning Results
Sample Effective Results for Teaching Faculty:
Leaders of the Classroom Learning System

- Classroom or course academic performance results are improving.
- Key measures and indicators of student performance show steady improvement.
- All-important learning and performance data are presented.
- Comparative data include other classrooms, courses, and comparable units.

7.2 Student- and Stakeholder-Focused Results (70 points)
Results Scoring

Summarize your organization's key student- and stakeholder-focused results, including student and stakeholder satisfaction. Segment your results by student and stakeholder groups and market segments, as appropriate. Include appropriate comparative data.

Provide data and information to answer the following questions:

a. Student- and Stakeholder-Focused Results

(1) What are your current levels and trends in key measures/indicators of current and past student and key stakeholder satisfaction and dissatisfaction, including comparisons with competitors' and/or comparable organizations' levels of student and stakeholder satisfaction?

(2) What are your current levels and trends in key measures/indicators of student- and stakeholder-perceived value, persistence, positive referral, and/or other aspects of building relationships with students and stakeholders, as appropriate?

Notes:

N1. Student and stakeholder satisfaction and dissatisfaction results (7.2a[1]) should relate to determination methods and data described in Item 3.2. Results data might include feedback from students and stakeholders and their overall assessment of education and operations. Examples of student and stakeholder satisfaction and dissatisfaction indicators are given in the notes for Item 3.2.

N2. Current levels and trends in key measures/indicators of student satisfaction relative to competitors and/or comparable schools (7.2a[1]) might include gains and losses of your students from or to other schools or alternative means of education, such as home schooling or corporate educational programs. Results also might include objective information and/or data from independent organizations and/or key stakeholders. Such objective information might include survey results, competitive awards, recognition, and ratings. The information and/or data should reflect comparative satisfaction (and dissatisfaction). Information on comparative performance of your students should be included in Item 7.1.

N3. Comparisons should include a brief description of how the appropriateness of each comparison is ensured. Comparable organizations might include those of similar types/sizes, as well as organizations serving similar populations of students.

This Item looks at the organization's student- and stakeholder-focused performance results, with the aim of demonstrating how well the organization has been satisfying students and stakeholders and delivering educational programs that lead to satisfaction and loyalty. Results are to be segmented by student and stakeholder groups and market segments, so results of specific efforts can be assessed.

Organizations must provide data to demonstrate current levels, trends, and appropriate comparisons for key measures and/or indicators of the following:

- Student and stakeholder satisfaction, dissatisfaction, and satisfaction relative to comparable organizations; and
- Student and stakeholder loyalty (retention), positive referral, and student/stakeholder-perceived value.

This Item focuses on the creation and use of all relevant data to determine and help predict the organization's performance as viewed by students and stakeholders:

- Relevant data and information include student and stakeholder satisfaction and dissatisfaction; retention, gains, and losses of students; student and stakeholder complaints; student/stakeholder-perceived value based on educational programs; and awards, ratings, and recognition from students and stakeholders and independent rating organizations.
- Performance results appropriate for recording in this Item might be based upon one or more of the following:
  - Internal (organizational) measurements
  - Field performance
  - Data collected by the organization or for the organization
  - Surveys on programs and services
  - Awards, ratings, and recognition

- The correlation between student learning and student/stakeholder satisfaction is a critical management tool for defining and focusing on the relationship between achievement and satisfaction. The correlation might reveal emerging or changing student segments, the changing importance of requirements, or even the potential obsolescence of program offerings.

7.2 Student- and Stakeholder-Focused Results

The organization's student and stakeholder satisfaction and dissatisfaction results, using indicators of current and past students, key stakeholders, and market segments.

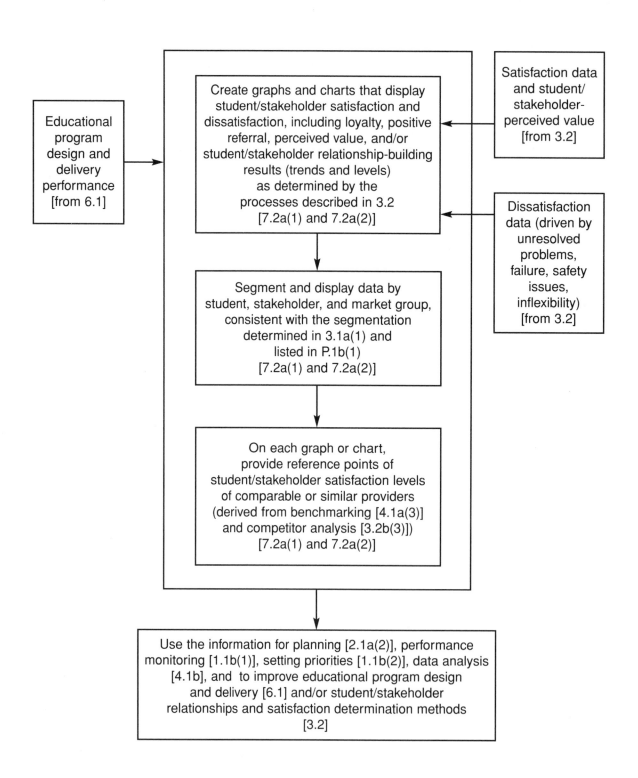

7.2 Student- and Stakeholder-Focused Results Item Linkages

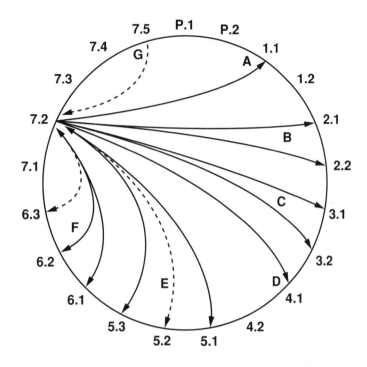

Nature of Relationship

A   Senior leaders [1.1b] use performance results data [7.2] to monitor organizational performance.

B   Student and stakeholder results [7.2] are considered in the strategic planning process [2.1] and in setting performance goals [2.2].

C   Student and stakeholder results [7.2] provide information to help determine student and stakeholder needs and expectations [3.1] as well as help determine contact requirements (service standards [3.2a]) and help in the design of satisfaction measurement instruments [3.2b]. Information about student and stakeholder needs and expectations, [3.1] as well as complaint data [3.2a], are reported in 7.2.

D   Student and stakeholder satisfaction data [7.2] are aggregated and analyzed [4.1] to assess performance and help leaders set priorities and make other management decisions.

E   Student and stakeholder results [7.2] are factors in reward and recognition [5.1], are used to help determine training and development needs [5.2], and can impact faculty and staff morale and well-being [5.3]. Similarly, systems to promote faculty and staff involvement and effectiveness [5.1], training and development [5.2], and morale and well-being [5.3] can produce higher levels of student and stakeholder satisfaction [7.2].

F   Student and stakeholder results [7.2] are factors that must be considered when designing and delivering education programs [6.1], student services [6.2], and related support services [6.3]. Similarly, design, development, and delivery of education programs [6.1], student services [6.2], and support services [6.3] contribute to student and stakeholder satisfaction [7.2].

G   Organizational effectiveness results [7.5] can provide predictive or leading indicators for student and stakeholder satisfaction results [7.2].

7.2 Student- and Stakeholder-Focused Results
Sample Effective Results

- Trends and indicators of student and stakeholder satisfaction and dissatisfaction (including complaint data), segmented by student and stakeholder groups, are provided in graph and chart form for all key measures. Multiyear data are provided.
- All indicators show steady improvement. Indicators include data collected in Item 3.2b, such as student and stakeholder assessments of education programs and offerings.
- All indicators compare favorably to competitors or similar providers.
- Student and stakeholder satisfaction graphs and information are accurate and easy to understand.
- Data are not missing.
- Results data are supported by student and stakeholder feedback, and overall assessments of education programs and offerings.
- Data are presented concerning student and stakeholder dissatisfaction for the most relevant program or service quality indicators collected through the processes described in Item 3.2b (some of which may be referenced in the Organizational Profile).

7.2 Student- and Stakeholder-Focused Results
Sample Effective Results for Teaching Faculty:
Leaders of the Classroom Learning System

- The level of student involvement and satisfaction results are improving steadily over time.
- Student and stakeholder satisfaction and dissatisfaction results indicate a positive trend.
- Data are not missing.
- Results data are consistent with student and stakeholder feedback.

7.3 Budgetary, Financial, and Market Results (40 Points)
Results Scoring

Summarize your organization's key budgetary, financial, and market performance results by segments, as appropriate. Include appropriate comparative data.

Provide data and information to answer the following questions:

a. Budgetary, Financial, and Market Results

  (1) What are your current levels and trends in key measures/indicators of budgetary and financial performance, including measures of cost containment, as appropriate?

  (2) What are your current levels and trends in key measures/indicators of market performance, including market share and new markets entered, as appropriate?

Notes:

N1. Responses to Item 7.3 might include measures such as instructional and general administration expenditures per student; income, expenses, reserves, and endowments; the tax rate; tuition and fee levels; cost per academic credit; annual grants/awards; program expenditures as a percentage of budget; annual budget increases or decreases; resources redirected to education from other areas; scholarship growth; the percentage of budget for research; and the budget for public service.

N2. New markets entered (7.3a[2]) might include offering Web-based services.

N3. Comparisons should include a brief description of how the appropriateness of each comparison is ensured.

This Item looks at the organization's budgetary, financial, and market results, with the aim of cost containment and increasing value.

Organizations should provide data demonstrating levels, trends, and appropriate comparisons for key budgetary, financial, and market indicators. Overall, these results should provide a complete picture of budgetary and financial performance:

- Measures reported in this Item are those usually tracked by senior leaders to assess organization-level performance.
- Appropriate budgetary and financial measures and indicators might include:
  - Administrative expenses
  - Expenditures per student
  - Income/expenses
  - Reserves/endowments
  - Tuition/fee levels
  - Cost per academic credit
  - Annual grants/awards
  - Program expenditures as a percentage of budget
  - Annual budget increase/decrease
  - Scholarship growth
  - Resources redirected to education
  - Budget for public service
- Appropriate market indicators might include:
  - Market share
  - Measures of growth or loss of students or programs
  - New Web-based and distance learning markets
  - Market position
  - Student transfers in or out of the organization, for example, charter schools, home schooling, or vouchers
  - New educational program offerings or delivery methods

7.3 Budgetary, Financial, and Market Results

Results of improvement efforts using key measures and/or indicators of budgetary, financial, and market performance.

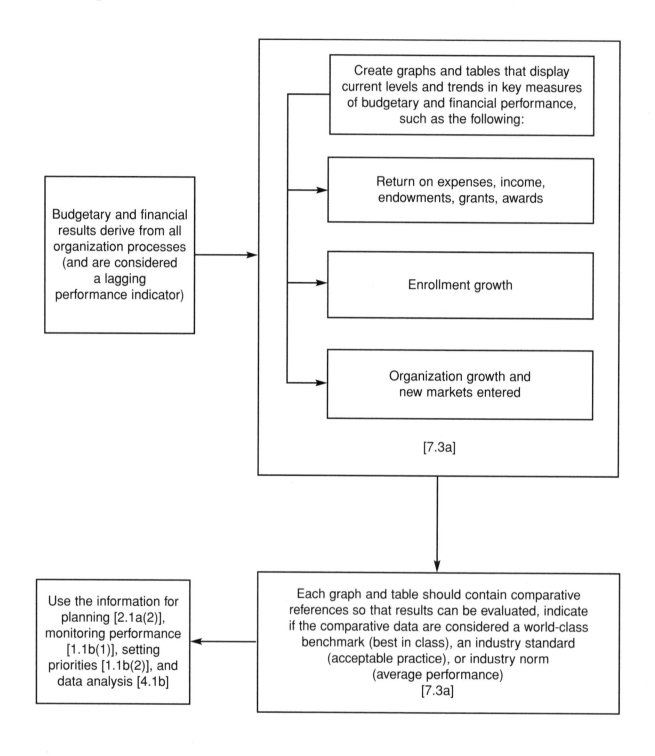

Budgetary and financial results derive from all organization processes (and are considered a lagging performance indicator)

Create graphs and tables that display current levels and trends in key measures of budgetary and financial performance, such as the following:

Return on expenses, income, endowments, grants, awards

Enrollment growth

Organization growth and new markets entered

[7.3a]

Each graph and table should contain comparative references so that results can be evaluated, indicate if the comparative data are considered a world-class benchmark (best in class), an industry standard (acceptable practice), or industry norm (average performance) [7.3a]

Use the information for planning [2.1a(2)], monitoring performance [1.1b(1)], setting priorities [1.1b(2)], and data analysis [4.1b]

7.3 Budgetary, Financial, and Market Results Item Linkages

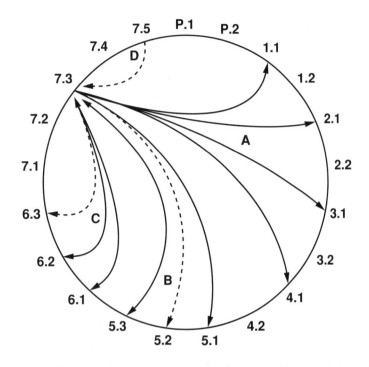

Nature of Relationship

A Budgetary, financial, and market results data [7.3] are used for strategic planning [2.1], understanding market requirements [3.1], leadership monitoring and decision making [1.1], and analysis [4.1].

B Budgetary, financial, and market data [7.3] are used, in part, as a basis for recognition and reward [5.1], setting training priorities [5.2], and can influence morale and well-being [5.3]. Similarly, human resource activities [Category 5] can impact budget, financial and market results [7.3].

C Budgetary, financial, and market results [7.3] impact design and development of programs [6.1], student services [6.2], and support processes [6.3]. Similarly, improvements in educational design and delivery processes [6.1], student services [6.2], and support processes [6.3] affect budgetary, financial, and market results [7.3].

D Organizational effectiveness results [7.5] can impact budgetary, financial, and market results [7.3].

7.3 Budgetary, Financial, and Market Results
Sample Effective Results

- Key measures and indicators of organization budgetary, financial, and market performance address the following areas:
  - Administrative expenses
  - Expenditures per student
  - Income/expenses
  - Reserves/endowments
  - Tuition/fee levels
  - Cost per academic credit
  - Annual grants/awards
  - Program expenditures as a percentage of budget
  - Annual budget increase/decrease
  - Scholarship growth
- Measures and indicators show steady improvement.
- Important budgetary and financial data are presented.
- Comparative data include industry best, best competitor, and other appropriate benchmarks.
- Market share increase from new program offerings, such as Web-based or long distance delivery.

7.4 Faculty and Staff Results (70 Points)
Results Scoring

Summarize your organization's faculty- and staff-related results, including faculty and staff well-being, satisfaction, development, and work system performance. Segment your results by types and categories of faculty and staff, as appropriate. Include appropriate comparative data.

Provide data and information to answer the following questions:

a. Faculty and Staff Results

  (1) What are your current levels and trends in key measures/indicators of faculty and staff well-being, satisfaction and dissatisfaction, and development?

  (2) What are your current levels and trends in key measures/indicators of faculty and staff work system performance and effectiveness?

Notes:

N1. Results reported in this Item should relate to activities described in Category 5. Your results should be responsive to key process needs described in Category 6 and to your organization's action plans and human resource plans described in Item 2.2.

N2. For appropriate measures of faculty and staff well-being and satisfaction (7.4a[1]), see Notes to Item 5.3. Appropriate measures/indicators of faculty and staff development might include innovation and suggestion rates, courses or educational programs completed, learning, on-the-job performance improvements, collaboration/teamwork, and cross-training rates.

N3. Appropriate measures/indicators of work system performance and effectiveness (7.4a[2]) might include use of teams; knowledge and skill sharing across work functions, units, and locations; and flexibility. Additional indicators for staff performance might be simplification of the job and of the job classification, as well as job rotation.

N4. Comparisons should include a brief description of how the appropriateness of each comparison is ensured.

This Item looks at the organization's human resource results, with the aim of demonstrating how well the organization has created, maintained, and enhanced a positive, productive, learning, and caring work environment.

Organizations should provide data demonstrating current levels, trends, and appropriate comparisons for key measures and/or indicators of faculty and staff well-being, satisfaction, dissatisfaction, and development. The organization should also provide data and information on the organization's work system performance and effectiveness:

- Results reported might include generic or organization-specific factors.

- Generic factors might include safety, absenteeism, turnover, satisfaction, and complaints (grievances). For some measures, such as absenteeism and turnover, local or regional comparisons may be most appropriate.

- Organization-specific factors related to faculty and staff research results might include factors that relate to faculty and staff well-being and satisfaction. These factors might include extent of training or cross-training and systems to promote the effectiveness of self-directed and empowered faculty and staff.

- Results measures reported for work system performance might include improvement in job classification, job rotation, work layout, and local decision making. Results reported might include input data, such as extent of training, but the main emphasis should be on data that show effectiveness of outcomes.

7.4 Faculty and Staff Results

Results of current levels and trends in key measures and/or indicators of faculty and staff well-being, satisfaction, development, and work system performance.

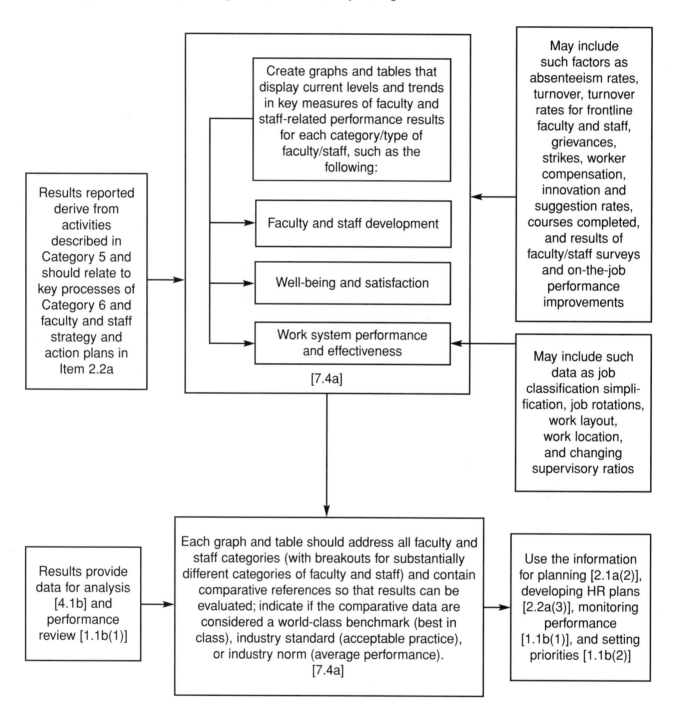

Results reported derive from activities described in Category 5 and should relate to key processes of Category 6 and faculty and staff strategy and action plans in Item 2.2a

Create graphs and tables that display current levels and trends in key measures of faculty and staff-related performance results for each category/type of faculty/staff, such as the following:

Faculty and staff development

Well-being and satisfaction

Work system performance and effectiveness

[7.4a]

May include such factors as absenteeism rates, turnover, turnover rates for frontline faculty and staff, grievances, strikes, worker compensation, innovation and suggestion rates, courses completed, and results of faculty/staff surveys and on-the-job performance improvements

May include such data as job classification simplification, job rotations, work layout, work location, and changing supervisory ratios

Results provide data for analysis [4.1b] and performance review [1.1b(1)]

Each graph and table should address all faculty and staff categories (with breakouts for substantially different categories of faculty and staff) and contain comparative references so that results can be evaluated; indicate if the comparative data are considered a world-class benchmark (best in class), industry standard (acceptable practice), or industry norm (average performance).
[7.4a]

Use the information for planning [2.1a(2)], developing HR plans [2.2a(3)], monitoring performance [1.1b(1)], and setting priorities [1.1b(2)]

7.4 Faculty and Staff Results Item Linkages

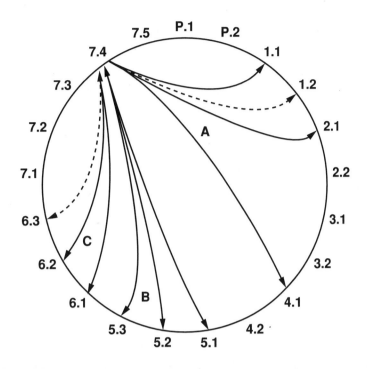

Nature of Relationship

A   Faculty and staff results data [7.4] are collected and used for planning [2.1], for leader decision making [1.1], to provide feedback through the leadership system [1.1], and for priority setting [4.1]. In addition, results in the area of faculty and staff safety [7.4] are used to ensure compliance with regulatory requirements [1.2].

B   Faculty and staff results derive from and are enhanced by improving work systems, enhancing flexibility, and strengthening faculty and staff recognition systems [5.1], training [5.2], and well-being and satisfaction [5.3]. In addition, faculty and staff results data [7.4] are monitored, in part, to assess work system effectiveness [5.1], training effectiveness [5.2], and improvements in faculty and staff satisfaction [5.3c].

C   Information about faculty and staff satisfaction [7.4] is used to target improvements in educational program design and delivery [6.1], student services [6.2], and support processes [6.3]. In addition, the effectiveness of these processes [Category 6] affects faculty and staff satisfaction results [7.4].

7.4 Faculty and Staff Results
Sample Effective Results

- The results reported in Item 7.4 derive from activities described in Category 5.
- Multiyear data are provided to show sustained performance.
- All results show steady improvement.
- Data are not missing—if faculty and staff results data are declared important, they are reported.
- Comparison data for benchmark or comparable organizations are reported.
- Trend data are reported for faculty and staff satisfaction with working conditions, safety, retirement package, and other faculty and staff benefits. Satisfaction with administration is also reported.
- Trends for declining absenteeism, grievances, faculty and staff turnover, strikes, and worker compensation claims are reported.
- Data are reported for all faculty and staff categories.

7.5 Organizational Effectiveness Results (70 Points)
Results Scoring

Summarize your organization's key performance results that contribute to opportunities for enhanced learning and/or the achievement of organizational effectiveness. Include appropriate comparative data.

Provide data and information to answer the following questions:

a. Organizational Effectiveness Results

(1) What are your current levels and trends in key measures/indicators of the performance of key education design and delivery processes, student services, and support processes that contribute to enhanced learning and/or operational effectiveness? Include school capacity to improve student performance, student development, the education climate, indicators of responsiveness to student or stakeholder needs, supplier/partner performance, and other appropriate measures of effectiveness and efficiency.

(2) What are your results for key measures/indicators of organizational strategy accomplishment?

b. Public Responsibility and Citizenship Results

What are your results for key measures/indicators of safety; regulatory, legal, and/or accreditation compliance; and support of key communities?

Notes:

N1. Results reported in 7.5a should address your key organizational requirements and progress toward accomplishment of your key organizational performance goals as presented in the Organizational Profile and in Items 1.1, 2.2, 6.1, 6.2, and 6.3. Include results of mission-specific research and outreach processes, as appropriate. Include results not reported in Items 7.1, 7.2, 7.3, and 7.4.

N2. Safety and regulatory, legal, and/or accreditation compliance results reported in 7.5b should address requirements described in Item 1.2.

N3. Results reported in Item 7.5 should provide key information for analysis (Item 4.1) and review (Item 1.1) of your organizational performance and should provide the operational basis for improved student learning results (Item 7.1); student- and stakeholder-focused results (Item 7.2); and budgetary, financial, and market results (Item 7.3).

N4. Comparisons should include a brief description of how the appropriateness of each comparison is ensured.

This Item looks at the organization's other key operational performance results, with the aim of achieving organizational effectiveness and enhanced learning.

Organizations should provide data in this Item if it does not belong in Items 7.1, 7.2, 7.3, or 7.4. Results expected in Item 7.5 should report on current levels, trends, and appropriate comparisons for key measures and/or indicators of operational and strategic performance that support the ongoing achievement of results reported in Items 7.1 through 7.4:

- This Item encourages the organization to develop and include unique and innovative measures to track educational program development and operational improvement. Levels and trends for key design, delivery, and support process performance should be included. However, all key areas of education and operational performance should be covered by measures that are relevant and important to the organization.

- Measures and/or indicators of operational effectiveness and efficiency might include organization capacity to improve student performance, student development, educational climate, and indicators of responsiveness.

Organization should also provide data and information on the results of its safety, accreditation, regulatory/legal and/or accreditation compliance, and citizenship activities:

- Measures should include safety, regulatory/ legal and accreditation compliance, and noteworthy achievements in these areas, as appropriate. Results also should include indicators of support for key communities and other public purposes.
- If the organization has received sanctions or adverse actions under law, regulation, or contract during the past three years, the incidents and current status should be summarized.

7.5 Organizational Effectiveness Results

Results of improvement efforts that contribute to achievement of enhanced learning or operational effectiveness and enhancement of public responsibility and citizenship.

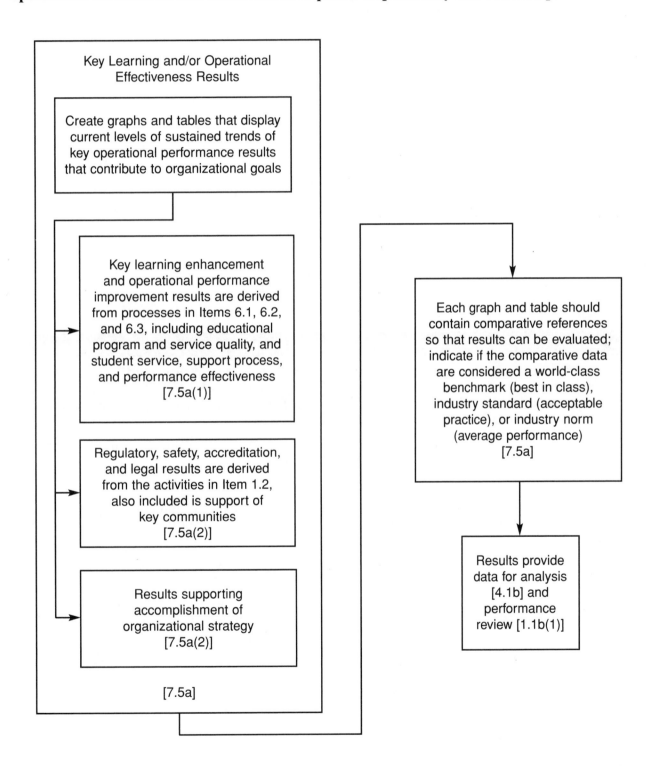

7.5 Organizational Effectiveness Results Item Linkages

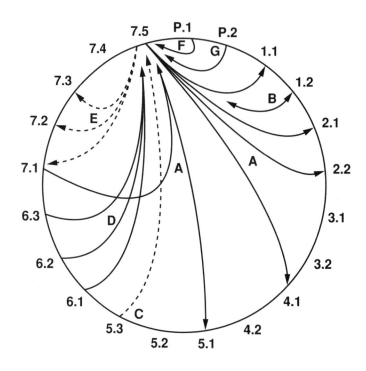

Nature of Relationship

A   Operational performance results data [7.5] are collected and used for planning [2.1]; goal setting [2.2]; management, monitoring, and decision making [1.1]; analysis [4.1]; and reward and recognition determination [5.1]. In addition, processes to improve student learning [7.1], faculty and staff initiative, and flexibility [5.1] can enhance performance results [7.5].

B   Regulatory, safety, accreditation, and legal results from the activities in Item 1.2 should be reported in Item 7.5. In addition, these results are monitored to determine if process changes are needed.

C   Faculty and staff morale and well-being [5.3] affect organizational results [7.5].

D   Designing and delivering educational, student services, and support programs to meet student and stakeholder requirements [6.1, 6.2, 6.3] improves student learning and educational program performance [7.1 and 7.5].

E   Organization effectiveness results [7.5] are often early or leading indicators of financial, budgetary, and market performance [7.3]; student learning [7.1]; and student and stakeholders' satisfaction [7.2].

F   The regulatory requirements described in P.1a(5), and the key suppliers and partners listed in P.1b(2) create an expectation that related performance results will be reported in 7.5b and 7.5a respectively.

G   Progress in achieving strategic challenges, as described in P.2b, should be reported in Item 7.5a(2). [Note that the strategic challenges identified in P.2b should be consistent with the strategic objectives in 2.1b(1).]

7.5 Organizational Effectiveness Results
Sample Effective Results

- Indices and trend data are provided in graph and chart form for all operational performance measures identified in Items 6.1, 6.2, 6.3, 1.2, relevant organizational goals (2.2), and the key factors identified in the profile and not reported elsewhere in Category 7.
- Multiyear data are reported.
- Most to all indicators show steady improvement.
- Results data reflect performance relative to specific performance requirements that relate closely to student and stakeholder satisfaction and student retention.
- Product and service measures and indicators address requirements, such as accuracy, timeliness, and reliability, and are key to predicting student and stakeholder behavior. Examples include defect levels, repeat services, meeting education program or offering delivery or response times, availability levels, and complaint levels.
- Operational performance measures address productivity, efficiency, and effectiveness, such as productivity indices, faculty and staff utilization, waste reduction, energy efficiency, cycle time reduction, and education design improvement measures cycle time reductions.
- Public responsibility and citizenship data include safety, regulatory, legal, and/or accreditation compliance and support of key communities.
- Comparative data include comparable best, best competitor, state/county average, and appropriate benchmarks. Data are also derived from independent surveys, studies, laboratory testing, or other sources.
- Data are not missing. (For example, do not show a steady trend from 1995 to 2000, but leave out 1996.)
- Data are not aggregated, since aggregation tends to hide poor performance by blending it with good performance. Break out and report trends separately.

Tips on Preparing a Baldrige Award Application

Applications are put together by every conceivable combination of teams, committees, and individual efforts, including consultants. There is no "right" or "best" way to do it. There are, however, lessons that have been learned and are worth considering because they contribute to people and organizations growing and improving.

The thoughts that follow are intended to generate conversation and learning. They are not intended to present a comprehensive treatment of the subject.

Getting the Fingerprints of the Organization on the Application

How do we put together a "good" application? To be "good" from a technical perspective, it must be both accurate and respond fully to the requirements of the criteria.

To be effective, the application must be more than technically accurate. The organization must feel a sense of commitment and ownership for the application. Ownership requires a role for people throughout the organization, as well as top leadership. The actual "putting of words on paper" can be accomplished in a variety of ways. However, ignoring this larger question of ownership exposes the organization to developing a sterile, disjointed, or unrecognizable document that discounts its value as a vehicle of growth.

The Spirit and Values in an Application

Like it or not, the team or individual that is responsible for developing an application will be closely watched by everyone in the organization. The people coordinating the development of the application need to be perceived as "walking the talk." They need to be seen as believers and role models for what is being written. In the midst of the pressure of putting together an application, a few values have to be continuously brought to the forefront:

- Continuous improvement must be fully embedded into all management processes and work processes.
- The application describes the system used to run the organization. This includes not just a description of the pieces but the linkages among the activities that make the organization function effectively.
- Put your best foot forward, but do not exaggerate—don't perfume the pig.

Core Values and Recurring Themes

In a document as complex and fact-filled as an application, make sure key messages are clearly communicated. There are 11 core values, and the application must address all of them. The organization needs to decide at the onset what key messages drive success. These key messages must pop out from each category and tie together the entire application. This is one of the reasons it becomes so important to design and write the organizational profile early and well. Don't ignore the importance of the new profile as an organizing tool. The profile must clearly identify those things that are important to the organization, its students and stakeholders, other partners, and to the future of the organization. These selected themes need to serve as a constant reminder as the application is developed. We are often asked, "How many themes should an organization focus on?" The answer really depends on how many the organization actually uses. Try developing three.

The Organizational Profile, and particularly the organizational challenges which are described in part two of the profile, are part of what examiners and judges use in all stages of application review, including the site visit.

Tests for Reasonableness

During the development of an application, there are "tests" that need to be conducted periodically with two groups of people: the senior executive team and contact faculty and staff.

With senior executive teams, the issue is the rate of growth of those Items undergoing intensive improvement efforts and under the direct sponsorship of senior executives. Every Baldrige application effort uses the occasion to drive significant process improvements throughout the organization. The development of an application offers an opportunity to review these initiatives. Each initiative is usually an improvement on an existing process and, therefore, a candidate for inclusion in an application to demonstrate progress.

At the faculty and staff level, the issue is a "reality check." Does the application as written reflect the way the organization is run? Several things happen at this level when people are given the opportunity to review a developing application:

- Faculty and staff should get an opportunity to comment on how closely the write-up reflects reality. It provides the writer(s) the opportunity to calibrate those words with reality.
- It helps the students and stakeholders to take a "roof top" view—which can be a learning experience in itself.
- It forces the writer to walk in the shoes of the individual contributor—again learning.

Test the Application

As an application comes together, a question asked by everyone—particularly the leadership team—is, "How well are we doing, and what's the score?" Although the real value of an application is continuous improvement, the competitive nature of people also comes to the forefront. After all, it's that spirit that helps drive us to higher levels of excellence. Nurture that spirit.

The best means of getting an objective review is to have people familiar with the Baldrige process examine the application. It is surprising how differently outsiders sometimes view the workings of the business we have just written about and know so well. The important aspect of this review is obviously the skill of the reviewers or examiners. The value to the organization is threefold:

- An early assessment—which sets expectations and eliminates surprises;
- An opportunity for an early start on improvement initiatives; and
- A test of understandability by outsiders—which every application ultimately has to pass.

Take Time to Celebrate/Continuously Improve

Developing an application is tough work. At the end of the day, it is: (1) a document highlighting the accomplishments and future aspirations of the organization, (2) a plan for getting there, and (3) an operations manual for new people entering the organization.

At key milestones in the development of an application, it is important to take time to celebrate the accomplishments just completed. The celebration should be immediate, inclusive, and visible. Such a celebration raises questions within the organization, it raises eyebrows, and it raises expectations—all of which are critical when trying to change and improve the overall performance of the organization. It also presents a perfect opportunity to promote improvement initiatives.

Some Closing Thoughts

In the words of David Kearns, former CEO of Xerox, Deputy Secretary of the U.S. Department of Education, and one of the greatest business and education leaders of Performance Excellence in the United States, "Quality is a journey without an end." Every organization today is faced with the struggle to bring about change—and the pace quickens each year. The Baldrige Criteria provided a mechanism that can help focus the energy for change in a most productive manner. Used properly, the criteria can help organizations break out of restrictive paradigms and continue on the journey to top levels of Performance Excellence.

Preparing the Organizational Profile

The Organizational Profile is a snapshot of your organization, the key influences on how you operate, and the key challenges you face. The Organizational Profile is intended to help examiners understand what is relevant and important to the organization and its performance.

The Organizational Profile is critically important for the following reasons:

- It is the starting point for self-assessment, writing and reviewing the application, helping to ensure focus on key education and management issues, and consistency in responses, especially in reporting educational performance results.
- It is used by the examiners and judges in the application review, including the site visit.
- It may be used by itself for an initial self-assessment for topics which are identified, but have little or no information available.

Guidelines for Preparing the Organizational Profile

The Organizational Profile consists of two items, divided into five sections.

Organizational Description

Organizational Environment

This section should provide information on the following:

- The nature of your organization's educational services.
- The size and location(s) of your organization and information on whether it is a public or private organization.
- Your organizational culture: purpose, vision, mission, and values, as appropriate.
- Your faculty and staff base, including number, types, educational level, and bargaining units.
- Your major technologies, equipment, facilities, and technologies used.
- The regulatory environment affecting you: health and safety, financial, district boundaries, and so on.

If your organization is a subunit of a larger organization, describe the following:

- The organizational relationship to your parent and percent of faculty and staff the subunit represents.
- How your services relate to those of your parent and/or other units of the parent organization.
- Key support services, if any, that your parent organization provides.

Organizational Relationships

This section should provide information on the following:

- Key student, stakeholder and/or market segment. Also, include key student and stakeholder requirements for services (for example, special accommodations, curriculum, class size, degrees available, student advising, and so on). Briefly describe all important requirements, and note significant differences, if any, in requirements among student and stakeholder groups. (Note any special relationships, such as partnerships with stakeholder groups.)
- Your major markets: local, regional, national, or international; and principal student types: advanced placement, special needs, traditional, nontraditional, and so on.
- Key supplier and partnering relationships and communication mechanisms. For example, include the types and numbers of other organizations with key linkages; the most important types of schools, businesses, or other organizations; any limitations, special relationships, or special requirements that may exist with some or all schools, businesses, or other organizations.

Organizational Challenges

Competitive Situation

This section should provide information on the following:

- Numbers and types of competitors.
- Your competitive position (relative size, growth) in the education sector.
- Principal factors that determine your competitive success, such as special or unique programs, leadership, services, e-services, and geographic proximity.
- Changes taking place that affect competition, such as new technologies, community size, or new employers and/or opportunities for collaboration.

Strategic Challenges

This section should provide information, as appropriate, on the following:

- Key strategic challenges, such as electronic communications with key stakeholders, better program cycle times, new markets or segments, changing demographics, student persistence, and faculty/staff retention.
- Education and Learning Challenges.
- Human Resource Challenges.
- Operational Challenges.
- Community Challenges.

Performance Improvement System

This section should provide information, as appropriate, on the following:

- Maintaining an organizational focus on performance improvement.
- Your approach to systematic evaluation and improvement of key processes.
- Your approach to fostering organizational learning and knowledge sharing.

Page Limit

The Organizational Profile is limited to five pages. These pages are not counted in the overall 50-page application limit.

The Organizational Profile should be prepared first and then used to guide the writing of the document used for assessment.

Guidelines for Responding to Approach/Deployment Items

The criteria focus on key educational performance results. However, results by themselves offer little help in diagnosing why performance is not at required levels. For example, if some results are poor or are improving at rates slower than comparable organizations, it is important to understand why this is so and what might be done to accelerate improvement.

The purpose of Approach/Deployment Items is to permit diagnosis of the organization's most important processes—the ones that enable fast-paced performance improvement and contribute to key organizational results. Diagnosis and feedback depend heavily upon the processes and systems that are in place. For this reason, it is important to respond to these Items by providing key process information.

Understand the Meaning of How

Items requesting information on approach include questions that begin with the word *how*. Responses should outline key process information, such as methods, measures, deployment, and evaluation, improvement, and learning factors. Responses lacking such information, or merely providing an example, are referred to in the scoring guidelines as anecdotal information and are worth little to nothing.

Show What and How

Describe your system for meeting the requirements of each Item. Ensure that methods, processes, and practices are fully described. Use flowcharts to help examiners visualize your key processes.

It is important to give basic information about what the key education and management processes are and how they work. Although it is helpful to include who performs the work, merely stating who does not permit effective communication or feedback. For example, stating that "parent satisfaction data are analyzed for improvement by the public relations department" does not set the stage for useful feedback, because potential strengths and weaknesses in the analysis cannot be identified from this very limited information. This makes it impossible to determine if a systematic process is in place.

Show That Activities Are Systematic

Ensure that the response describes a systematic approach, not merely an anecdotal example.

Systematic approaches are repeatable, predictable, and involve the systematic use of data and information for cycles of improvement. In other words, the approaches are consistent over time, build-in learning and evaluation, and show maturity. Scores above 50 percent rely on clear evidence that approaches are systematic.

Show Deployment

Ensure that the response gives clear and sufficient information on deployment. For example, one must be able to distinguish from a response whether an approach described is used in one, some, most, or all parts of the organization. Is it used in one school or college or the whole organization?

Deployment can be shown compactly by using summary tables that outline what is done in different parts of the organization. This is particularly effective if the basic approach is described in a narrative.

Show Focus and Consistency

The response demonstrates that the organization is focused on key processes and on improvements that offer the greatest potential to improve organization performance and accomplish organization action plans.

There are four important factors to consider regarding focus and consistency: (1) the Organizational Profile should make clear what is important; (2) the Strategic Planning Category, including the strategy and action plans, should highlight areas of greatest focus and describe how deployment is accomplished; (3) descriptions of organization-level analysis (Items 4.1 and 1.1) should show how the organization analyzes and reviews performance information to set priorities; and (4) the Process Management Category should highlight processes that are key to overall organization performance.

Focus and consistency in the Approach/Deployment Items should yield corresponding results reported in Results Items.

Respond Fully to Item Requirements

Ensure that the response fully addresses all important parts of each Item and each Area to Address. Missing information will be interpreted by examiners as a gap in approach and/or deployment. All areas should be addressed and checked in final review. Individual components of an Area to Address may be addressed individually or together.

Cross-Reference When Appropriate

Organizations should try to make each Item response self-contained. However, some responses to different Items might be mutually reinforcing. It is then appropriate to reference responses to other Items, rather than to repeat information. In such cases, applicants should use area designators, for example, "see Area 3.2a(1)."

Use a Compact Format

Organizations should make the best use of the 50 application pages permitted. Whenever possible, organizations should use flowcharts, tables, and "bulleted" lists.

Refer to the Scoring Guidelines

The evaluation of Item responses is accomplished by consideration of the criteria Item requirements and the maturity of the organization's approaches, breadth of deployment, and strength of the improvement process relative to the scoring guidelines. Therefore, organizations need to consider both the criteria and the scoring guidelines in preparing responses. In particular, remember that in order to score over 50 percent, organizations must demonstrate consistent evaluation and corresponding improvements. The Scoring Guidelines make this requirement applicable to *all* Items in Categories 1 through 6. Even if the details of the Item do not ask for a description of techniques, it will help the examiners give you full credit for your processes if an explanation is provided to show how the processes are evaluated and refined.

Guidelines for Responding to Results Items

The Baldrige Education Criteria place great emphasis on results. Items 7.1, 7.2, 7.3, 7.4, and 7.5 call for results related to all key requirements, students, stakeholders, markets, faculty/staff, and goals.

Focus on Reporting Critical Results

Results reported should cover the most important requirements for education success, highlighted in the Organization Profile and the Strategic Planning Categories and included in responses to other Items, such as Faculty and Staff Focus (Category 5) and Process Management (Category 6).

Four key requirements for effective presentation of results data include the following:

1. Trends show directions of results and rates of change.
2. Performance levels show performance on some meaningful measurement scale.
3. Comparisons show how trends or levels compare with those of other, appropriately selected, organizations.
4. Breadth of results shows completeness of deployment of improvement activities.

No Minimum Time

No minimum period of time is required for trend data. However, results data might span five years or more for some results. Trends might be much shorter for some of the organization's improvement activities. Because of the importance of showing deployment and focus, new data should be included even if trends and comparisons are not yet well-established.

Compact Presentation

Presenting many results can be done compactly by using graphs and tables. Graphs and tables should be labeled for easy interpretation. Results compared with others should be "normalized"—presented in a way (such as use of ratios) that takes into account various size or inflation factors. For example, if an organization's faculty and staff has been growing, reporting safety results in terms of accidents per 100 employees would permit more meaningful trend data than in terms of the total number of accidents.

Link Results with Text

Discussion of results and the results themselves should be close together in the report. Use figure numbers that correspond to Items. For example, the third figure for Item 7.2 would be 7.2–3. (See Figure 19.)

The graph in Figure 19 illustrates data that might be presented in this manner as part of a response to Item 7.2, Student- and Stakeholder-Focused Results.

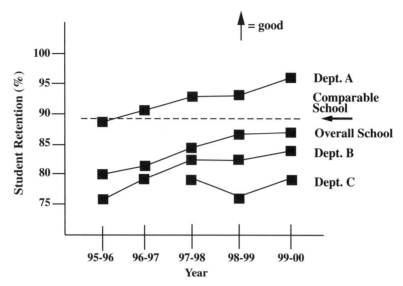

Figure 7.2–3 Student- and Stakeholder-Focused Results

Figure 19

Using the graph, the following characteristics of clear and effective data presentation are illustrated:

- Trend lines report data for a key mission objective.
- Both axes and units of measure are clearly labeled.
- Results are presented for several years.
- Meaningful comparisons are clearly shown.
- The organization shows, using a single graph, that its departments separately track retention rates.

To help interpret the scoring guidelines, the following comments on the graphed results would be appropriate:

- The overall organization performance level is excellent. This conclusion is supported by the comparison with comparable organizations.
- The organization exhibits an overall excellent improvement record.
- Department A is the current performance leader—showing sustained high performance well above comparable organizations and a positive trend. Department B shows rapid improvement. Its current performance is near that of comparable organizations.
- Department C—a new division—is having early problems. The applicant has analyzed and explained the early problems in the application text. Its current performance is not yet at the level of the other departments or comparable organizations.

Complete Data

Be sure that results data are displayed for all relevant students and stakeholders, financial concerns, faculty and staff, operational performance, and other performance characteristics. If you identify relevant performance measures and goals in other parts of the analysis, (for example, Items 1.1, 1.2, 2.1, 2.2, 3.1, 3.2, 4.1, 4.2, 5.1, 5.2, 5.3, 6.1, 6.2, and 6.3), be sure to include the results of these performance characteristics in Category 7. As each relevant performance measure is identified in the assessment process, create a blank chart and label the axes. Define all units of measure, especially if they are organization-specific or unique to the organization. As data are collected, populate the charts. If expected data are not provided in the application, examiners may assume that the trends or levels are not good. Missing data drive the score down in the same way that poor trends do. Be sure to provide comparative data. Without comparative data, as in Figure 20, it is difficult to judge the "goodness" of the performance.

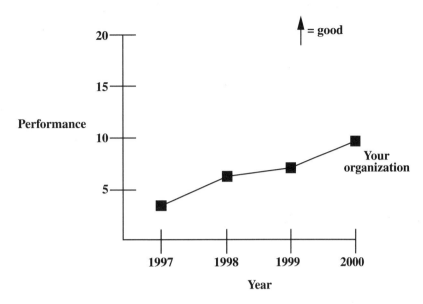

Chart lacking comparative data

Figure 20

Break Out Data

Avoid aggregating the data. Where appropriate, break data into meaningful components. If the organization serves several different student and stakeholder groups, display performance and satisfaction data for each group. As Figure 21 demonstrates, only one of the three trends is positive, although the average is positive. Examiners will seek component data when aggregate data are reported. Only presenting aggregate data instead of meaningful component data could reduce the score.

The Importance of Criteria Notes

Several Items are followed by one or more notes that offer some insight and explanation about the Item. Often these notes suggest activities or measures that other organizations have used to meet the requirements of the Item. There are many ways to manage a high-performance system that are not included in the notes. Notes should be considered suggestions and not requirements.

Data and Measures

Comparison data are required for all Items in Category 7. These data are designed to demonstrate how well the organization is performing. To judge Performance Excellence, one must possess comparison data. In Figure 20, performance is represented by the line connecting the squares. Clearly, the organization is improving, but how "good" is it? Without comparison data, answering that question is difficult.

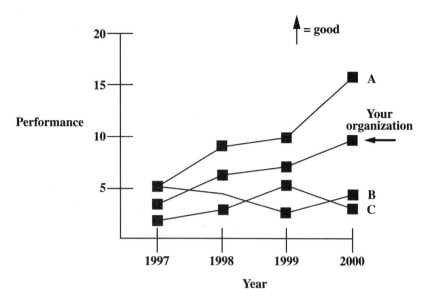

Chart with comparative data included

Figure 21

Now consider the chart with comparison data added (Figure 21). Note the position of three hypothetical comparisons, represented by the letters *A, B,* and *C*.

Consider the following two scenarios:

1. If *A* represents a state/county average and both *B* and *C* represent area competitors, examiners would conclude that the organization's performance was substandard, even though it is improving.

2. If *A* represents a best-in-class (benchmark) organization and *B* represents a state/county average, examiners would conclude that organizational performance is very good.

In both scenarios, the organizational performance remained the same, but the examiner's perception of it changed.

Measures

Agreeing on relevant measures is a difficult task for organizations in the early phases of quality and performance improvement. The task is easier if the following guidelines are considered:

- Clearly define student and stakeholder requirements. Clear requirements are easier to measure. Clearly defined student and stakeholder requirements require probing and suggesting. For example, the student wants better test results reporting. After probing to find what better means, we discover that: (1) the student wants the grade, as well as specific teacher comments; (2) better also means quicker results—the next school or class day; and (3) students want an opportunity within two weeks to retake the test and raise their grades.

- For each of the three requirements defined, identify a measure. For example, since the students are concerned with turnaround time for test results, we must assess how long it took the teacher to grade, comment on, and return the test. Measures include time in hours, days, and minutes to produce "better" test results reporting.

- Collect and report data. Several charts might be required to display these factors.

Scoring System

The scoring of organization responses to criteria Items and feedback are based on three evaluation dimensions: approach, deployment, and results. Organizations need to furnish information relating to these dimensions. Specific factors for these dimensions are described as follows.

Approach

Approach refers to how the organization addresses the Item requirements—the method(s) used. The factors used to evaluate approaches include the following:

- Appropriateness of the methods to the requirements.
- Effectiveness of use of the methods. This includes the degree to which the approach is systematic, integrated, and consistently applied; embodies evaluation, improvement, and learning cycles; and is based on reliable information and data.
- Evidence of innovation and/or significant and effective adaptations of approaches used in other types of organizations.

Deployment

Deployment refers to the extent to which the organization's approach is applied to all requirements of the Item. The factors used to evaluate deployment include the following:

- Use of the approach in addressing organization and Item requirements; and
- Use of the approach by all appropriate work units.

Results

Results refers to outcomes in achieving the purposes given in the Item. The factors used to evaluate results include the following:

- Current performance;
- Performance relative to appropriate comparisons and/or benchmarks;
- Rate, breadth, and importance of performance improvements;
- Demonstration of sustained improvement and/or sustained high-level performance; and
- Linkage of results measures to key performance measures identified in the Organizational Profile and in Approach/Deployment Items.

Item Classification and Scoring Dimensions

Items are classified according to the kinds of information and/or data those seeking assessment are expected to furnish relative to the three evaluation dimensions.

The two types of Items and their designations are: (1) Approach/Deployment, and (2) Results.

Approach and deployment are linked to emphasize that descriptions of approach should always indicate the deployment—consistent with the specific requirements of the Item. Although approach and deployment dimensions are linked, feedback reflects strengths and/or areas for improvement in either or both dimensions.

Results Items call for data showing performance levels and trends on key measures and/or indicators of organizational performance. However, the evaluation factor, "breadth" of performance improvements, is concerned with how widespread the improvement results are. This is directly related to the deployment dimension. That is, if improvement processes are widely deployed, there should be corresponding results. A score for a Results Item is thus a composite based upon overall performance, taking into account the breadth of improvements and their importance (see next section).

Importance as a Scoring Factor

The three evaluation dimensions previously described are critical to evaluation and feedback. However, evaluation and feedback must also consider the importance of improvements in approach, deployment, and results to the organization. The areas of greatest importance should be identified in the Organization Profile, and in such Items as 2.2, 3.1, 6.1, 6.2, 7.1, and 7.5. Of particular importance are the key student requirements, key strategies, and action plans.

Assignment of Scores to Responses

The following guidelines should be observed in assignment of scores to responses:

- All relevant Areas to Address should be included in the Item response. Also, responses should reflect what is important to the organization.

- In assigning a score to an Item, an examiner first decides which scoring range (for example, 40 to 60 percent) best fits the overall Item response. Overall "best fit" does not require total agreement with each of the statements for that scoring range. Actual score within the range depends upon an examiner's judgment of the closeness of the Item response in relation to the statements in the next higher and next lower scoring ranges.

- An Approach/Deployment Item score of 50 percent represents an approach that meets the basic objectives of the Item and that is deployed to the principal activities covered in the Item. Higher scores reflect maturity (cycles of improvement), integration, and broader deployment.

- A Results Item score of 50 percent represents a clear indication of improvement trends and/or good levels of performance in the principal results areas covered in the Item. Higher scores reflect better improvement rates and/or levels of performance and better comparative performance, as well as broader coverage and integration with organizational requirements.

	Approach/Deployment	Results
0%	• No systematic approach is evident; information is anecdotal	• There are no results or poor results in areas reported
10% to 20%	• The beginning of a systematic approach to the basic purposes of the Item is evident • Major gaps exist in deployment that would inhibit progress in achieving the basic purposes of the Item • Early stages of a transition from reacting to problems to a general improvement orientation are evident	• There are some improvements and/or early good performance levels in a few areas • Results are not reported for many to most areas of importance to your key organizational requirements
30% to 40%	• An effective, systematic approach, responsive to the basic purposes of the Item, is evident • The approach is deployed, although some areas or work units are in early stages of deployment • The beginning of a systematic approach to evaluation and improvement of basic Item processes is evident	• Improvements and/or good performance levels are reported in many areas of importance to your key organizational requirements • Early stages of developing trends and obtaining comparative information are evident • Results are reported for many to most areas of importance to your key organizational requirements
50% to 60%	• An effective, systematic approach, responsive to the overall purposes of the Item and your key organizational requirements, is evident • The approach is well-deployed, although deployment may vary in some areas or work units • A fact-based, systematic evaluation and improvement process is in place for improving the efficiency and effectiveness of key processes • The approach is aligned with your basic organizational needs identified in the other criteria categories	• Improvement trends and/or good performance levels are reported for most areas of importance to your key organizational requirements • No pattern of adverse trends and no poor performance levels are evident in areas of importance to your key organizational requirements • Some trends and/or current performance levels—evaluated against relevant comparisons and/or benchmarks—show areas of strength and/or good to very good relative performance levels • Organizational performance results address most key student/stakeholder, market, and process requirements
70% to 80%	• An effective, systematic approach, responsive to the multiple requirements of the Item and your current and changing educational service needs, is evident • The approach is well deployed, with no significant gaps • A fact-based, systematic evaluation and improvement process and organizational learning/sharing are key management tools; there is clear evidence of refinement and improved integration as a result of organizational-level analysis and sharing • The approach is well integrated with your organizational needs identified in the other criteria categories	• Current performance is good to excellent in areas of importance to your key organizational requirements • Most improvement trends and/or current performance levels are sustained • Many to most trends and/or current performance levels—evaluated against relevant comparisons and/or benchmarks—show areas of leadership and very good relative performance levels • Organizational performance results address most key student/stakeholder, market, process, and action plan requirements
90% to 100%	• An effective, systematic approach, fully responsive to all the requirements of the Item and all your current and changing educational service needs, is evident • The approach is fully deployed without significant weaknesses or gaps in any areas or work units • A very strong, fact-based, systematic evaluation and improvement process and extensive organizational learning/sharing are key management tools; strong refinement and integration, backed by excellent organizational-level analysis and sharing, are evident • The approach is fully integrated with your organizational needs identified in the other criteria categories	• Current performance is excellent in most areas of importance to your key organizational requirements • Excellent improvement trends and/or sustained excellent performance levels are reported in most areas • Evidence of education sector and benchmark leadership is demonstrated in many areas • Organizational performance results fully address key student/stakeholder, market, process, and action plan requirements

Supplementary Scoring Guidelines

Authors' note: Many examiners and organizations have found the official scoring guidelines to be vague, although they have been improved considerably this year. The guidelines, presented in 20 percent increments, may increase the difficulty of reaching consensus on a score and increase scoring variation. To resolve this problem, we developed the following supplemental scoring guidelines. Many state award programs have used these guidelines for several years and found that they make the consensus process easier and produce comparable scores.

Approach/Deployment

1. For each Approach/Deployment Item, first determine the appropriate level on the approach scale. This sets the upper possible score the applicant may receive on the Item.

2. Then read the corresponding level on the deployment scale. For example, if the approach level is 40 percent, read the 40 percent standard on the deployment scale where one would expect "several work units are in the early stages of deployment," and "progress in achieving the primary purposes of the Item is not inhibited." If that is the case, the final score is 40 percent.

3. However, if the deployment score is lower than the approach score, then it establishes the lower range of possible final scores for the Item. The actual final score will be between the low and high scores. For example, if "many major gaps exist and progress is significantly inhibited," the lowest possible score would be 10 percent. This final score must be between 40 and 10 percent (for example, 10, 20, 30, or 40 percent).

4. Never increase an approach score based on better deployment.

5. Scoring Approach/Deployment Items are presented on the pages immediately following this scoring section.

Results

1. For Results Items, base your assessment only on the standards described on the results scale. *Do not consider approach or deployment standards at all.*

2. Determine the extent to which performance results are positive, complete, and at high levels relative to competitors or similar providers or an industry standard.

3. To determine the extent to which all important results are reported, examiners should develop a list of the key measures the applicant indicates are important. Start with the measures listed in the Profile section. Then add to the key measures list based on key data reported in Item 2.1 and the goals in Item 2.2, as well as measures that may be mentioned in Categories 5 and 6. Key measures can be reported anywhere in an application.

Score	Approach	Deployment
0%	No systematic approach evident; anecdotal information.	Anecdotal, undocumented.
10%	Early beginning of a systematic approach consistent with the basic purposes of the Item is somewhat evident. Mostly reactive approach to problems. Many key requirements of the Item not addressed. In the earliest stages of transitioning from reacting to problems to a general improvement orientation.	Many major gaps exist in deployment. Progress in achieving basic purposes of Item is significantly inhibited.
20%	A partially systematic but beginning approach consistent with the basic purposes of the Item is evident. Generally reactive to problems. Some key requirements of the Item not addressed. In the early stages of transitioning from reacting to problems to a general improvement orientation.	Some major gaps exist in deployment. Progress in achieving basic purposes of Item is noticeably inhibited.
30%	An effective, systematic approach responsive to the basic purposes of the Item is somewhat evident. A few key requirements of the Item not addressed. Beginning of a systematic approach to evaluation but little if any improvement of basic Item processes is evident. Random improvements may have been made.	The approach is generally deployed, although several units are in the earliest stages of deployment. Progress in achieving primary purposes of Item is minimally inhibited.
40%	An effective, systematic approach responsive to the basic purposes of the Item is clearly in place. Several minor requirements of the Item are not addressed. Beginning of a systematic approach to evaluation and improvement of basic Item processes is evident. Random improvements may have been made.	The approach is deployed, although several units are in the early stages of deployment. Progress in achieving primary purposes of Item is not inhibited.
50%	An effective, systematic approach responsive to the overall purposes of the Item is fully developed. Some minor requirements of the Item are not addressed. Fact-based improvement system is in place for basic Item processes that includes process evaluation in key areas (but no refinements are in place). Random improvements may have been made. The approach is aligned with some basic school needs identified in the other criteria categories.	No major gaps in deployment exist that inhibit progress in achieving primary purposes of Item, although deployment may vary in some areas or work units. Some work units are still in the early stages of deployment.
60%	An effective, systematic approach responsive to the overall purposes of the Item is clearly in place. A few minor requirements of the Item not addressed. Fact-based improvement system is in place for the basic requirements of the Item, including at least one evaluation and improvement cycle completed, and some systematic refinement based on the evaluation in key areas. The approach is aligned with most basic school needs identified in the other criteria categories.	No major gaps in deployment exist that inhibit progress in achieving primary purposes of Item, although deployment may vary in some areas or work units. A few work units may still be in the early stages of deployment.
70%	An effective, systematic approach, responsive to many of the multiple purposes of the Item, is clearly in place and fully developed. Organizational learning and sharing are frequently used management tools at many levels. Some systematic evaluation and evidence of refinements and improved integration result from organization-level analysis and learning. The approach is aligned and well-integrated, with many overall school needs identified in the other criteria categories.	Approach is well-deployed, with some work units in middle or advanced stages. No significant gaps exist that inhibit progress in achieving the purposes of the Item.
80%	An effective, systematic approach, responsive to most of the multiple purposes of the Item, is clearly in place and fully developed. Organizational learning and sharing are frequently used management tools at most levels. Considerable systematic evaluation and evidence of refinements and integration result from organization-level analysis and learning. The approach is aligned and well-integrated with most overall school needs identified in the other criteria categories.	Approach is well-deployed, with many work units in the advanced stages. No gaps exist that inhibit progress in achieving the purposes of the Item.
90%	An effective, systematic approach, responsive to all of the multiple purposes of the Item, is in place. Considerable systematic evaluation and extensive refinements and improved organizational sharing and learning are key management tools at most levels. Some innovative processes are evident, with strong refinement and integration supported by substantial organization-level analysis and sharing.	Approach is fully deployed, with most work units in the advanced stages. No significant gaps or weaknesses exist in any areas or work units.
100%	An effective, systematic approach, fully responsive to all of the multiple purposes of the Item, is clearly in place. Considerable systematic evaluation and clear evidence of extensive refinements and improved organizational sharing and learning are key management tools at all levels. Many innovative processes are evident, with strong refinement and integration supported by excellent organization-level analysis and sharing.	Approach is fully deployed, with most to all work units in the advanced stages. No significant gaps or weaknesses exist in any areas or work units.

Score	Scoring Results
0%	No results or poor results in areas reported.
10%	Results not reported for most areas of importance to the organization's key requirements. Limited positive results and/or limited good performance levels are evident for a few areas.
20%	Results not reported for many areas of importance to the organization's key requirements. Some positive results and/or early good performance levels are evident for a few of these areas.
30%	Results are reported for many areas of importance to the organization's key requirements. Improvements and/or good performance levels are evident for many areas of importance to the organization's key requirements. Early stages of developing trends but little or no comparative information has been obtained.
40%	Results are reported for most key areas of importance to the organization's key requirements. Improvements and good performance levels are evident for many areas of importance to the organization's key requirements. Early stages of developing trends and obtaining comparative information.
50%	Results are reported for most key student, other stakeholder, process, and action plan requirements. Some positive trends and/or good performance levels—evaluated against relevant comparisons or benchmarks— show a few areas of strength or good relative performance levels. No pattern of adverse trends and no poor performance levels in areas of importance to key organization requirements.
60%	Results are reported for most key student, other stakeholder, process, and action plan requirements. Many positive trends and/or good performance levels—evaluated against relevant comparisons and benchmarks—show some areas of strength and good relative performance levels. No pattern of adverse trends and no poor performance levels in areas of importance to key organization requirements.
70%	Results are reported for most key student, other stakeholder, process, and action plan requirements. Current performance is good in many areas important to key organization requirements. Most improvement trends and/or current performance levels are sustained, and many of these—evaluated against relevant comparisons and/or benchmarks—show some areas of leadership and very good relative performance levels.
80%	Results are reported for most key student, other stakeholder, process, and action plan requirements. Current performance is excellent in many areas important to key organization requirements. Most improvement trends and/or current performance levels are sustained, and most of these—evaluated against relevant comparisons and/or benchmarks—show areas of leadership and very good relative performance levels.
90%	Results fully address key student, other stakeholder, process, and action plan requirements. Current performance is excellent in most areas important to key organization requirements. Most improvement trends or current performance levels are sustained, and most of these—evaluated against relevant comparisons or benchmarks—show areas of education-sector leadership or benchmark leadership in many areas.
100%	Results fully address key student, other stakeholder, process, and action plan requirements. Current performance is excellent in most areas important to key organization requirements. Excellent improvement trends and current performance levels are sustained and—evaluated against relevant comparisons and benchmarks—show education sector-leadership or benchmark leadership in many areas.

Approach/Deployment Terms

Systematic

Look for evidence of a system—a repeatable, predictable process that is used to fulfill the requirements of the Item. Briefly describe the system. Be sure to explain how the system works. You must communicate the nature of the system to people who are not familiar with it. This is essential to achieve the 30 percent scoring threshold.

Integrated

Determine the extent to which the system is integrated, or linked, with other elements of the overall management system. Show the linkages across categories for key themes, such as those displayed earlier for each Item.

Consider the extent to which the work of senior leaders is integrated. For example:

1. Senior leaders (Item 1.1) are responsible for shaping and communicating the organization's vision, values, and expectations throughout the leadership system and workforce.
2. They develop relationships with key students and stakeholders (Item 3.2) and monitor student and stakeholder satisfaction (Item 7.2) and organizational performance (Item 7.5).
3. This information, when properly analyzed (Item 4.1), helps them plan better and make more informed decisions to optimize student and stakeholder satisfaction and operational and financial performance.
4. With this in mind, senior leaders participate in strategy development (Item 2.l) and ensure the alignment of the workplace to achieve organizational goals (Item 2.2).
5. Senior leaders may also become involved in supporting new structures to improve faculty and staff performance (Item 5.1), training effectiveness (Item 5.2), and faculty and staff well-being and satisfaction (Item 5.3).

Similar relationships (linkages) exist between other Items. Highlight these linkages to demonstrate integration.

Prevention-Based

Prevention-based systems are characterized by actions to minimize or prevent the recurrence of problems. In an ideal world, all systems would produce perfect products and flawless service. Since that rarely happens, high-performing organizations are able to act quickly to recover from a problem (fight the fire) and then take action to identify the root cause of the problem and prevent it from surfacing again. The nature of the problem, its root cause, and appropriate corrective action is communicated to all relevant faculty and staff so that they can implement the corrective action in their areas before the problem arises.

Continuous Improvement

Continuous improvement is a bedrock theme. It is the method that helps organizations keep their competitive edge. Continuous improvement involves evaluation and improvement of processes crucial to organizational success. Evaluation and improvement completes the high-performance management cycle. Continuous improvement evaluations can be complex, data-driven, statistical processes, or as simple as a focus group discussing what went right, what went wrong, and how it can be done better. The key to optimum performance lies in the pervasive evaluation and improvement of all processes. By practicing systematic, pervasive, continuous improvement, time becomes the organization's ally. Consistent evaluation and refinement practices with correspondingly good deployment can drive the score to 60 percent or 70 percent, and higher.

Complete

Each Item contains one or more Areas to Address. Many Areas to Address contain several parts. Failure to address all areas and parts can push the score lower. If an Area to Address or part of an area does not apply to your organization, it is important to explain why. Otherwise, examiners may conclude that the system is incomplete.

Anecdotal

If your assessment describes a process that is essentially anecdotal and does not systematically address the criteria, it is worth very little (0 to 10 points).

Deployment

The extent to which processes are widely used by organization units affects scoring. For example, a systematic approach that is well-integrated, evaluated consistently, and refined routinely may be worth 70 percent to 90 percent. However, if that process is not in place in all key parts of the organization, the 70 percent to 90 percent score will be reduced, perhaps significantly, depending on the nature and extent of the gap.

Major gaps are expected to exist at the 0 to 20 percent level. At the 30 percent and higher levels, no major gaps exist, although some units may still be at the early stages of development. At the 70 percent to 80 percent level, no major gaps exist and the approach is well integrated with organizational needs identified in other parts of the criteria.

Summary

For each Item examined, the process is rated as follows:

- Anecdotal: 0 to 10 percent
- Systematic: 10 percent to 30 percent
- Fully developed: 40 percent
- Prevention-based and evaluated: 50 percent
- Integrated: 50 percent to 100 percent
- Refined: 60 percent to 80 percent
- Widely used, with no gaps in deployment: 70+ percent

Systematic, integrated, prevention-based, and continuously improved systems that are widely used are generally easier to describe than undeveloped systems. Moreover, describing numerous activities or anecdotes does not convince examiners that an integrated, prevention-based system is in place. In fact, simply describing numerous activities and anecdotes suggests that an integrated system does not exist. However, by tracing critical success threads through the relevant Items in the criteria, the organization demonstrates that its system is integrated and fully deployed.

To demonstrate system integration, pick several critical success factors and show how the organization manages them. For example, trace the leadership focus on performance:

- Identify performance-related data that are collected to indicate progress against goals (Item 4.1).
- Show how performance data are analyzed (Item 4.1) and used by leaders to set work priorities (Item 1.1).
- Show how performance effectiveness is considered in the planning process (Item 2.1) and how work at all levels is aligned to increase performance (Item 2.2).
- Demonstrate the impact of human resource management (Item 5.1) and training (Item 5.2) on performance and show how both tie to the strategy and faculty/staff resource plans (Item 2.2).
- Show how educational design, development, delivery, student, and support processes (Items 6.1, 6.2, 6.3) are enhanced to improve results.
- Report the results of improved performance (Items 7.1, 7.2, 7.3, 7.4, and 7.5).
- Determine how improved performance affects student and stakeholder satisfaction levels (Item 7.2).
- Show how student and stakeholder concerns (Item 3.1 and 3.2) are used to drive the selection of key measures (Item 4.1) and affect design and delivery processes (Item 6.1).

Note that the application is limited to 50 pages, not including the 5-page Organizational Profile. This may not be sufficient to describe in great detail the approach, deployment, results, and systematic integration of all of your critical success factors, goals, or key processes. Thus, you must pick the most important few, indicate them as such, then thoroughly describe the threads and linkages throughout the application.

Comparing Assessment for Performance Improvement and Accreditation

I. Introduction

This section provides a brief discussion of the relationship between assessment based on the Baldrige framework and accreditation processes that are in widespread use in education. For this purpose, we will focus on the diagnostic uses of the Baldrige framework to guide and drive performance improvement and leave the Baldrige Award as a form of recognition in the background.

Assessment and accreditation are both about quality in education. The approaches have a number of themes in common, but important differences remain. This section contains a brief discussion of these two topics. Where concrete illustrations of criteria will be useful, we will compare the Baldrige Education Criteria to the criteria of the Southern Association of Colleges and Schools (Commission on Colleges or, SACS). The Southern Association provides regional accreditation services for 11 U.S. southern states, and these accreditation services operate at the institutional level, rather than with a specialized focus on a particular academic unit or program. As the term *regional* implies, the remainder of the United States is divided into regions, each of which has its own accrediting agency and process. While these processes differ in details, they operate in fundamentally similar ways. In choosing the SACS for this discussion, we imply no value judgment regarding its relationship to other regional accreditation processes. We will use the 2001 Baldrige Criteria and the 1998 SACS Criteria (the most recent version).

Table 1   Comparison of Baldrige-Based Assessment and Accreditation from a Process Perspective

Stage	Baldrige Assessment	Accreditation
Preparation	Written award application or other compilation of information and data.	Institutional self-study prepared by the faculty, staff, and administration.
Evaluation	Use of Baldrige Criteria to assess the approaches and results of the institution. This can involve a site visit by a team of outside people.	Use of accreditation standards to evaluate the self-study. This is a peer review process conducted by a visiting team.
Feedback	Identification of strengths and areas for improvement. An assessment score on a defined scale is also often produced as a product of the evaluation.	Identification of areas of conformity and nonconformity to the standards (criteria) and a statement regarding whether the institution is in sufficient compliance with the standards to warrant accreditation.
Response	The institution identifies priorities for actions to improve approaches currently in use.	The institution develops a plan for removal of any nonconformity in order to improve the institution's degree of compliance with the standards.
Frequency	Whatever the institution chooses but rarely more often than annual.	Rarely more often than every five years and typically less frequent than that.

II. Assessment and Accreditation Cycles

Table 1 compares Baldrige-based assessment and accreditation from a process perspective.

The underlying philosophy of a Baldrige-based assessment is that the results an institution produces are the consequences of the approaches (systems, processes, measurements, and actions focused on improvement) that it employs to accomplish its purposes. The purpose of a Baldrige-based assessment is to produce or obtain a diagnosis that can be used as an input to a planning process from which priorities and action plans emerge. This approach is well-adapted to any institution that wishes to apply regular, systematic effort to year-over-year improvement in its processes and results.

Accreditation has historically played a quality assurance role with regard to external stakeholders of an institution. The underlying notion is that compliance with accreditation standards assures students, families, and sponsors that the institution has met a basic test of the quality of what the institution does. Since accreditation decisions can essentially be characterized as pass/fail decisions (or sometimes "pass with conditions"), it seems clear that the orientation is to achieving a threshold that is sufficient to warrant or earn accreditation. In addition, the burden of preparing a self-study means that accreditation is done relatively infrequently and, consequently, is rarely used as a tool to drive efforts to make improvements. When an institution is on the road to achieving accreditation for the first time, emphasis is on achieving the necessary threshold. When an institution is in its first cycles of reaccreditation, emphasis is on ensuring that the levels necessary to clear the threshold are maintained. Once an institution has become a "mature" accredited institution, the accreditation decision is frequently incidental to other issues that an institution might discover about itself in the course of the accreditation cycle.

Table 2   Comparison of Baldrige and SACS Criteria

MBNQA Education Criteria	SACS (Colleges) Criteria
• Organization Overview	• Institutional Purpose
• Leadership	
• Strategic Planning	
	• Administrative Processes
• Student and Stakeholder Focus	
• Faculty and Staff Focus	• Educational Program
• Educational and Support Process Management	• Educational Support Services
• Information and Analysis	
• Organizational and Performance Results	• Institutional Effectiveness

III. Assessment and Accreditation Criteria

Table 2 provides a high-level, side-by-side comparison of the Baldrige and SACS Criteria. Insofar as possible, the criteria sections are aligned in the table to show the primary areas of overlap. The purpose here is not to conduct an exhaustive comparison of the two sets of criteria, but to provide enough information to permit some comparative statements. Hence, this presentation is at the "category" level of the Baldrige Criteria and the "section" level of the SACS Criteria.

Table 2 suggests that Baldrige and accreditation criteria have a considerable degree of overlap. While this is true in some general sense, the comments that follow indicate that there are some underlying differences in perspective.

Accreditation criteria focus on program elements and resources (human, physical, technological, and other). These are often stated as requirements ("musts" in SACS terminology). While it is often not a trivial achievement to comply with each of the "musts" in the criteria, the presumption is that this is a sufficient condition (demonstration of the indicators of quality) to warrant accreditation. Accreditation also typically looks carefully at governance of the institution, in order to permit a determination of whether the institution is free of influences that would damage academic freedom.

The Baldrige Education Criteria focus on the approaches that an institution uses to plan, deliver, evaluate, and improve its educational activities. The Baldrige Criteria framework also addresses the results that a high-performing educational institution should achieve. We will return to the issue of results.

Table 2 also indicates respects in which the two types of criteria differ. The Baldrige Categories on leadership and strategic planning have no direct counterparts in the SACS accreditation criteria. As discussion elsewhere in this book indicates in more detail, these two portions of the Baldrige Criteria investigate how the institution considers stakeholder needs in setting its strategic direction, how senior leaders set values and expectations for the institution, and how the institution's performance is reviewed. No exact counterpart is present in the SACS accreditation criteria. The section on administrative processes addresses organization and administration, institutional advancement (alumni affairs and fund raising), financial resources, physical resources, and externally funded grants and contracts. The emphasis here is more on structure and resources than on process and evaluation.

Table 3   Comparison of Baldrige Organization Performance Results Category and the SACS Institutional Effectiveness Section

Organizational Performance Results (MBNQA Education Criteria)	Institutional Effectiveness (SACS Criteria)
• Student Performance Results • Student- and Stakeholder-Focused Results	• Planning and Evaluation: Educational Programs
• Budgetary, Financial, and Market Results • Faculty and Staff Results	• Planning and Evaluation: Administrative and Educational Support Services
• Organizational Effectiveness Results	• Institutional Research

There is an important overlap between the two sets of criteria that is not evident from the level of summary in Table 2. The section on Educational Programs in the SACS Criteria addresses academic program requirements and explores many aspects of faculty development and involvement in educational programs. This review typically reveals how the faculty of an institution is involved in academic planning. The titles of the Baldrige Categories do not examine this same information quite so directly. However, within the Process Management Category, the first fundamental Item deals with Education Design and Delivery.

We will conclude this section with a comparison of the Baldrige Category on Organizational Performance Results to the SACS section on Institutional Effectiveness. Table 3 provides a useful summary.

These two sections of the respective criteria deal with the results that an institution is achieving. Table 3, like Tables 1 and 2, not surprisingly indicates significant areas of overlap. Here, the differences are of interest. The underlying notion of this category of the Baldrige Criteria is to provide a comprehensive compilation of data in support of evaluation of institutional performance. In general, the Baldrige Criteria set a broad agenda, but the institution must decide what metrics to employ.

The Baldrige Item on student- and stakeholder-focused results seeks indications of whether students and other stakeholders (for example, alumni and employers of graduates) think well of what the institution is doing and whether they would recommend enrollment to prospective students. The SACS Criteria do not require such results to be gathered. The Baldrige Item on faculty and staff results seeks indications of the levels of satisfaction, well-being, and performance of faculty and staff. The SACS Criteria call for information about the credentials of faculty and about criteria and procedures for evaluation.

The topics that comprise the agenda for the Baldrige Category on organizational results provide a comprehensive scorecard that serves as a foundation for fact-based decisions regarding where to deploy resources and effort for improvement.

IV. Conclusion

Assessment and accreditation both aim at quality in education. The latter emphasizes program design, structure, and inputs; evaluates compliance with standards; and occurs relatively infrequently. Assessment emphasizes approaches and related results, diagnoses strengths and areas for improvement, and can be used frequently enough to be a powerful tool for improving an institution's performance.

References

2001 Education Criteria for Performance Excellence, (Gaithersburg, MD: Baldrige National Quality Program, National Institute of Standards and Technology).

Criteria for Accreditation, (Atlanta, GA: Commission on Colleges of the Southern Association of Colleges and Schools, 1998).

"What Accreditation and the Baldrige Can Learn from Each Other," in *High Performing Colleges,* D. Seymour. (Maryville, MO: Prescott Publishing Company, 1996).

Self-Assessments of Educational Organizations and Management Systems

Baldrige-based self-assessments of organization performance and management systems take several forms, ranging from rigorous and time intensive, to simple and somewhat superficial. This section discusses the various approaches to organizational self-assessment and the pros and cons of each. Curt Reimann, the first director of the Malcolm Baldrige National Quality Award office and the closing speaker for the Tenth Quest for Excellence Conference, spoke of the need to streamline assessments to get a good sense of strengths, areas for improvement, and the vital few areas to focus leadership and drive organizational change. Three distinct types of self-assessment will be examined: (1) the written narrative, (2) the Likert scale survey, and (3) the behaviorally anchored survey.

Full-Length Written Narrative

The Baldrige application development process is the most time-consuming organizational self-assessment process. To apply for the Baldrige Award, applicants must prepare a 50-page written narrative to address the requirements of the Performance Excellence Criteria. In the written self-assessment, the applicant is expected to describe the processes and programs it has in place to drive Performance Excellence. The Baldrige application process serves as the vehicle for self-assessment in most state-level quality awards. The process has not changed since the national quality award program was created in 1987 (except for reducing the maximum page limit from 85 to 50 pages).

Over the years, three methods have been used to prepare the full-length, comprehensive written narrative self-assessment:

1. The most widely used technique involves gathering a team of people to prepare the application. The team members are usually assigned one of the seven categories and asked to develop a narrative to address the criteria requirements of that category. The category writing teams are frequently subdivided to prepare responses Item by Item. After the initial draft is complete, an oversight team consolidates the narrative and tries to ensure processes are linked and integrated throughout. Finally, top leaders review and scrub the written narrative to put the best spin on the systems, processes, and results reported.

2. Another technique is similar to that previously described. However, instead of subdividing the writing team according to the Baldrige Categories, the team remains together to write the entire application. In this way, the application may be more coherent and the linkages between educational program design and processes are easier to understand. This approach also helps to ensure the consistency and integrity of the review processes. However, with fewer people involved, the natural "blind spots" of the team may prevent a full and accurate analysis of the management system. Finally, as with the first method described, top leaders review and scrub the written narrative.

3. The final method of preparing the written narrative is the least common and involves one person writing for several days to produce the application. Considering the immense amount of knowledge and work involved, it is easy to understand why this method is used so rarely.

With all three methods, external experts are usually involved. Baldrige Award recipients usually reported that they hired consultants to help them finalize their application by sharpening its focus and clarifying linkages.

Pros

- Baldrige-winning organizations report that the discipline of producing a full-length written self-assessment (Baldrige application) helped them learn about their organization and identify areas for improvement before the site visit team arrived. The written narrative self-assessment process clearly helped focus leaders on their organization's strengths and areas for improvement—provided that a complete and honest assessment was made.

- The written narrative self-assessment also provides rich information to help examiners conduct a site visit (the purpose of which is to verify and clarify the information contained in the written self-assessment).

Cons

- Written narrative self-assessments are extremely time and labor intensive. Organizations that use this approach for Baldrige or state applications or for internal organizational review report that it requires between approximately 2000 and 4000 person-hours of effort—sometimes much more. People working on the self-assessment are diverted from other tasks during this period.

- Because the application is closely scrutinized and carefully scrubbed, and because of page limits, it may not fully and accurately describe the actual management processes and systems of the organization. Decisions based on misleading or incomplete information may take the organization down the wrong path.

- Although the written self-assessment provides information to help guide a site visit, examiners cannot determine the depth of deployment because only a few points of view are represented in the narrative.

- Finally, and perhaps most importantly, the discipline and knowledge required to write a meaningful narrative self-assessment is usually far greater than that possessed within the majority of organizations. Many Baldrige winners hire expert consultants to help them prepare and refine their written narrative.

Short Written Narrative

Two of the most significant obstacles to writing a useful full-length written narrative self-assessment are poor knowledge of the Performance Excellence Criteria and the time required to produce a meaningful assessment. If people do not understand the criteria, it takes significantly longer to prepare a written self-assessment. In fact, the amount of time required to write an application/assessment is inversely related to the knowledge of the criteria possessed by the writers. The difficulty associated with writing a full-length narrative has prevented many organizations from participating in state, local, or organization award programs.

To encourage more organizations to begin the performance improvement journey, many state award programs developed progressively higher levels of recognition, ranging from "commitment" at the low-end, through "demonstrated progress," to "achieving excellence" at the top of the range. However, even with progressive levels of recognition, the obstacle of preparing a 50-page written narrative prevented many from engaging in the process. To help resolve this problem, several state programs permit applicants who seek recognition at the lower levels to submit a 7- to 20-page "short" written narrative self-assessment. (Most states still require applicants for the top-level award to complete a full-length written self-assessment.) The short form ranges from requiring a one-page description per category to one-page per Item (hence the 7- to 20-page range in length).

Pros

- It clearly takes less time to prepare the short form.
- Because of the reduced effort required to complete the self-assessment, states find more organizations are beginning the process of assessing and improving their performance.

Cons

- The short form provides significantly less information to help examiners prepare for the site visit. Although it does take less time to prepare than the full-length version, the short form still requires several hundred hours of team preparation.
- The short form is usually closely scrutinized and carefully scrubbed just as its full-length cousin. This reduces accuracy and value to both the organization and examiners.
- The knowledge required to write even a short narrative prevents organizations in the beginning stages from preparing an accurate and meaningful assessment.
- Finally, there is not enough information presented in the short form to understand the extent of deployment of the systems and processes covered by the criteria.

The Likert Scale Survey

Just about everyone is familiar with a Likert scale survey. These surveys typically ask respondents to rate, on a scale of 1 to 5, the extent to which they strongly disagree or strongly agree with a comment.

The following is an example of a simple Likert scale survey Item:

Senior leaders effectively communicate values and a focus on student learning.

1	2	3	4	5
Strongly Disagree				**Strongly Agree**

A minor variation on the simple Likert scale survey Item has been developed in an attempt to improve consistency among respondents. Brief descriptors have been added at each level as shown in the following descriptive Likert scale survey Item:

Senior leaders effectively communicate values and a focus on student learning.

1	2	3	4	5
None	**Few**	**Some**	**Many**	**Most**

Pros

- The Likert scale survey is quick and easy to administer. People from all functions and levels within the organization can provide input.

Cons

- Both the simple and the descriptive Likert scale survey Items are subject to wide ranges of interpretation. One person's rating of 2 and another person's rating of 4 may actually describe the same systems or behaviors. This problem of scoring reliability raises questions about the accuracy and usefulness of both the simple and the descriptive survey techniques for conducting organizational self-assessments. After all, a quick and easy survey that produces inaccurate data still has low value. That is the main reason why states have not adopted the Likert scale survey as a tool for conducting the self-assessments, even for organizations in the beginning stages of the quality journey.

The Behaviorally Anchored Survey

A behaviorally anchored survey contains elements of a written narrative and a survey approach to conducting a self-assessment. The method is simple. Instead of brief descriptors, such as "strongly agree/strongly disagree" or "none-few-some-many-most," a more complete behavioral description is presented for each level of the survey scale. Respondents simply identify the behavioral description that most closely fits the activities in the organization. A sample is shown below:

Making Improvements Based on Performance Reviews [1.1b(2 and 3)]

1F How do leaders use the results of performance reviews?

1 **Not Evident** ☑	Leaders do not use performance reviews to spot areas that need improvement.
2 **Beginning** ☐	A few leaders use performance reviews to spot areas that need improvement.
3 **Basically Effective** ☐	Some leaders use performance reviews to spot areas that need improvement.
4 **Mature** ☐	Many leaders use performance reviews to spot areas that need improvement. They sometimes check the accuracy of their reviews.
5 **Advanced** ☐	Most leaders use performance reviews to spot areas that need improvement. They sometimes share findings with feeder schools, key partners, and students and stakeholders to help them improve. They regularly check the accuracy of their reviews. They constantly make improvements.
6 **Role Model** ☐	Nearly all leaders use performance reviews to spot areas that need improvement. They regularly share findings with feeder schools, key partners, and students and stakeholders to help them improve. They regularly check the accuracy of their reviews. They constantly make improvements.
Not Applicable ☐	I do not have enough information to answer this question.

Describe how your leaders use performance review findings to improve organizational performance. Suggest ways they can improve.

Improving Leadership and Management Effectiveness [1.1b(4)]

1G How well do leaders and managers use performance data and faculty and staff feedback to improve their own effectiveness?

1 **Not Evident** ☐	Leaders only use test performance results, not faculty and staff feedback, to improve their own effectiveness.
2 **Beginning** ☑	Leaders mostly use test performance results, and very little faculty and staff feedback, to improve their own effectiveness. Sometimes they use this information to set personal improvement goals. They have made few, if any, actual improvements in their effectiveness.
3 **Basically Effective** ☐	Some leaders use some key performance results, as well as faculty and staff feedback, to evaluate their own effectiveness. Some use this information to set personal improvement goals. Some actually make improvements in their own effectiveness.
4 **Mature** ☐	Many leaders use many key performance results, as well as faculty and staff feedback, to evaluate their own effectiveness. Many use this information to set personal improvement goals. Sometimes they make improvements in their own effectiveness.
5 **Advanced** ☐	Most leaders use most key performance results, as well as faculty and staff feedback, to evaluate their own effectiveness. Most use this information to set personal improvement goals. Usually, they make improvements in their own effectiveness.
6 **Role Model** ☐	Nearly all leaders use all key performance results, as well as faculty and staff feedback, to evaluate their own effectiveness. They nearly all use this information to set personal improvement goals. They constantly make improvements in their own effectiveness.
Not Applicable ☐	I do not have enough information to answer this question.

Describe ways that your leaders and managers use faculty and staff feedback or performance results to improve their own effectiveness. Suggest ways they can improve.

Since the behavioral descriptions in the survey combine the requirements of the criteria with the standards from the scoring guidelines, it is possible to produce accurate Baldrige-based scores for Items and categories for the entire organization and for any subgroup or division.

Figure 22 provides sample scores for the entire organization and for two job classifications. It also shows the percent scores, on a 0 to 100 scale, for each Item. This helps users determine at a glance the relative strengths and weaknesses.

Sample Organization
Overall Percent Scores by Item

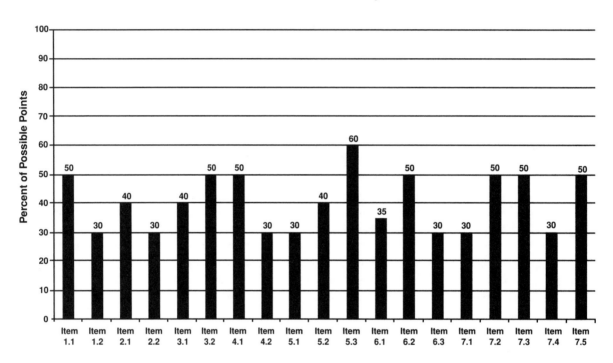

Figure 22

Figure 23 shows the ratings by subgroup, in this case, position of senior leaders and supervisors. In Figure 22, Item 1.1, Organizational Leadership, reflected a rating of 50 percent. However, according to the breakout in Figure 23, administrators believe the processes are much stronger (over 60 percent) than faculty and staff (less than 35 percent). This typically indicates incomplete systems development or poor deployment of existing systems and processes required by the Item.

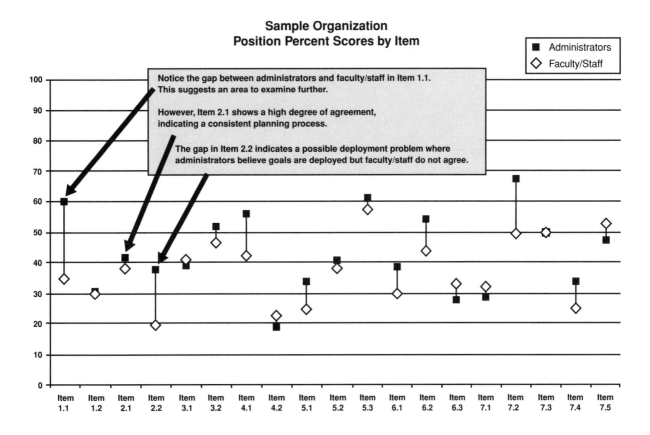

Figure 23

The Pareto diagram in Figure 24 presents data reflecting the areas respondents believed were most in need of improvement. Continuing with the leadership example, it is clear that respondents believe that leaders need to do a better job of setting clear high-performance expectations (Theme D), communicating vision and performance expectations (Theme E), and assessing and improving leadership performance and accountability (Theme G). This helps examiners focus on which areas in leadership may be the most important opportunities for improvement.

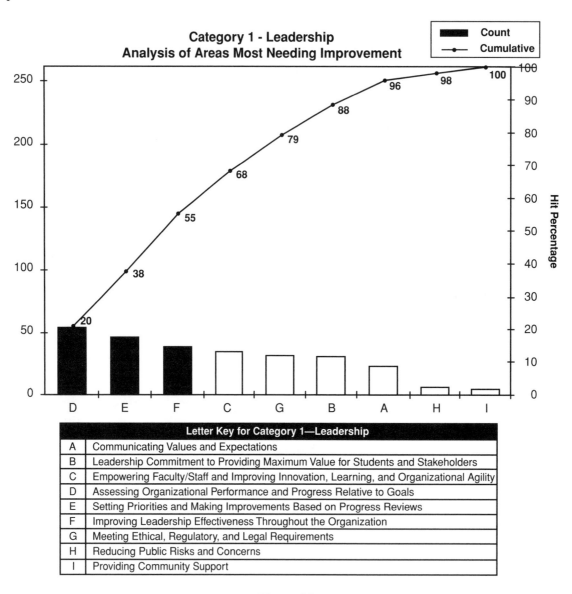

Figure 24

Priority Improvement Counts and Percentages — By Position for Leadership Category

1. Leadership

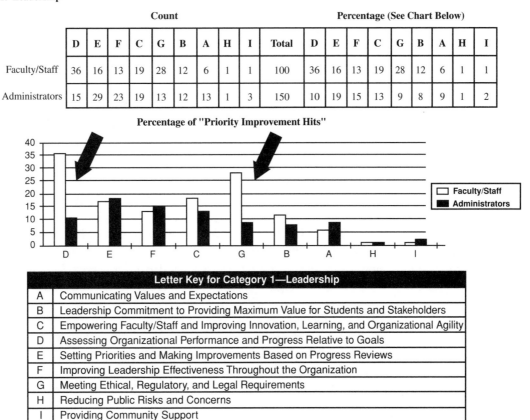

	Count										Percentage (See Chart Below)								
	D	E	F	C	G	B	A	H	I	Total	D	E	F	C	G	B	A	H	I
Faculty/Staff	36	16	13	19	28	12	6	1	1	100	36	16	13	19	28	12	6	1	1
Administrators	15	29	23	19	13	12	13	1	3	150	10	19	15	13	9	8	9	1	2

Percentage of "Priority Improvement Hits"

	Letter Key for Category 1—Leadership
A	Communicating Values and Expectations
B	Leadership Commitment to Providing Maximum Value for Students and Stakeholders
C	Empowering Faculty/Staff and Improving Innovation, Learning, and Organizational Agility
D	Assessing Organizational Performance and Progress Relative to Goals
E	Setting Priorities and Making Improvements Based on Progress Reviews
F	Improving Leadership Effectiveness Throughout the Organization
G	Meeting Ethical, Regulatory, and Legal Requirements
H	Reducing Public Risks and Concerns
I	Providing Community Support

Figure 25

Figure 25 shows by chart information that allows examiners to determine what type of employee (in this case administrator or faculty/staff) identified the various improvement priorities. Look at Themes D and G, and you will see that faculty/staff identified the need to improve these areas by a 3-to-1 margin. This tends to indicate a deployment gap and suggests that administrators are not perceived to be as effective as they believe.

Finally, a complete report of the comments and explanations of the respondents can be prepared and used by examiners and organization leaders for improvement planning.

Pros

- Descriptive behavioral anchors increase the consistency of rating. That is, one respondent's rating of 2 is likely to be the same as another respondent's rating of 2.

- Although completing a behaviorally anchored survey requires more reading than a Likert scale survey, the amount of time and cost required to complete it is still less than 20 percent of the time and cost required to prepare even a short written narrative.

- Because it is easy and simple to use, the behaviorally anchored survey does not impose a barrier to participation as does the written narrative. States and organizations that use surveys with properly written behavioral anchors find the accuracy of the assessment to be as good and in many cases better than that achieved by the narrative self-assessment, and significantly better than Likert scale assessments. By obtaining input from a cross-section of functions and levels throughout the organization, a performance profile can be developed which not only identifies strengths and areas for improvement, but deployment gaps as well—something the written narrative assessments rarely provide.

- For organizations doing teaching or researching throughout the world, the behaviorally anchored survey—translated into the native language of respondents—permits far greater input than the written narrative.

- Modern techniques involving surveying through Internet access created an easy way to survey a large, global organization.

- Accurate survey data, based on behavioral anchors, can be used to compare or benchmark organizations within and among industries, and can also support longitudinal performance studies.

- Finally, examiners report that the effort required to analyze survey data and plan a site visit is about 50 percent less than the amount of effort required to analyze and prepare for a site visit based on a written narrative. Moreover, they report better information regarding deployment.

Cons

- Organizations with highly developed performance management systems that seek to apply for top state or national recognition may prefer to practice developing the full-length narrative self-assessment because it is usually required.

- Examiners who are comfortable with the Baldrige application review process, which requires 25 or more hours to conduct an individual review of a full-length narrative self-assessment, initially find it disconcerting to develop comments and plan a site visit based on data gathered from a survey. Different training for examiners is required to develop skills at using survey data to prepare feedback and plan site visits.

NOTE: The preceding report of a behaviorally anchored self-assessment survey is administered by the National Council for Performance Excellence, Winooski, Vermont. Readers may contact them by calling Wendy Steager at (802) 655-1922 or by writing to NCPE, One Main Street, Winooski, VT 05404. The Vermont Council for Quality, Minnesota Council for Quality, and Florida Sterling Award and their boards of examiners use this survey technique to assess schools, government agencies, and businesses. The behaviorally anchored survey has completely replaced the written narrative self-assessment as the application for the Vermont Quality Award, as well as the Aruba National Quality Award. Examiners successfully use survey data to plan and conduct site visits in numerous organizations as well. At the same time, organization leaders use survey data for improvement planning. The Florida Sterling Award and the Minnesota Quality Award use the behaviorally anchored survey approach for organizations in various stages of developing Performance Excellence systems. In addition, many private sector organizations are using this type of assessment for internal business evaluations.

In Conclusion

- The full-length written narrative self-assessment is costly. It provides useful information both to examiners and the organizations completing it. The process of completing the written self-assessment can help more advanced organizations to focus and work together as a team.

- The usefulness of the short form written self-assessment is marginal, especially for beginning organizations; little useful information is provided to examiners and administrators/faculty and staff of the organization. However, because it takes less time to complete, one of the barriers to participation is lowered.

- Concerns over the accuracy and interrater reliability of the simple and descriptive Likert scales make their use in conducting effective organizational assessments of management systems questionable.

- The behaviorally anchored survey combines the benefits of survey speed with the accuracy and completeness of a well-developed written narrative self-assessment. In addition, the behaviorally anchored survey can identify gaps in deployment unlike the written narrative self-assessment and is less costly and faster to administer than the written narrative.

A complete copy of many business, education, and health care surveys can be obtained from the National Council for Performance Excellence, One Main Street, Winooski, VT 05404, (802) 655-1922. Following are two sample surveys.

Baldrige In Depth For Education
2001 Organizational Self-Assessment Sample

Customized Demographic Profile

Each participating organization completes a customized demographic profile (a generic sample follows). In this way, survey data can be analyzed by these variables to help pinpoint specific areas needing improvement. This allows the extent of use (deployment) of management systems to be examined.

Please circle one selection from EACH column below to indicate your position within the organization.

Position	Location	Function	Org.	Years of Service
– Board Member	– North	– Instruction	– 1	– 0 < 1
– Executive Leadership	– South	– Administration	– 2	– 1 < 3
	– East	– Faculty and Staff	– 3	– 3 < 5
– Department Manager or Supervisor	– West	– Resources	– 4	– 5 < 10
	– Central Administration	– Finance/Legal	– 5	– 10+
– Faculty/ Staff		– Support Staff	– Other	
– Student		– Staff Training		
		– Instructional Design and Supervision		
		– Information Technology		
		– Other		

The Performance Improvement Assessment is a confidential assessment. Do not write your own name or other personally identifiable information on this questionnaire. **We will compile performance information feedback results. This assessment will be used to help evaluate the progress of your organization toward developing high-performance systems.**

DO NOT PROCEED UNTIL YOU HAVE CIRCLED THE APPROPRIATE SELECTIONS ABOVE.

Baldrige In-Depth *Instructions*

This survey consists of 63 themes or questions that relate to the 2001 Baldrige Education Performance Excellence Criteria. It is organized into seven "sections," one for each of the seven Performance Excellence Criteria Categories.

- To the best of your knowledge, select a rating (1 to 6) that describes the level of development in your organization. **Note that all of the elements of a statement must be true before you can select that level. If one or more is not true, you must go to a lower level.** After you have selected the rating level, please enter the value in the empty box to the right of the row of statements.

➡ *Accuracy Tip: The rating scale involves your assessment about the extent of use of the required management processes. The following definitions should help you rate this consistently:*

- ✔ Few . . . . less than 15%
- ✔ Some . . . . 15% to less than 30%
- ✔ Many . . . . 30% to less than 50%
- ✔ Most . . . . 50% to less than 80%
- ✔ Nearly All . . . . 80% to less than 99%
- ✔ All 100%

✦ *Time-saving Tip: Start reading at level 2. If all parts of the statement are true, go to level 3, if not, drop back to read level 1. After a few answers, save even more time by starting at the number you select most often. Don't waste time by reading from row 1 each time (unless most of your answers are 1).*

- **If you do not know an answer, enter NA (Not Applicable/Does Not Apply) or ? (Don't Know).** If you are unsure of the meaning of a word or phrase, please check the glossary at the end of this booklet.

- After all statements in the first category (Leadership) have been rated, go to the last page in the Leadership category. Follow the directions and **identify two areas you believe most need improvement** in your organization now. Then, go back to the space below each row of statements you identified as vital to improve. **Describe briefly the activities your organization conducts that relate to the topic. Also, please suggest steps that your organization or its leaders could take to improve the processes.** Your thoughtful comments are as helpful as the rating itself. If you want to comment on more themes, please do so.

- Continue in the same way to complete all seven categories.

Summary of Category 1: Leadership

This sample assessment looks at one question in the Leadership category. The full-length assessment of Leadership contains nine questions covering the following themes:

The first part (six questions 1A through 1F) looks at how senior leaders set directions and seek future opportunities to help guarantee the long-term success of the organization. Senior leaders should express clear values and set high-performance expectations that address the needs of all students and stakeholders.

- You are asked how senior leaders set directions, communicate and deploy values and performance expectations, and take into account the expectations of students and stakeholders. This includes how leaders create an environment that promotes ethical values, equity, empowerment, innovation, safety, organizational agility, and organizational and faculty/staff learning. You also are asked how senior leaders review organizational performance, what key performance measures they regularly review, and how review findings are used to drive improvement and change, including your leaders' effectiveness.

The second part (three questions 1G through 1I) looks at how well the organization meets its responsibilities to the public and how the organization practices good citizenship.

- You are asked how the organization addresses current and future impacts on society in a proactive manner and how it ensures ethical practices in all student and stakeholder interactions. The impacts and practices are expected to cover all relevant and important areas — services and operations.

- You also are asked how the organization, senior leaders, and faculty/staff identify, support, and strengthen key communities as part of good citizenship practices.

Leadership Commitment to Providing Maximum Value for Students and Stakeholders

1B   *How serious are top leaders about providing maximum value to students and stakeholders? Do they make it clear that producing value for students and stakeholders is critical for success?*

Not Evident

1   Leaders focus on short-term issues, *not* on value for students and stakeholders.

Beginning

2   A *few* leaders are just beginning to focus on value for students and stakeholders.

Basically Effective

3   *Some* leaders focus occasionally on value for students and stakeholders through their written and verbal communication.

Mature

4   *Many* leaders focus the organization on providing maximum value to students and stakeholders. They *sometimes* check on the effectiveness of activities that focus on student and stakeholder value.

Advanced

5   *Most* leaders and managers focus on providing maximum value to students and stakeholders. They *regularly* check on the effectiveness of activities that focus on student and stakeholder value. They *sometimes* make improvements.

Role Model

6   *Nearly all* leaders and managers focus on providing maximum value to students and stakeholders. They *frequently talk* with students and stakeholders and *regularly* check on the effectiveness of activities that focus on value. They make *ongoing* improvements.

NA   **Not Applicable**
        I do not have enough information to answer this question.

Comments: Describe how the leaders commit to providing value to students and stakeholders. How widely is this done? Describe improvements to this process, if any.

Summary of Category 2: Strategic Planning

This sample assessment looks at one question in the Strategic Planning Category. The full-length assessment of Strategic Planning contains seven questions covering the following themes:

The first part (three questions 2A through 2C) looks at how the organization develops its strategic plans. The category stresses that key student and stakeholder needs and operational performance excellence are key strategic issues that need to be integral parts of the organization's overall planning. Specifically:

- Student/stakeholder-driven performance is a strategic view. The focus is on the drivers of student/ stakeholder satisfaction, and enhancing performance relative to comparable schools— key factors in competitiveness, performance, and educational success; and

- Operational performance improvement contributes to short- and longer-term productivity, growth, and value. Building operational capability—including speed, responsiveness, and flexibility—represents an investment in strengthening competitive fitness.

The second part (four questions 2D through 2G) looks at the way educational processes support the organization's strategic directions, to help make sure that priorities are carried out.

- The organization must translate its strategic objectives into action plans to accomplish the objectives. The organization must also be able to assess the progress of action plans. The aim is to ensure that strategies are understood and followed by everyone in the organization to help achieve goals.

Developing Action Plans Based on Strategic Objectives

2D   *How well do the organization's action plans support its strategic objectives? Do the action plans help all parts of the organization pull together (align) to carry out its strategic objectives? Are appropriate resources allocated to carry out the actions?*

Not Evident

1   The organization *does not* develop specific action plans to support strategic objectives.

Beginning

2   The organization has developed action plans to support a *few* strategic objectives. Resources *are not* allocated to achieve desired actions.

Basically Effective

3   The organization has developed action plans to support *some* strategic objectives. Resources are *generally* allocated to achieve desired actions.

Mature

4   The organization has developed action plans to support *many* strategic objectives in regards to its services, operations, markets, faculty/staff requirements, and resource allocation. Resources are allocated to achieve desired actions. The action plans and resources are *sometimes* checked to see how well they support objectives.

Advanced

5   The organization has developed action plans to support *most* strategic objectives in regards to its services, students and stakeholders/markets, faculty/staff requirements, and resource allocation. Resources are specifically allocated to achieve desired actions. The action plans and resources are *regularly* checked to see how well they support objectives and improvements are *sometimes* made.

Role Model

6   The organization has developed action plans to support *all* strategic objectives in regards to its services, students and stakeholders/markets, faculty/staff requirements, and resource allocation. Resources are specifically allocated to achieve desired actions. The action plans and resources are *regularly* checked to see how well they support objectives. They are *consistently* improved to strengthen key educational services.

NA   **Not Applicable**
      I do not have enough information to answer this question.

Comments: Describe how action plans are created and resources are allocated to carry out strategic objectives. How widely is this done? Describe improvements to this process, if any.

Summary of Category 3: Student, Stakeholder, and Market Focus

This sample assessment looks at one question in the Student, Stakeholder, and Market Focus category. The full-length assessment of Student, Stakeholder, and Market Focus contains 11 questions covering the following themes:

The first part (four questions 3A through 3D) looks at how the organization tries to understand what the student, stakeholders, and the marketplace wants. The organization must learn about student, stakeholders, and markets to help make sure it understands new requirements, offers the right services, and keeps pace with changing student and stakeholder demands and increasing competition.

- You are asked how the organization determines key student and stakeholder groups and how it segments the markets.
- You are asked how the organization determines the most important service features.
- Also, you are asked how the organization improves the way it listens and learns from students and stakeholders so that it keeps current with changing educational service needs.

The second part (seven questions 3E through 3K) looks at how well the organization builds good relationships with students and stakeholders to earn loyalty and positive referrals. You are also asked how the organization gets data on student and stakeholder satisfaction and dissatisfaction for its current and competitors' students and stakeholders.

- You are asked how the organization makes it easy for existing potential students and stakeholders to get information or assistance and/or to comment and complain.
- You are asked how the organization gathers, analyzes, and learns from complaint information to increase student and stakeholder satisfaction and loyalty.
- You are asked how the organization builds relationships with students and stakeholders, since success depends on maintaining close relationships.
- You are asked how the organization determines the satisfaction and dissatisfaction for different student, stakeholder, and market groups to increase positive referrals.
- Finally, you are asked how the organization follows up with students and stakeholders, and how it determines satisfaction relative to competitors so that it may improve future performance.

Understanding What Students and Stakeholders Value Most in Educational Services

3D   *How well does the organization determine what educational service features students and stakeholders value the most? How do you know what features drive their enrollment decisions?*

Not Evident

1   The organization *does not* know the preferences of its students or stakeholders.

Beginning

2   The organization *does not* collect data on why students or stakeholders choose educational programs.

Basically Effective

3   The organization collects and analyzes data to determine why *some* students/stakeholders make educational decisions and what service features they value.

Mature

4   The organization collects and analyzes data to determine why *many* students/stakeholders make educational decisions and what service features they value. It *sometimes* checks how well the process works.

Advanced

5   The organization collects and analyzes data to determine why *most* students and stakeholders make educational decisions and what service features these students and stakeholders value for *most* services. It *often* checks how well the process works and *sometimes* makes improvements.

Role Model

6 The organization collects and analyzes data to determine why *nearly all* students and stakeholders make educational decisions and what service features these students and stakeholders value for all *services*. It *regularly* checks how well the process works and makes *ongoing* improvements.

NA **Not Applicable**

I do not have enough information to answer this question.

Comments: Describe how you determine what drives student/stakeholder decisions and what educational service features they value the most throughout their association with the institution. How widely is this done? Describe improvements to this process, if any.

Summary of Category 4: Information and Analysis

This sample assessment looks at one question in the Information and Analysis Category. Information and Analysis is the "brain center" of an effective management system. Appropriate information and analysis are used to improve decision making at all levels to achieve high levels of student and operational performance. Effective measures, properly deployed, also help align the organization's operations to achieve its strategic goals.

The full-length assessment of Information and Analysis contains nine questions covering the following themes:

The first part (six questions 4A through 4F) looks at the selection, management, use, and analysis of data and information to support effective decision making at all levels. Data and information guide decision making to help the organization improve student and operational performance at all levels and parts of the organization.

- The organization must build an effective performance measurement system. It must select and integrate the right measures for tracking daily operations and use those measures for monitoring overall organizational performance. The organization must also make sure that data and information are accurate and reliable.

- Competitive comparisons and benchmarking (best practices) information should be used to help drive performance improvement.

- The organization should evaluate and improve the performance measurement system to keep it current with changing educational service needs.

- Data and information concerning processes and results (outcomes) from all parts of the organization must be analyzed to support the senior leaders' assessment of overall organizational health, organizational planning, and daily operations.

- Analyses must be communicated to support decision making at all levels of the organization.

- Finally, these analyses must be closely aligned with key student and operational performance results and strategies to ensure the analysis is relevant to support effective decision making.

The second part (three questions 4G through 4I) looks at how the organization ensures the quality and availability of data and information to support effective decision making for students and stakeholders, faculty and staff, and suppliers and partners.

- The organization must ensure data and information are available, accessible, reliable, accurate, timely, secure, and confidential, as appropriate.

- For data that are captured, stored, analyzed, and/or accessed through electronic means, the organization must ensure hardware and software reliability and user friendliness.

All of these systems must be evaluated and enhanced to ensure they remain current with changing educational service needs and directions.

Selecting Measures to Track Daily Operations, Educational Climate, and Overall Organizational Performance

4B   *How well does the organization select appropriate measures throughout the organization to effectively track daily operations, educational climate, and overall performance?*

Not Evident

1   The organization *does not* collect data to track how well it performs.

Beginning

2   The organization collects data to track overall student learning but very *few* other areas of performance.

Basically Effective

3   The organization collects data to understand *some* areas of organizational performance, such as overall student learning, budgetary, and operational.

Mature

4   The organization collects data to understand *many* areas of organizational performance, such as student learning, market, budgetary, student and stakeholder satisfaction, operational, and faculty/staff resources. The organization *sometimes* checks usefulness of data.

Advanced

5   The organization collects data to understand <u>most</u> areas of organizational performance, such as financial, market, student and stakeholder satisfaction, operational, and faculty and staff resources. The organization *regularly* checks how well the data enable tracking and promote alignment at the different levels and *sometimes* makes improvements.

Role Model

6   The organization collects data to understand *nearly all* areas of organizational performance, including financial, market, student and stakeholder satisfaction, operational, and faculty and staff resources. The organization *regularly* checks how well the data enable tracking and promote alignment throughout the organization and makes *ongoing* improvements.

NA   **Not Applicable**

I do not have enough information to answer this question.

Comments: Describe how you determine what data need to be collected to track performance and ensure effective decision making. How widely is this done? Describe improvements to this process, if any.

Summary of Category 5: Faculty and Staff Focus

This sample assessment looks at one question in the Faculty and Staff Focus Category. The full-length assessment of Faculty and Staff Focus contains 11 questions covering the following themes:

The first part (six questions 5A through 5F) looks at how well the organization's systems for work and job design, compensation, motivation, recognition, and hiring help all faculty and staff reach peak performance.

- You are asked how the organization designs work and jobs to empower faculty/staff to exercise initiative, innovation, and decision making, resulting in high performance.

- You are asked how the organization compensates, recognizes, and rewards faculty/staff to support its high performance objectives (strategic objectives) as well as ensuring a student/stakeholder and learning focus.

- Finally, you are asked how the organization recruits and hires faculty/staff who will meet its expectations and needs. The right workforce is an enabler of high performance.

The second part (two questions 5G through 5H) looks at how well education and training meets the needs of faculty/staff.

- You are asked how education and training are designed, delivered, reinforced on the job, and evaluated.
- You are also asked about how well the organization provides training in performance excellence, which includes succession planning and leadership development, at all levels.

The third part (three questions 5I through 5K) looks at the organization's work environment, its support climate, and how the organization determines faculty/staff satisfaction, with the aim of fostering faculty/staff well-being, satisfaction, and motivation.

- You are asked how the organization's work environment for all faculty/staff is safe and healthful.
- You are asked how the organization enhances well-being, satisfaction, and motivation for all faculty/staff groups.
- Finally, you are asked how the organization assesses faculty/staff well-being, satisfaction, and motivation, and how it relates assessment findings to key educational results to set improvement priorities.

Providing Feedback, Compensation, and Recognition to Support High-Performance Goals and a Student/Stakeholder Focus

5D   *How well do educational leaders at all levels provide feedback to faculty/staff and make sure pay, reward, and recognition support high performance and student/stakeholder focus? [Note that compensation and recognition might include promotions and bonuses based on performance, skills acquired, and other factors contributing to high-performance goals. Recognition may be provided to individuals and/or groups and includes monetary, nonmonetary, formal, and informal techniques.]*

Not Evident

1   The organization *does not* provide effective feedback to faculty/staff.

Beginning

2   The organization provides effective feedback about performance to a *few* faculty/staff.

Basically Effective

3   The organization provides effective feedback about performance to *some* faculty/staff. It ties pay and recognition to *some* high performance.

Mature

4   The organization provides effective feedback about performance to *many* faculty/staff. It ties pay and recognition to *many* high-performance goals. The organization *sometimes* checks these processes.

Advanced

5   The organization provides effective feedback about performance to *most* faculty/staff. It ties pay and recognition to most high-performance, student and stakeholder focus, and educational service goals and strategies. The organization *regularly* checks the effectiveness of its feedback and compensation processes and improvements are *sometimes* made.

Role Model

6   The organization provides effective feedback about performance to *nearly all* faculty/staff. It ties pay and recognition to *nearly all* high-performance, student and stakeholder focus, and educational service goals and strategies. The organization *regularly* checks its feedback and compensation processes and makes *ongoing* improvements.

NA   Not Applicable

I do not have enough information to answer this question.

Comments: Describe how educational leaders make sure pay, reward, and recognition are aligned to support performance goals and objectives. How widely is this done? Describe improvements to this process, if any.

Summary of Category 6: Process Management

This sample assessment looks at one question in the Process Management Category. The full-length assessment of Process Management contains 11 questions covering the following themes:

Process Management is the focal point for all key processes. The first part (six questions 6A through 6F) looks at the organization's educational programs and offerings design and delivery processes.

- You are asked how curriculum and instructional design and delivery processes ensure educational programs and offerings address student needs, high standards, and active learning.
- Design/delivery processes must work consistently. Performance measures should be designed to get an early alert of potential problems so prompt action can be taken to correct the problem.
- You are asked how design processes address sequencing, linkages among offerings, transfer of learning from the past and across the organization, new technology, cycle time, and other efficiency/effectiveness factors.
- You are asked how formative and summative assessments are used to measure and improve program design and delivery.
- You are asked how you ensure that faculty and staff are prepared to implement educational programs and offerings.
- Finally, you are asked how the organization improves its design/delivery processes to achieve better processes and educational services.

The middle part (two questions 6G through 6H) examines the management of key student services, such as counseling, advising, and tutoring, registration, financial aid, and food services.

- You are asked how key student service processes are determined using input from students and stakeholders, faculty/staff, and suppliers, as appropriate.
- You must effectively control and improve these student service processes using in-process measures and student, stakeholder, and supplier feedback, as appropriate.
- Finally, you are asked how the organization improves its student service processes to achieve better performance.

The last part (three questions 6I through 6K) examines the organization's key support processes, with the aim of improving overall operational performance.

- You are asked how key support processes are designed to meet all the requirements of internal and external students and stakeholders.
- The day-to-day operation of key support processes should meet the key requirements. In-process measures and internal student and stakeholder feedback should be used to get an early alert of problems.
- Finally, you are asked how the organization improves its key support processes to achieve better performance.

Designing Educational Programs and Offerings

6A   *How well does the organization design educational programs, offerings and related delivery systems that meet ongoing student needs? To what extent does the organization incorporate changing student, stakeholder, and market requirements into program designs and into related delivery (instructional) systems? How well do related delivery (instructional) systems address student needs, high standards, and active learning?*

Not Effective

1   The organization *does not* have a standard design process.

Beginning

2   The organization uses a standard design process for a *few* key programs. The design process *is not* responsive to changing students, stakeholders, and market requirements.

Basically Effective

3   The organization uses a standard design process for *some* key programs and offerings. The design process is a response to *a few* changing students, stakeholders, and market requirements.

Mature

4   The organization uses a standard design process for *many* programs and offerings and related delivery (instructional) processes. The design process is responsive to *many* changing students, stakeholders, and market requirements. The effectiveness of these processes is *sometimes* checked to make sure they meet *many* requirements.

Advanced

5   The organization uses a standard design process for *most* programs, offerings, and related delivery (instructional) processes. The design process is responsive to *most* changing students, stakeholders, and market requirements. The effectiveness of these processes is *regularly* checked to make sure they meet *most* requirements and improvements are *sometimes* made.

Role Model

6   The organization uses a standard process for designing *nearly all* key programs and offerings and related delivery (instructional) processes. The design process is rapidly responsive to *nearly all* changing students, stakeholders, and market requirements. The effectiveness of these processes is *regularly* checked to make sure they meet *nearly all* key requirements and *ongoing* improvements are made.

NA   Not Applicable

I do not have enough information to answer this question.

Comments: Describe how the organization designs programs and offerings and makes sure current and changing student and stakeholder requirements are included. Also describe how students and stakeholders are involved in the design process. Define the processes used to ensure that design and delivery systems work effectively to meet key performance requirements. How widely are these processes used? Describe improvements to this process, if any.

Summary of Category 7: Organizational Performance Results

This sample assessment looks at one theme in the Organizational Performance Results Category. The full-length assessment of Organizational Performance Results contains five questions covering the following themes:

The Organizational Effectiveness Results Category looks for the results produced by the management systems. Results range from lagging performance outcomes, such as student and stakeholder satisfaction, budgetary, financial, and market performance to predictive or leading outcomes, such as internal operating measures and faculty and staff resource results. Together, these lagging and leading results create a set of balanced indicators of organizational health, commonly called a "balanced scorecard."

- The first theme (question 7A) looks at key student learning results.
- The second theme (question 7B) looks at student and stakeholder satisfaction and dissatisfaction.
- The third theme (question 7C) looks at the strength of the organization's budgetary, financial, and market results.
- The fourth theme (question 7D) looks at how well the organization has been creating and maintaining a positive, productive, learning, and caring work environment for faculty and staff.
- The fifth theme (question 7E) looks at the organization's other key operational performance results, to determine the strength of its organizational effectiveness and compliance with applicable laws and regulations. It also looks at public responsibility and citizenship.

Student- and Stakeholder-Focused Results

7B   *What are the trends and results for student and stakeholder satisfaction and dissatisfaction? These include student and stakeholder loyalty indicators, measures of student- and stakeholder-perceived value, student and stakeholder retention, positive referral, and product and service performance. [Results data may come from surveys, awards, ratings, and internal measures, as well as data from students, stakeholders, and independent organizations such as The College Board, National Assessments, and so on.]*

Not Evident
1   No results or poor results.

Beginning
2   Key results are *not reported*. Good performance levels and improvement in a *few* areas.

Basically Effective
3   *Many* key results are reported and address *many* areas important to student and stakeholder satisfaction. Good performance levels or improvement in *some* areas. Beginning to develop trends and get comparison data.

Mature
4   *Most* key results are reported and address *most* areas important to student and stakeholder satisfaction. Good performance levels or improvement in *many* areas when compared to industry average.

Advanced
5   *Most* key results are reported and address *most* areas important to student and stakeholder satisfaction for *most* student, stakeholder, and market segments. No adverse trends or poor performance in *key* areas. Good to very good performance levels or improvement in *most* areas when compared to benchmarks or industry average.

Role Model
6   *Nearly all* key results are reported and address *nearly all* areas important to student and stakeholder satisfaction for *nearly all* student, stakeholder, and market segments. Good to excellent performance levels and sustained improvement in *nearly all* areas when compared to benchmarks. Leads the industry in *some* areas.

NA   Not Applicable
I do not have enough information to answer this question.

Comments: Give examples of your key student and stakeholder satisfaction, loyalty, student- and stakeholder-perceived value, student and stakeholder retention, positive referral, and product/service performance trends and show how you compare with competitors and/or providers of similar products and services.

2001 Safety and Security
Organizational Self-Assessment Sample

Safety and Security Survey Sample Introduction and Instructions

This survey consists of sample themes or questions that relate to the Safety and Security requirements of the 2001 Baldrige Criteria for Performance Excellence in Education. It is organized into the seven Baldrige categories. Results of the full survey can be used to identify what seems to be working and how your organization can improve its management system to improve safety and security. Comparisons can be made from one survey cycle to the next, between different groups taking the survey (for example, K–12 verses high school or faculty versus administrators). The overall score is purely an internal indicator that is based on the Baldrige Criteria, not on the Baldrige scoring guidelines.

This includes a sample comment and suggestion for improvement. Sample comments are from various levels and types of educational organizations.

To the best of your knowledge, select a rating (1–6) that describes the level of development in your organization. **Note that *all* of the elements of a statement must be true before you can select that level. If one or more is not true, you must go to a lower level.** After you have selected the rating level, circle the appropriate number.

If you do not know an answer, enter NA (Not Applicable) or (?). If you are unsure of the meaning of a word or phrase, please check the glossary at the end of this booklet.

After all statements in the first category (Leadership) have been rated, go to the last page in the Leadership chapter. Follow the directions, and **identify two areas you believe most need improvement** in your organization now. Then, **go back to the space below each row of statements** you identified as vital to improve. **Describe briefly the activities your organization conducts that relate to the topic. Also, please suggest steps that your organization or its leaders could take to improve the processes.** Your thoughtful comments are as helpful as the rating itself. If you want to comment on more themes, please do so.

Continue in the same way to complete all seven categories.

Category 1: Leadership

Leaders understand the values and expectations of students and stakeholders for a safe learning environment. They promote clear values, such as respect, fairness, equity, and tolerance. They create a learning environment where all feel safe and secure. They have a clear societal responsibility to consider all risks associated with school operations.

1A *Leaders promote ethical values through words and actions.*							
NA	**?**	**1**	**2**	**3**	**4**	**5**	**6**
It does not apply.	I don't know.	They don't do it.	**Beginning** A few do it, but they do not do it well.	**Basically Effective** Some do this well.	**Mature** Many do it well. They sometimes check their effectiveness.	**Advanced** Most do it well. They usually check their effectiveness and sometimes improve.	**Role Model** Nearly all do it well. They regularly check their effectiveness and constantly improve.

Comments: Give an example of how your leaders communicate goals and set performance expectations. Suggest ways they can improve. *[Baldrige ref. 1.1a(2)]*

Example Comments: Our superintendent and her top staff are fully involved in the community. They have made sure that the core values of our district—respect, caring, responsibility, and healthy lifestyles—are also the values of community organizations, such as the YMCA, Rotary, Civic Clubs, Chamber of Commerce, and our local Soup Kitchen.

Improvement Opportunity—Sometimes the top leaders know that staff has not been fair in such areas as grading, discipline, or application of policies. They need to back parents and students up in these instances, or students will think they are not following their own values.

Category 2: Strategic Planning

The strategic planning process considers faculty, staff, student, and stakeholder needs and expectations for a safe and secure learning environment. This includes potential threats, such as safety concerns, that affect school performance.

	2A *All parts of your organization support its safety improvement strategy with concrete action plans.*						
NA	**?**	**1**	**2**	**3**	**4**	**5**	**6**
It does not apply.	I don't know.	They don't do it.	**Beginning** A few do it, but they do not do it well.	**Basically Effective** Some do this well.	**Mature** Many do it well. They sometimes check their effectiveness.	**Advanced** Most do it well. They usually check their effectiveness and sometimes improve.	**Role Model** Nearly all do it well. They regularly check their effectiveness and constantly improve.

Comments: Describe action plans that support the school safety strategy. Suggest ways to improve. *[Baldrige ref. 2.2a]*

Example Comments: A cross-organizational committee was selected and convened (students, parents, top administrators, board members, faculty, and staff) to develop a strategy and action plan to prevent violence in the school district. Resources were allocated to carry out the plans.

Improvement Opportunity—Some safety improvement strategies have plans that have not worked. For example, although many steps over the past year have been taken to stop "graffiti" threats in bathrooms, they have not decreased their occurrence. The strategy needs to be revisited more frequently to respond to problems.

Category 3: Student, Stakeholder, and Market Focus

The school uses a variety of listening and learning methods to determine and anticipate student and stakeholder needs and concerns. It uses student input to determine the relevance of student and educational services and develops new ones based on this input. It builds and improves positive relationships with students and stakeholders using a variety of methods. It uses satisfaction and dissatisfaction data to target improvement strategies.

3A *All parts of your organization ask students in many different ways what is most important to them.*							
NA	**?**	**1**	**2**	**3**	**4**	**5**	**6**
It does not apply.	I don't know.	They don't do it.	**Beginning** A few do it, but they do not do it well.	**Basically Effective** Some do this well.	**Mature** Many do it well. They sometimes check their effectiveness.	**Advanced** Most do it well. They usually check their effectiveness and sometimes improve.	**Role Model— Best in Class** Nearly all do it well. They regularly check their effectiveness and constantly improve.

Comments: Give examples of how your organization listens to students about important expectations. Suggest ways they can improve. *[Baldrige ref. 3.1(1&2)]*

Example Comments: Last year, there was a lot of anxiety about graduation at our college because of increased school violence and threats. The college officials met with many students and listened to their fears and concerns. Then, based on the meetings, college officials developed and distributed written letters detailing extra security measures to prevent violence and allay fears of students, parents, and others. It was very thorough and addressed policies and actions so no weapons, drugs, alcohol, etc., were part of campus graduation activities.

Improvement Opportunity—Have regular and frequent open meetings where faculty, staff, and students could talk about safety concerns and how to act together to address the concerns. There is some concern that the college is overreacting in some areas and not doing anything about other serious issues related to safety.

Category 4: Information and Analysis

The school uses data and information to improve the school environment, including school safety. It determines needs of stakeholders. It gives data users (including students, staff, and faculty) access, confidentiality, and ongoing reliability. It provides data on safety and schoolwide performance.

4A *All parts of your organization effectively track overall progress on school safety.*							
NA	?	1	2	3	4	5	6
It does not apply.	I don't know.	They don't do it.	**Beginning** A few do it, but they do not do it well.	**Basically Effective** Some do this well.	**Mature** Many do it well. They sometimes check their effectiveness.	**Advanced** Most do it well. They usually check their effectiveness and sometimes improve.	**Role Model** Nearly all do it well. They regularly check their effectiveness and constantly improve.

Comments: Describe how your organization tracks progress on school safety. Suggest ways to improve. *[Baldrige ref. 4.1a(1)]*

Example Comments: We have a goal to decrease the incidence of fights in the school. Each month results are tracked on a bulletin board at the school's entrance. Results are used by the school safety committee for making recommendations to improve school safety.

Improvement Opportunity—This has been done for six months and it is working well, but could be improved by analyzing the data over the six-month period to produce trends if possible.

Category 5: Faculty and Staff Focus

The school's work systems promote cooperation and capability to respond to changing student needs. The school provides training, education, and support for faculty and staff. It assesses safety, health, and well-being through a variety of methods and indicators. It maintains a safe, healthful, and secure work environment.

5A *All parts of your organization support a cooperative work environment.*							
NA	**?**	**1**	**2**	**3**	**4**	**5**	**6**
It does not apply.	I don't know.	They don't do it.	**Beginning** A few do it, but they do not do it well.	**Basically Effective** Some do this well.	**Mature** Many do it well. They sometimes check their effectiveness.	**Advanced** Most do it well. They usually check their effectiveness and sometimes improve.	**Role Model— Best in Class** Nearly all do it well. They regularly check their effectiveness and constantly improve.

Comments: Give examples of cooperation in your work environment. Suggest ways to improve cooperation. *[Baldrige ref. 5.1a(1)]*

Example Comments: Our school just dedicated space for a faculty/staff lounge where we can eat lunch, work, and plan in teams. This has facilitated our level of teamwork and strengthened morale.

Improvement Opportunity—Different schedules prevent some faculty/staff from attending our meetings, and this has resulted in gaps in program planning.

Category 6: Process Management

The school's educational support systems address student well-being needs. The school provides programs to ensure faculty and staff are prepared to deal with special situations that may involve safety and security. The school's plants and facilities, information services, student services, and other support services must promote safety and security.

6A *All parts of your organization design all programs to focus on active learning.*							
NA	**?**	**1**	**2**	**3**	**4**	**5**	**6**
It does not apply.	I don't know.	They don't do it.	**Beginning** A few do it, but they do not do it well.	**Basically Effective** Some do this well.	**Mature** Many do it well. They sometimes check their effectiveness.	**Advanced** Most do it well. They usually check their effectiveness and sometimes improve.	**Role Model** Nearly all do it well. They regularly check their effectiveness and constantly improve.

Comments: Give an example of how your organization designs programs to focus on active learning. Suggest ways they can improve. *[Baldrige ref. 6.1a(2)]*

Example Comments: Our program in microelectronics has a clean room, and students learn in an environment similar to the one they will be working in. We also have a world-class co-op program requirement that adds meaning and value to student learning.

Improvement Opportunity—There are far too many lectures (and boring ones) that could be transformed into active learning programs. This is frustrating to students and decreases their commitment.

Category 7: Organizational Performance Results

The school tracks trends and results related to safety, security, and well-being of students, faculty, and staff. It uses data on satisfaction and dissatisfaction and well-being to improve the school climate. Specific improvements in school safety are reported and tracked.

7A *All parts of your organization have improved its student satisfaction.*							
NA	**?**	**1**	**2**	**3**	**4**	**5**	**6**
It does not apply.	I don't know.	They don't do it.	**Beginning** A few do it, but they do not do it well.	**Basically Effective** Some do this well.	**Mature** Many do it well. They sometimes check their effectiveness.	**Advanced** Most do it well. They usually check their effectiveness and sometimes improve.	**Role Model** Nearly all do it well. They regularly check their effectiveness and constantly improve.

Comments: Give an example of how your organization has improved student satisfaction. *[Baldrige ref. 7.2(2)]*

Example Comments: Our middle school house tracks student satisfaction with accessibility of faculty for tutoring and extra help. Satisfaction has improved over the last two years steadily.

Improvement Opportunity—Measure more classroom satisfaction, such as fairness and how interesting instructors are.

The Site Visit

Introduction

Many educators and educational organizations have asked about how to prepare for site visits. This section is intended to help answer those questions and prepare the educational organization for an on-site examination. It includes rules of the game for examiners and what they are taught to look for. As we all know, the best preparation for this type of examination is to see things through the eyes of the trained examiner.

Before an organization can be recommended to receive the Malcolm Baldrige National Quality Award, it must receive a visit from a team of education assessment experts from the National Board of Examiners. Approximately 25 to 30 percent of all organizations applying for the Baldrige Award in recent years have received these site visits.

The Baldrige Award site visit team usually includes two senior examiners—one of whom is designated as team leader—and four to seven other examiners. In addition, the team is accompanied by a representative of the National Quality Award office and a representative of the American Society for Quality (ASQ), which provides administrative services to the Baldrige Award office under contract.

The site visit team usually gathers at a hotel near the organization's central office on the Sunday morning immediately preceding the site visit. During the day, the team makes final preparations and plans for the visit.

Each team member is assigned lead responsibility for one or more categories of the award criteria. Each examiner is usually teamed with one other examiner during the site visit. These examiners usually conduct the visit in pairs to ensure the accurate recording of information.

Site visits usually begin on a Monday morning and last one week. By Wednesday or Thursday, most site visit teams will have completed their on-site review. They retire to the nearby hotel to confer and write their reports. By the end of the week, the team must reach consensus on the findings and prepare a final report for the panel of judges.

Purpose of Site Visits

Site visits help clarify uncertain points and verify self-assessment (that is, application) accuracy. During the site visit, examiners investigate areas most difficult to understand from self-assessments, such as the following:

- Deployment—how widely a process is used throughout the organization
- Integration—whether processes fit together to support Performance Excellence
- Process ownership—whether processes are broadly owned, simply directed, or micromanaged
- Student engagement and focus
- Faculty and staff involvement—whether the extent to which faculty and staff's participation in managing processes of all types is optimized
- Continuous improvement maturity—the number and extent of improvement cycles and resulting refinements in all areas of the organization and at all levels

Characteristics of Site Visit Issues

Examiners look at issues that are an essential component of scoring and role model determination. They have a responsibility to do the following:

- Clarify information that is missing or vague
- Verify significant strengths identified from the self-assessment
- Verify deployment of the practices described in the self-assessment

Examiners will do the following:

- Concentrate on crosscutting issues
- Examine data, reports, and documents
- Interview individuals and teams
- Receive presentations from the applicant organization

Examiners are not permitted to conduct their own focus groups or surveys with students, parents, or faculty and staff, or to disrupt educational processes. Conducting focus groups or surveys would violate the confidentiality agreements, as well as be statistically unsound.

Typically Important Site Visit Issues

- Role of senior administration in leading and serving as a role model
- Degree of involvement and self-direction of students, faculty, and staff
- Comprehensiveness and accessibility of the information system
- Utility and validity of available data
- Extent that facts and data are used in decision making
- Degree of emphasis on student and stakeholder satisfaction
- Extent of systematic approaches to organization processes
- Deployment and integration of high-performance principles and processes
- Training effectiveness
- Use of compensation, recognition, and rewards to promote key values
- Extent that strategic plans align educational work
- Extent of the use of measurable goals at all levels in the organization
- Evidence of evaluation and improvement cycles in all organization processes and in system effectiveness
- Improvement levels in cycle times and other operating processes
- Extent of integration of all operational and support processes
- Level of maturity of improvement initiatives
- Extent of ability to make meaningful comparisons to other organizations
- Uncovering improvements since the submission of the application (self-assessment) and receiving up-to-date performance results

Discussions with the Applicant Prior to the Site Visit

Prior to the site visit, all communication between the organization and its team must be routed through their respective single points of contact. Only the team leader may contact the organization on behalf of the site visit team prior to the site visit. This helps ensure consistency of message and communication for both parties. It prevents confusion and misunderstandings.

The team leader should provide the organization with basic information about the process. This includes schedules, arrival times, and equipment and meeting room needs.

Organizations usually provide the following information prior to the site visit team's final site visit planning meeting at the hotel on the day before the site visit starts:

- List of key contacts
- Organization chart
- Facility layout
- Performance data requested by examiners

The team leader, on behalf of team members, will ask for supplementary documentation to be compiled (such as results data brought up-to-date) to avoid placing an undue burden on the organization at the time of the site visit.

The site visit team will select sites that allow them to examine key issues and check deployment in key areas. This information may or may not be discussed with the organization prior to the site visit. Examiners will need access to all areas of the organization.

Conduct of Site Visit Team Members (Examiners)

Examiners are not allowed to discuss findings with anyone but team members. Examiners may not disclose the following to the organization:

- Personal or team observations and findings
- Conclusions and decisions
- Observations about the organization's performance systems, either in a complimentary or critical way

Examiners may not discuss observations about other organizations or the names of other award program organizations with anyone.

Examiners may not accept trinkets, gifts, or gratuities of any kind (coffee, cookies, rolls, breakfast, and lunch are okay), so organizations should not offer them. At the conclusion of the site visit, examiners are not permitted to leave with any of the organization's materials, including logo items or catalogs—not even items usually given to visitors. Examiners will dress in appropriate attire for the organization.

Opening Meeting

An opening meeting will be scheduled to introduce all parties and set the structure for the site visit. The meeting is usually attended by senior administrators and the self-assessment writing team. The opening meeting usually is scheduled first on the initial day of the site visit (8:30 or 9:00 A.M.). The team leader generally starts the meeting, introduces the team, and opens the site visit. Overhead slides and formal presentations are usually unnecessary.

The organization usually has one hour to present any information it believes important for the examiners to know. This includes time for a tour, if necessary.

Immediately after the meeting, examiners are likely to want to meet with senior leaders and those responsible for preparing sections of the self-assessment (application).

Conducting the Site Visit

The team will follow the site visit plan, subject to periodic adjustments according to its findings.

The site visit team will need a private room to conduct frequent caucuses. Organization representatives are not present at these caucuses. The team will also conduct evening meetings at the hotel to review the findings of the day, reach consensus, write comments, and revise the site visit report.

If, during the course of the site visit, someone from the organization believes the team or any of its members are missing the point, the designated point of contact should inform the team leader or the Baldrige Award office monitor. Also, someone who believes an examiner behaved inappropriately should inform the designated point of contact, who will inform the team leader or the award office monitor.

Faculty and staff should be instructed to mark every document given to examiners with the name and work location of the person providing the document. This will ensure that it is returned to the proper person. Records should be made of all material given to team members.

Organization personnel may not ask examiners for opinions and advice. Examiners are not permitted to provide any information of this type during the site visit.

Team Leader's Site Visit Checklist

The following checklist provides a summary of activities required of site visit team leaders:

Preparation

- Size of team and length of visit is determined, with starting and ending date and time selected.
- All team members receive copies of consensus report.
- Team is notified of starting and ending times and locations.
- Background information on new team members (if any) is received.
- Category lead and team pairing assignments are made for each team member.
- New team members complete review of narrative.
- Site visit notebooks are prepared.
- Individual team members prepare assigned site visit issues.
- Subteam members exchange site visit issues for comments.
- Revised site visit issues are received from subteams.
- Site visit issues are reviewed by team leader and comments sent to subteams.
- Team is asked to revise site visit themes or issues (as appropriate).

Previsit Meeting

- Examiner introductions are made.
- Site visit issues and themes are reviewed and approaches outlined.
- Sites are selected to visit and logistics reviewed.
- Specific requests for the first day are listed (interviews and data).
- Caucus plans are established.

Conduct of Visit

- Conducted opening presentation.
- Followed site visit plan.
- Revised plan as required.
- Caucused frequently.
- Maintained records of findings.
- Maintained records of organization documents received.
- Answered all selected site visit issues; developed information on site visit themes.
- Conducted closing meeting.

Site Visit Report

- Team completed site visit issues.
- Team completed Item and category summary forms.
- Completed overall summary form.
- Team initiated report.
- Report copied; original given to award office representative before leaving site.
- Leader kept copy, narrative, and other notes (or a backup person has material).
- Collected and returned all material to organization prior to leaving site.
- Collected all narratives, materials, and notes; sent or given to award office.

Feedback Report

- Senior examiner/feedback author collected feedback points during site visit.
- Senior examiner/feedback author reviewed feedback points with team during site visit report writing session.
- Reviewed feedback report completed before leaving site and sent to award office.

Generic Site Visit Questions

Examiners must verify or clarify the information contained in an application, whether or not the examiners have determined a process to be a strength or an area for improvement. Examiners must verify the existence of strengths, as well as clarify the nature of each significant area for improvement.

Before and during the site visit review process, examiners formulate a series of questions based on the Baldrige Education Performance Excellence Criteria. Because the site visit must verify or clarify all significant aspects of the organization's performance management systems against the criteria, it is possible to identify a series of generic questions that examiners are likely to ask during the site visit process. These questions are presented in the following section to help prepare applicants for the assessment process.

Category 1: Leadership

1. Describe the process your organization used in developing your mission, vision, and values. To top leaders: Who was involved with that process? How do you create future opportunities for the organization?
   - Please share with us the mission, vision, and values of this organization.
   - What are your organization's top priorities?
   - How do you ensure that all your faculty and staff know this?
   - How do you know how effective you are at communicating your commitment to the vision and values?

2. How do you, as a leader, see your role in supporting processes to ensure Performance Excellence?
   - How do you role model the behaviors you want your administrators and other faculty and staff to emulate?
   - What do the leaders do personally to lead this organization? What do you do that visibly displays to faculty and staff throughout the organization your personal involvement and commitment to the vision and values? How do you promote improvement?
   - What percentage of your time is spent on performance review and improvement activities?
   - What is your process for evaluating the effectiveness of the leadership system? How do you include or use faculty and staff feedback in the evaluation?
   - Please identify specific examples where the senior leadership improved the leadership system as a result of these evaluations. How do administrators evaluate and improve their own personal leadership effectiveness? How is faculty and staff feedback used here?

3. What are the criteria for promoting administrators within the organization?

   • How are you making administrators accountable for performance improvement, faculty and staff involvement, and student and stakeholder satisfaction objectives?

   • What measures do you personally use to track progress toward achieving the organization's key educational results drivers? How often do you monitor these measures?

   • Can we see a copy of an administrator's evaluation form?

   • How have you improved the process over the years of evaluating administrators?

4. Share with us what you feel are the most important requirements of your key students and stakeholders.

   • (Pick one of the requirements.) Which department is responsible for delivering this?

   • Please show us evidence of continuous improvement within that department.

5. What is the process used to monitor the performance of your organization? How does it relate to the organization's strategic business plan?

   • Do measurable goals exist?

   • How were the goals established?

   • How are they monitored? How often?

   • How are they key to your students' and stakeholders' primary needs and expectations?

   • What are the key success factors (or key results areas or critical success factors) for your organization, and how do you use them to drive Performance Excellence?

6. As a responsible citizen, what is your process for contributing to and improving the environment and society?

   • What do you do to anticipate public concerns over the possible impact of your organization? What are some examples? How do you measure progress?

   • What are some ways your organization ensures that faculty and staff act in an ethical manner in all organization-related matters and activities? How is this monitored to ensure compliance?

   • Tell me about your involvement in the community. How do you promote this involvement to the faculty and staff?

   • Do you have plans or processes in place for systematic evaluation and improvement?

Category 2: Strategic Planning

1. When was the last time the strategic plan was updated? How recent is it? Can we review a copy?

2. How did you develop this plan? What factors did you consider in the development of your strategic plan?

   • How does your strategic plan address faculty and staff capabilities?

   • What role do your students and their expectations play in the development of the strategic plan?

   • How do you identify resources needed to prepare for new opportunities and requirements?

   • What are the objectives for your organization that are derived from this plan? If they are not from the plan, where do they come from?

3. How do you plan for the development, education, and training needs of the organization? What are the organization's faculty and staff development plans (long- and short-term)?

   • Summarize the organization's plans related to work design, flexibility, rapid response, compensation and recognition, faculty and staff development and training, health, safety, ergonomics, special services, and faculty and staff satisfaction.

   • How do these plans optimize the use of faculty and staff?

   • How do these plans align with the strategic plan?

   • What are examples of changes based on inputs from the strategic planning in the following areas: recruitment, training, compensation, rewards, incentives, fringe benefits, and programs?

4. How do you deploy these goals, objectives, and action plans throughout the organization to ensure that work is aligned and action is taken to achieve the plan?
   • How do you ensure that organization, work unit, and individual goals and plans are aligned?
   • How do you ensure that partner goals are aligned with your strategic plan?

5. Please summarize your process for evaluation and improvement of the strategic planning and plan deployment processes, including the faculty and staff planning process.
   • What are examples of improvements made as a result of this evaluation process? When did they occur?

6. How is performance relative to the plan tracked?

7. Who do you consider to be your top competitors, and how does your planned performance compare to theirs?
   • How do you determine who your competitors are?

8. What are your specific goals and objectives? Please provide a copy of your long-range performance projections. How did you go about establishing these projections? How do these projections compare with your competitors' projections for the same time period?

9. Based on challenges identified in your organizational profile, how do your strategic objectives and goals address these challenges?

Category 3: Student, Stakeholder, and Market Focus

1. How do you know what your former, current, and future students expect of you? How does your organization determine their short- and long-term requirements?
   • How do you engage students in their learning goals and activities?
   • How do you differentiate key requirements from less important requirements and prepare to meet them? How do you anticipate requirements?
   • How do you evaluate and improve processes for determining student, stakeholder, and market requirements?

2. How do you provide easy access for your stakeholders to obtain information and assistance, or make complaints? What do you expect to learn from their complaints?
   • What is your process for handling student and stakeholder complaints? Do you monitor or track complaint data? What do you do with the information?
   • What percent of complaints are resolved at first contact? Describe the training you provide to student- and stakeholder-contact faculty and staff.
   • Describe your process for follow-up with stakeholders. What do you do with their feedback regarding programs and offerings? What triggers action?
   • What are the key objectives of relationships with your stakeholders? What are their needs? How were they determined? How do you know if they are being met?
   • How do you evaluate and improve the stakeholder relationship process?
   • What are some improvements you have made to the way you determine student and stakeholder requirements? How did you decide they were important to make, and when were they made?

3. How often do senior administrators talk to students and stakeholders? What do they do with this information?

4. What are your key measures for student and stakeholder satisfaction and dissatisfaction? How do these measures provide information on likely future behavior (loyalty, enrollment, budget votes, and referrals)?

   - How do you measure student and stakeholder satisfaction and dissatisfaction? Do you measure satisfaction/dissatisfaction for all key student and stakeholder groups/segments? What are your groups or segments? How do you determine them? How do you differentiate them in regard to programs, offerings, and services you offer? What process do you use to ensure the objectivity and validity of student and stakeholder satisfaction data?

   - What do you do with the information?

   - How do you disseminate satisfaction and dissatisfaction information to your faculty and staff? What action do they take as a result?

   - How do you know appropriate action is taken?

   - How do you go about improving the way you determine student and staff satisfaction? Please provide some examples of how you have improved it over the past several years. When were the requirements made?

5. What processes do you use to build loyalty, positive referral, and lasting relationships with students and staff?

   - How do you differentiate these processes according to student and stakeholder groups?

6. How do you evaluate the effectiveness of processes for building stakeholder relationships? What improvements have resulted from this evaluation? When were they made?

7. How does your organization work with partners, such as other community organizations, to ensure smooth transitions for students entering and leaving your organization?

Category 4: Information and Analysis

1. What are the major performance indicators critical to running your organization?

2. How do you determine whether the information you collect and use for decision making is complete, timely, reliable, accessible, confidential, and accurate? What is the process you use to determine the relevance of the information to organization goals and action plans?

   - How do you ensure that all data collected support the management of organization processes?

   - Describe how you obtain feedback from the users of the information. How is this feedback used to make improvements?

3. You have told us what your top priorities are.
   How do you use comparative information against these? Please describe how needs and priorities for selecting comparisons and benchmarks are determined. Share an example of the process of prioritization.

   - How do you use competitive or comparative performance data generally?

   - How are the results of your comparison efforts used to set stretch targets?

   - How are the results of your comparison efforts used to improve work processes and stimulate innovation?

   - How do you evaluate and improve your comparative and benchmarking processes?

   - Show us samples of comparative studies. Picking some at random, determine the following: Why was the area selected? How were comparison data selected and obtained? How were data in the example used?

4. Please share with us an example of analysis of information important to your students and stakeholders and your own organization's success.

   - How are data analyzed to determine relationships between student and stakeholder information and academic performance, or between operational data and student or stakeholder satisfaction?

   - What data and analyses do you use to understand your faculty and staff, your students and stakeholders, and your community?

   - Are these analyses widely used for decision making? What actions are you taking to extend the analysis across all parts of the organization?

   - What are you doing to improve the analysis process? What are some improvement examples? When were they made?

5. Please tell us about the process used to review progress relative to your action plans.

   - Can you show us some examples of improvements made as a result of the reviews? When were they made?

   - What measures are reviewed? How often? Who is the principal reviewer(s)?

   - How do you use the findings from the review to prioritize improvements, identify innovation opportunities, and allocate resources? Can you give us some examples? How are they deployed throughout the organization?

   - What are you doing to improve the review process? Do you have examples of improvements made? What were they and when did they occur?

6. How available is data to you for your needs?

   - How "user friendly" is your computer hardware and software for your needs?

   - What is being done to improve "user friendliness" of hardware and software?

Category 5: Faculty and Staff Focus

1. Do faculty and staff know and understand organization/department priorities? How do you determine this?

   - What do you do to ensure effective communication among faculty, staff, and departments?

   - What authority do faculty and staff have to direct their own actions and make educational decisions?

   - (To faculty and staff.) What authority do you have to make decisions about resolving problems, changing processes, and communications across departments?

   - What is the process you have used to evaluate and enhance opportunities for faculty and staff to take individual initiative and demonstrate self-directed responsibility in designing and managing their work? Show examples of actions taken and improvements made. When were they made?

2. How does the organization link recognition, reward, and compensation to reinforce overall organization objectives for performance improvement, student learning, and faculty and staff development? Describe your approach to faculty and staff recognition and compensation. How does your compensation and recognition differ for different categories of faculty and staff?

   - (General question for faculty and staff.) Do you feel that your contributions to the organization are recognized? How have you been recognized for contributing to achieving the organization's action plans?

   - What specific reward and recognition programs are utilized?

3. What ongoing training is provided for your faculty and staff?

- How is your training curriculum designed and delivered? How do you integrate faculty and staff, chair or team leaders, and administrator feedback into the design of your training program? What methods are used?

- How does your training program affect operational performance goals? How do you know your training improves your academic results? Show examples.

- What training and education do you provide to ensure that you meet the needs of all categories of faculty and staff? What training do new faculty and staff receive to obtain the knowledge and skills necessary for success and high performance, including leadership development of faculty and staff at all levels?

- If applicable, how do faculty and staff in remote locations participate in training programs?

- What is your system for improving training? Please give us some examples of improvements made and when they were made.

4. What are your targets or measures for faculty and staff health and safety? Does your approach to health and safety address the needs of all faculty and staff groups?

- How do you determine that you have a safe and healthy work environment? How do you measure this?

- How are you performing against those measures?

- What are your procedures for systematic evaluation and improvement?

5. How do your senior administrators, chairs, team leaders, and supervisors encourage faculty and staff to develop and put to use their full potential?

6. How is faculty and staff satisfaction measured? What do you do with the information?

- What are the key areas of concern? What do you do to improve faculty and staff satisfaction systematically? Please give us some examples of improvements.

- (To faculty and staff) What does the organization do to enhance your career development?

- What special services, facilities, activities, and opportunities does your organization provide faculty and staff?

Category 6: Process Management

1. What is your process for designing new educational programs and offerings to ensure that student and stakeholder requirements are met?

- How do students, stakeholders, and support organizations participate in the design process?

- How are design changes handled and methods used to ensure that all changes are included?

- How do you ensure that faculty is properly prepared before new programs and offerings are introduced?

- How do you evaluate and improve the process for designing new programs and offerings? Please provide some examples of improvements and when they were made.

2. How do you know that your ongoing programs and offerings are meeting design requirements? What observations, indicators, and performance measures are used and who uses them?

- What steps have you taken to improve the effectiveness/efficiency of key organization delivery processes?

- What are the processes by which you deliver these programs and offerings to ensure that student and stakeholder expectations will be met or exceeded?

- Once you determine that a process, such as for student services or support may not be meeting measurement goals or performing according to expectations, what process do you use to determine root cause and to bring about process improvement?

3. Please give an example of how an observation of a student or stakeholder request or complaint resulted in an improvement of a current process or the establishment of a new process.

4. Please share with us your list of key student and support processes, requirements, and associated process measures, including in-process measures.
   - How is performance of student and support services systematically evaluated and refined? Please provide some examples and when they occurred.
   - What are the steps you have taken to design your key student and support processes? How do you determine the types of services needed? How do your support services interact with and add value to your educational design and delivery processes?
   - How does your organization maintain the performance of key support services? Share some examples of processes used to determine root causes of support problems and how you prevent recurrence of problems.

5. How does your organization work with partners, such as other community organizations, to ensure student services meet requirements?

Category 7: Organizational Performance Results

1. What are the student learning trends and performance levels at this time?
   - Please show a breakout of data by student groups.
   - How do these trends compare with comparable organizations or selected student populations?

2. What are the student and stakeholder satisfaction trends and performance levels at this time? [Links to Item 3.2]
   - Please show a breakout of data by student and stakeholder group or segment.
   - How do these student and stakeholder satisfaction trends and levels compare with those of comparable organizations or similar educational providers?

3. What are the current levels and trends showing the effectiveness of your faculty and staff practices? [Links to Category 5]
   - Please provide data on key indicators, such as safety/accident record, absenteeism, turnover by category and type of faculty/staff and administrator, grievances, and related litigation.
   - How do these trends compare with those of comparable organizations or similar providers?

4. How do you measure results that contribute to enhanced learning?
   - Please show us your performance data from your design and delivery processes, regulatory requirements, and any cost-effectiveness measures.
   - How do you know which factors are most important to your students and stakeholders? [Links to Item 3.1]
   - How does your performance on these key indicators compare to comparable organizations or other educational providers?

5. How do you measure support and student service effectiveness and efficiency? [Links to Item 6.2 and 6.3]
   - Please show us your performance data.
   - How do you know what the key performance indicators should be?
   - How does your performance on these key indicators compare to comparable organizations or other educational providers?
   - What are your results and trends for public responsibility and citizenship?

General Crosscutting Questions Examiners Are Likely To Ask Faculty, Staff, and Administrators

- Who are your key stakeholders and markets?
- What are the organization's mission, vision, and values? What are your goals?
- What is the strategic plan for the organization? What are the organization's goals, and what role do you play in helping to achieve the goals?
- What kind of training do you receive? Is it useful?
- How are you involved in the work and decision making of the organization?
- Is this a good place to work? Why or why not?
- What activities are recognized or rewarded?

Summary of Eligibility
Categories and Restrictions

This category is open to for-profit and not-for-profit public, private, and government organizations and some subunits—including U.S. subunits of foreign organizations—that provide education services in the United States and its territories. Eligibility is intended to be as open as possible. Eligible organizations include elementary and secondary schools and school districts; colleges, universities, and university systems; schools or colleges within universities; professional schools; community colleges; and technical schools. Departments within schools or colleges are ineligible.

A subunit is a unit or division of a larger (parent) organization. Subunits of organizations may be eligible. To be eligible, the subunit must be self-sufficient enough to be examined in all seven criteria categories, and it must be recognizable as a discrete entity that is easily distinguishable from the parent and its other subunits. It cannot be primarily a support function (for example, student advising units, counseling units, food services, health services, housing, libraries, safety, finance and accounting, human resources, public relations, and purchasing).

Fees

Eligibility Determination Fee: $150
Application Fee:

- All not-for-profit institutions: $300
- For-profit institutions with more than 500 employees: $5000
- For-profit institutions with 500 or fewer employees: $2000

Multiple-Application Restrictions

A subunit and its parent may not both apply for awards in the same year; only one subunit of an educational institution may apply for an award in the same year in the same eligibility category. A subunit applicant must be self-sufficient in all seven categories and must have a clear definition of the organization to apply. Subunits must be discreet from the parent organization.

Site Visit Review Fees

Site visit review fees will be set when the visits are scheduled. Fees depend upon the number of examiners assigned and the duration of the visit.

Site visit review fees for for-profit education organizations with fewer than 500 employees are one-half the rate for for-profit education organizations with more than 500 employees. Nominal fees will be charged to not-for-profit education organizations selected for site visits. These fees are paid only by those applicants reaching the site visit stage.

Feedback

All applicants receive a feedback report. The feedback report—a tool for continuous improvement—is an assessment written by a team of leading U.S. educational performance experts.

Applicants receive a specific listing of strengths and areas for improvement based on the Baldrige Award Criteria. It is used by organizations as part of their strategic planning processes to focus on their customers and to improve productivity. The report does not provide suggestions or ideas on how to improve.

The feedback report contains the Baldrige Award evaluation team's response to the written application. Length varies according to the detail presented in the written responses to the Baldrige Award Criteria. The report includes the following components:

- Background
- Application review process
- Scoring
- Distribution of numerical scores for all applicants
- Overall scoring summary of applicant
- Criteria category scoring summary of applicant
- Details of the applicant's strengths and areas for improvement (feedback reports often contain more than 150 strengths and areas for improvement)

Strict confidentiality is observed at all times and in every aspect of application review and feedback.

A survey of recent Baldrige Award applicants conducted by the National Quality Award office showed that more than 90 percent of respondents used the feedback report in their strategic and business planning processes.

Information about current and past winners and their achievements was drawn from the award office Web page. General information on the National Institute of Standards and Technology and the Baldrige Award program is available on the World Wide Web at http://www.nist.gov.

State Award Recipients of Educational Excellence Awards

Most states (over 85 percent) have quality or performance awards that recognize Performance Excellence at different levels. Most recognize education performance as part of the award. The few states that do not are beginning to define criteria for this year. Therefore, we have included all states with Baldrige-based awards and information about any education recipients with which we were provided. Because many states offer progressive or tiered awards that recognize different levels of achievement, we have noted the levels of awards for each state.

[The following is based on current information received and is used with permission of Quantum Performance Group, Inc. In some cases, the year of recognition was not available.]

Alabama

Alabama Productivity Center
University of Alabama
249 Bidgood Hall
P.O. Box 870318
Tuscaloosa, AL 35487-0318
Contact: Linda Vincent
Telephone: (205) 348-8994
Fax: (205) 348-9391
E-mail: Linda@proctr.cba.ua.edu
Web site: proctr.cba.ua.edu/index.html

Award Levels:
  Education Recipient

1998 Winner
Mountain Brook City Schools
Dr. Tim Norris, Personnel Director
Mountain City Schools
P. O. Box 130040
Mountain Brook, AL 35213-0040
Telephone: (205) 871-4608
Fax: (205) 877-8303

Arizona

Arizona Quality Alliance
3737 N. 7th Street
Suite 157
Phoenix, AZ 85014-5079
Telephone: (602) 636-1383
Fax: (602) 636-1377
E-mail: aqa@Arizona-Excellence.com
Web site: www.arizona-excellence.com

Arizona's Pioneer and Governor's Award for Quality
Award Levels:
  Pioneer Award
  Governor's Award for Quality

1993 Pioneer Award
Rio Salado Community College

1998 Pioneer Award
Arizona had three Pioneer Award winners for 1998. They are as follows:
Cyprus Miami Mining Corporation
Richard Dana
P. O. Box 4444
Claypool, AZ 85532
Voice Mail: (520) 473-7214
Fax: (520) 473-7339

Arizona Department of Economic Security
Gloria Diaz
1140 E. Washington
Phoenix, AZ 85034
Voice Mail: (602) 229-2800
Fax: (602) 254-9378

University of Phoenix—Phoenix Campus
Richard Wagner
4605 E. Elwood Street, Suite 445
Phoenix, AZ 85040
Voice Mail: (602) 557-2237
Fax: (602) 929-7414
E-mail: rpwagner@apollogrp.edu

Arkansas

Arkansas Quality Award
1111 West Capitol Avenue
Room 1013
Little Rock, AR 72201-3005
Telephone: (501) 373-1300
Fax: (501) 373-1976
E-mail: arkansasquality@compuserve.com
Web site: www.arkansas-quality.org

Award Levels:
    Quality Interest
    Quality Achievement

1995 Quality Achievement Award

Westark Community College, Business and Industrial Institute

California

Governor's Golden State Quality Awards
CalQED
P.O. Box 1929
Danville, CA 94526-6929
Telephone: (925) 210-9766
E-mail: quality@calqed.org
Web site: www.calqed.org

Award Levels:
    Commitment
    Achievement
    Excellence

Eureka Award for Quality and Service Excellence
Contact: Barbara Blalock
Telephone: (510) 210-9766
E-mail: calqed@dnai.com

1995 Eureka Award—Bronze

Marvin Avenue School
    Best-in-Class

Cuesta College
    Silver Level—1998
    Best-in-Class
    Silver Level—1996
    Best-in-Class

Colorado

Colorado Performance Excellence
1750 Hawthorn Place
Boulder, CO 80304
Michael Chapman
Telephone: (303) 442-0715
Fax: (303) 546-0616
E-mail: cpex@att.net

Three levels of awards with first awards to be presented in the spring of 2002.

Connecticut

Connecticut Award for Excellence
Walt Cederholm, Executive Director
Telephone: (860) 285-2578
E-mail: walt.t.cederholm@us.abb.com

Award Levels:
    Nutmeg
    Charter Oak
    Genius (top level)

1996 Nutmeg

Regional School District No. 14—
    Woodbury/Bethlehem
Joseph Sabetella, Superintendent of Schools
    Woodbury, CT 06798
Telephone: (203) 263-4339

1996 Nutmeg

Litchfield Center and Elementary Schools,
    Grades K–6
Ann Mirizzi, Principal, Litchfield
    Intermediate School
Andrienne Longobucco, Principal,
    Litchfield Center School
Litchfield, CT 06749
Telephone: (860) 567-7520

Delaware

Delaware Quality Consortium
99 Kings Highway
Dover, DE 19901
Contact: Zena Tucker
Telephone: (302) 739-4271
E-mail: ztucker@state.de.us
Web site: www.delawarequalityaward.com

Award Levels:
   Delaware Quality Award
   Award of Merit

1995 Award Of Merit
New Castle County Vocational Technical
   School District
Dr. Donald C. James
Director, Pupil Services/Quality Management
1417 Newport Road
Wilmington, DE 19807
Voice Mail: (302) 995-8030
Fax: (312) 995-8196

Florida
The Florida Sterling Council
P.O. Box 13907
Tallahassee, FL 32317-3907
Telephone: (850) 922-5316
Fax: (850) 488-7579
E-mail: dlowman@floridasterling.com
Web site: www.floridasterling.com

Award Levels:
   Governor's Sterling Award
   Sterling Quality Achievement Recognition

1993
Pinellas County Schools
Dr. J. Howard Hinesley, Superintendent
Telephone: (727) 588-6295

1998
Marjorie Kinnan Rawlings Elementary School
Shirley Lorenzo, Principal
Telephone: (813) 547-7828

Georgia

1999 Oglethorpe Award
U.S. Army Infantry School & Center,
   Fort Benning
Sara Hodges
Quality Management Division
Directorate of Resource Management
Telephone: (706) 545-1018
E-mail: HodgesS@benning.army.mil

Hawaii
Hawaii State Award of Excellence
Pacific Region Institute for Service
   Excellence (PRISE)
Chamber of Commerce of Hawaii
1132 Bishop Street, Suite 200
Honolulu, HI 96813
Telephone: (808) 545-4394
Fax: (808) 545-4309
E-mail: norm@cochawaii.org

Award Levels:
   Gold – Score of 700 and above
   Red – Significant levels of excellence generally
      achieving excellence scores between 600–700.
   Purple – High levels of excellence generally
      achieving excellence scores between 500–600.
      A special award level for small business.

Kaiser Permanente Hawaii
Amy Watts
Telephone: (808) 263-9562
Fax: (808) 263-9560
E-mail: amywatts@gte.net

Idaho
Idaho Quality Award
Idaho Department of Commerce
700 West State Street
P.O. Box 83720
Boise, ID 83720-0093
Telephone: (208) 334-2470 or (800) 842-5858
Fax: (208) 334-2631
E-mail: info@idoc.state.id.us
Web site: www.idahoworks.com/iqa.html

Award Levels:
   Idaho Quality Award (Baldrige-based)
   Recognition level

Illinois
Walter Reilly, President
Lincoln Foundation for Business Excellence
Co-Executive Directors:
   Donna Connolly
   Maria Wrobel
820 W. Jackson Blvd., 7th Floor
Chicago, IL 60607
Telephone: (312) 258-5301
Fax: (312) 258-4066
E-mail: info@lincolnaward.com
Web site: www.lincolnaward.org

Award Levels:
  Commitment to Excellence
  Progress Toward Excellence
  Lincoln Award for Excellence (highest level)

1996
Dr. Julio A. Rivera
Charles G. Hammond Elementary School
2819 West 21st Place
Chicago, IL 60623
Telephone: (773) 535-4580
Fax: (773) 535-4579

1996
Dr. Normand R. Wentzel
Community Unit School District #300
300 Cleveland Avenue
Carpentersville, IL 60110
Telephone: (847) 426-1300 ext. 306
Fax: (847) 426-1209

1996
Mr. Bruce E. Andersen
Davea Career Center
301 South Swift Road
Addison, IL 60101-1499
Telephone: (630) 691-7591
Fax: (630) 691-7596

1996
Dr. Linda Helton
Lake Country High Schools, Technology Campus
19525 West Washington
Grayslake, IL 60030
Telephone: (847) 223-5989
Fax: (847) 223-7363

1996
Ms. Ann Elizabeth Shorey
Louisa May Alcott Elementary School
2625 North Orchard Street
Chicago, IL 60614
Telephone: (773) 534-5460
Fax: (773) 534-5789

1996
Mr. Raymond Buniak
Thomas Kelly High School
4136 South California
Chicago, IL 60632
Telephone: (773) 535-4900
Fax: (773) 535-4841

1996
Dr. David VanWinkle
Valley View Community Unit School District
  #364-U
755 Luther Drive
Romeoville, IL 60446
Telephone: (815) 886-7246
Fax: (815) 886-7294

1996
Dr. Kenneth B. Allen
Waubonsee Community College
Route 47 at Harter Road
Sugar Grove, IL 60554
Telephone: (630) 466-7900
Fax: (630) 466-9406

1997
Mr. Philip Hunsberger
Community Unit School District #5
410 East LeFevre Road
Sterling, IL 61081
Telephone: (815) 626-5050
Fax: (815) 622-4111

1997
Dr. John Conyers
Community Consolidated School District #15
580 North First Bank Drive
Palatine, IL 60067
Telephone: (847) 934-2809
Fax: (847) 934-2719

1997
Dr. Donald E. Weber
Naperville Community Unit School District #203
203 West Hillside Road
Naperville, IL 60540
Telephone: (630) 420-6311
Fax: (630) 420-1066

1998
Dr. Joseph Dockery-Jackson
Black Hawk College
6600 34th Avenue
Moline, IL 61265
Telephone: (309) 796-1311 ext. 13587
Fax: (309) 792-5976

1998
Dr. Robert M. Karp
Highland Community College
2998 West Pearl City Road
Freeport, IL 61032
Telephone: (815) 235-6121 ext. 374
Fax: (815) 235-6130

1998
Dr. Susan Scribner
McKendree College
701 College Road
Lebanon, IL 62254
Telephone: (618) 537-6860
Fax: (618) 537-6417

Indiana
Indiana Quality Improvement Award
Indiana Business Modernization &
   Technical Corporation
One North Capitol Avenue, Suite 925
Indianapolis, IN 46204-2242
Telephone: (317) 635-3058 ext. 246
Fax: (317) 231-7095
E-mail: qualityaward@bmtadvantage.org
Web site: www.bmtadvantage.org

Iowa
Iowa Recognition for Performance Excellence
Woods Quality Center
4401 6th Street, SW
Cedar Rapids, IA 52404
Contact: Gary Nesteby, Program Executive Director
Telephone: (319) 399-6583
E-mail: info@wqc.org
Web site: www.wqc.org

Kansas
Kansas Award for Excellence
P.O. Box 128
Tecumseh, KS 66542
John Shoemaker, Ph.D., Director
Tina Shoemaker, CHE, Associate Director
Telephone: (800) 743-6767
Fax: (785) 379-5047
E-mail: kae@Qof.com
Web site: www.kae.myassociation.com

Award Levels:
   Level 1—Commitment to Excellence Award
   Level 2—Performance in Quality Award
   Level 3—Kansas Excellence Award

Kentucky
Kentucky Quality Council
P.O. Box 1342
Frankfort, KY 40602
Nan Harice
Telephone: (502) 695-0066
Fax: (502) 695-6824
E-mail: Contact@kqc.org
Web site: www.kqc.org

Commonwealth of Kentucky Quality Award
   Award Levels:
   Level 1 – Quality Interest
   Level 2 – Quality Commitment
   Level 3 – Quality Achievement
   Level 4 – Governor's Gold Quality Award

Louisiana
Louisiana Quality Foundation
Louisiana Productivity Center
c/o The Louisiana Productivity Center
P.O. Box 44172
Lafayette, LA 70504-4172
Corinne Dupuy, LQF Administration
Telephone: (318) 482-6422
Fax: (318) 262-5472
E-mail: cad8292@usl.edu
Web site: www.laqualityaward.com

Maine
Margaret Chase Smith Marine State Quality Award
7 University Drive
Augusta, ME 04330-9412
Andrea Jandebeur, Program Administrator
Telephone: (207) 621-1988
Fax: (207) 282-6081
E-mail: mqc@Maine-Quality.org
Web site: www.Maine-Quality.org

Award Levels:
   Level 1—Commitment
   Level 2—Progress
   Level 3—Excellence

Gardner Regional Middle School
 Arthur Warren
Telephone: (207) 582-1326

Maryland

Maryland Quality Award
College Park Office
4511 Knox Road, Suite 102
College Park, MD 20740
Telephone: (301) 403-4413
Fax: (301) 403-4478
Web site: www.umcaps.umd.edu/umcqp/

Award Levels:
  Gold
  Silver
  Bronze

Quality Achievement (Silver)
Kettering Middle School (Education)
65 Herrington Drive
Upper Marlboro, MD 20772
Marian White-Hood
Telephone: (301) 808-4060

Massachusetts

MassExcellence
c/o Massachusetts Council for Quality
Center for Industrial Competitiveness
600 Suffolk Street (5th Floor)
Lowell, MA 01854
Tyler Fairbank
Telephone: (978) 934-2733
Fax: (978) 934-4035
E-mail: info@massescellence.com
Web site: www.massescellence.com

Massachusetts Quality Award
Award Levels:
  Level 1—Self-Assessment
  Level 2—Examiner Assessment
  Level 3—State Quality Award

Michigan

Michigan Quality Council
Michigan Quality Leadership Award
Oakland University
525 O'Dowd Hall
Rochester, MI 48309-4401
William Kalmar, Director
Telephone: (248) 370-4552
Fax: (248) 370-4628
E-mail: kalmar@oakland.edu
Web site: www.michiganquality.org

Award Levels:
  Michigan Quality Leadership Award
  Honor Roll

2000 Honor Roll
Montabella Middle School
Edmore, Michigan

1999 Honor Roll
Montabella Middle School
Edmore, Michigan

1995 Silver
Whitehall Shoreline Elementary School

1995 Muskegon Quality Award – Gold
Muskegon Community College

Minnesota

Minnesota Council for Quality
2850 Metro Drive, Suite 519
Bloomington, MN 55425
Telephone: (952) 851-3181
Fax: (952) 851-3183
E-mail: MC4quality@aol.com

Minnesota Quality Award Process
  Bronze – Commitment Level
  Silver – Advancement Level
  Gold – Achievement Level
  Crystal – Minnesota Quality Award

1998 Education Bronze
University of Minnesota, Duluth
Academic Services and Student Life
Bruce Gildseth, Vice chancellor
297 DA&B
10 University Drive
Duluth, MN 55812
Telephone: (218) 726-8501
Fax: (218) 726-6577

1997 Education Silver
Eden Prairie Schools, District #272
William Gaslin, Superintendent
8100 School Road
Eden Prairie, MN 55344-2292
Telephone: (612) 975-7010
Fax: (612) 975-7012

Mary Bollinger
Executive Director of Human Resources
8100 School Road
Eden Prairie, MN 55344-2292
Telephone: (612) 975-7101
Fax: (612) 975-7112

1996 Education Silver
Rochester Community and Technical College
Dave Weber, Director of Communications
851 Southeast 30th Avenue
Rochester, MN 55904-4999
Telephone: (507) 285-7212
Fax: (507) 280-3531

1996 Education Gold
Alexandria Technical College
Larry Shellito, President
1601 Jefferson Street
Alexandria, MN 56308
Telephone: (320) 762-0221
Fax: (320) 762-4501

David Trites, TQM Coordinator
Alexandria Technical College
1601 Jefferson Street
Alexandria, MN 56308
Telephone: (320) 762-4415
Fax: (320) 762-4421

Mississippi
Mississippi Quality Award Program
State Board for Junior & Community Colleges
3825 Ridgewood Road
Jackson, MS 39211
Duane Hamill
Telephone: (601) 982-6349
Fax: (601) 982-6363
E-mail: dhamill@sbcjc.cc.ms.us
Web site: www.sbcjc.cc.ms.us/progs.html

Award Levels:
   Governor's Award
   Excellence Award
   Quality Commitment
   Quality Interest

1995 Quality Interest
Itawamba Community College (Tupelo Campus)

Missouri
Excellence in Missouri Foundation
Missouri Quality Award
205 Jefferson St., 14th Floor
P.O. Box 1085
Jefferson City, MO 65102
John Politi, Director
Telephone: (573) 526-1725
Fax: (573) 526-1729
E-mail: jpoliti@mail.state.mo.us
Web site: www.mqa.org

1998 Winner
Missouri School for the Blind
Dr. Yvonne Howze, Superintendent
3815 Magnolia
St. Louis, MO 63110
Fax: (314) 772-1561
E-mail: Yhowze@msb.k12.mo.us

1997 Winner
Northwest Missouri State University
Contact: John Jasinski
Chair, Department of Mass Communications
Wells Hall 238
Maryville, MO 64468
Telephone: (660) 562-1333
Fax: (660) 562-1521
E-mail: jazz@acad.nwmissouri.edu

1995 Winner
University of Missouri-Rolla
Contact: Dr. John T. Park, Chancellor
1870 Miner Circle
Rolla, MO 65409-0910
Telephone: (573) 341-4116
Fax: (573) 341-6306
E-mail: parkj@umr.edu

Nebraska
The Edgerton Quality Award
Nebraska Dept. of Economic Development
301 Centennial Mall South
Lincoln, NE 68509-4666
Rich Stites
Telephone: (402) 471-4167
Fax: (402) 471-3778
E-mail: rstites@neded.org
Web site: assist.neded.org/edge2/eqa/home.htm

Award Levels:
Edgerton Award of Commitment
Edgerton Award of Progress
Edgerton Award of Excellence

New Hampshire

Granite State Quality Council
P.O. Box 29
Manchester, NH 03105-0029
Telephone: (603) 223-1312
Fax: (306) 223-1299
E-mail: quality@gsqc.com
Web site: www.gsqc.com

Granite State Quality Award

New Jersey

New Jersey Governor's Award for Performance
Excellence
Mary G. Roebling Building
P.O. Box 827
Trenton, NJ 08625-0827
Ken Biddle, Managing Director
Telephone: (609) 777-0940
Fax: (609) 777-2798
E-mail: kbiddle@qnj.org
Web site: www.qnj.org

Award Levels:
Gold
Silver
Bronze

1999 Governor's Award Commitment to Excellence

Manville School District
Francis X. Heelan, Ed.D., Superintendent
100 North 13th Avenue
Manville, NJ 08835
Telephone: (908) 231-8545
E-mail: fxheel@aol.com

1999 Governor's Award Commitment to Excellence

Rutgers College Student Centers and Student
Activities
Tricia Nolfi Torok, Assistant Dean
613 George Street
New Brunswick, NJ 08901
Telephone: (732) 932-6978
E-mail: tnolfi@rci.rutgers.edu

New Jersey Quality Achievement Award
Award Levels:
Quality Discoverer
Quality Explorer
Areas of Excellence Awards
NJ Quality Achievement

1998 Governor's Award for Performance Excellence Gold

Hunterdon Central Regional High School
Ray Farley, Superintendent
Route 31
Flemington, NJ 08822
Telephone: (908) 284-7135
E-mail: rfarley@star.hcrhs.hunterdon.k12. nj.us

New Mexico

New Mexico Quality Awards
Quality New Mexico
6501 Americas Parkway
Suite 700
Albuquerque, NM 87110
Mailing Address:
P.O. Box 25005
Albuquerque, NM 87105
Telephone: (505) 944-2001
Fax: (505) 944-2002
E-mail: BethE@quality-newmexico.org
Web site: www.quality-newmexico.org

Award Levels:
Pinon (Commitment)
Roadrunner (Progress)
Zia (Excellence)

Pinon

Aztec High School
University of Phoenix – New Mexico Campus
Workforce Training Center of the Albuquerque
  Technical Vocational Institute

Roadrunner

University of New Mexico – Gallup Campus
Western New Mexico University

1995 Pinon

Del Norte High School

1995 Pinon

Dona Ann Branch Community College

1995 Pinon
Juan de Onate Elementary School

1995 Pinon
New Mexico State University, Business Admin. &
  Economics

1995 Pinon
Petroglyph Elementary School

1995 Pinon
Western New Mexico University

1994 Pinon
Grants Cibola Co. Schools
Mt. Taylor Elementary School

1994 Pinon
Del North High School

1994 Pinon
Western NM University

1994 Pinon
Luna Vocational Technical Institute

1994 Roadrunner
San Juan College

New York
Barbara Ann Harms
Empire State Advantage: Excellence at Work
11 Computer Drive West, Suite 212
Albany, NY 12205
Telephone: (518) 482-1747
Fax: (518) 482-2231
info@esaprograms.org
Web site: www.esaprograms.org

Award Levels:
   The Governor's Award for Excellence—New York
     State's highest level of recognition for quality
   The ESA Program—Empire State Gold
     Registration/Certification
   Empire State Silver Registration/Certification

1999 Silver Certification
Berkshire Union Free School District
Arthur Walton, Superintendent
12640 Route 22
Canaan, NY 12029
Telephone: (518) 781-3500 ext. 576
Fax: (518) 781-4890

1999 Silver Certification
Madison-Oneida BOCES
Dr. Edward A. Shafer, District Superintendent
4937 Spring Road
Verona, NY 13478-0168
Telephone: (315) 361-5510
Fax: (315) 361-5517
E-mail: eshafer@mohawk.moric.org

1999 ESA Partners
East Islip School District
Michael J. Capozzi, Superintendent
Craig B. Gariepy Avenue
Islip Terrace, NY 11752
Telephone: (516) 581-1600 ext. 200
Fax: (516) 581-1617

1998 ESA Partners
Genesee-Livingston-Steuben-Wyoming BOCES
Michael Wesner, Assistant Superintendent
80 Munson Street
LeRoy, NY 14482
Telephone: (716) 768-9540 ext. 258
Fax: (716) 768-9633

1998 ESA Partners
School District of the City of Niagara Falls
Carmen A. Granto, Superintendent
607 Walnut Avenue
Niagara Falls, NY 14301
Telephone: (716) 286-4205
Fax: (716) 286-4283

1997 Silver Certification
Binghamton City Schools
Michael Melamed, Assistant Superintendent
98 Oak Street
Binghamton, NY 13905
Telephone: (607) 762-8124
Fax: (607) 762-8112

1997 Silver Certification
Skaneateles Central School
Kathryn Carlson
Assistant Superintendent, Pupil Personnel
  Services and Special Programs
49 Elizabeth Street
Skaneateles, NY 13152
Telephone: (315) 685-8361
Fax: (315) 685-0347

1997 Silver Certification

West Babylon Union Free School District
Melvin S. Noble, Superintendent
Ten Farmingdale Road
West Babylon, NY 11704-6289
Telephone: (516) 321-3142
Fax: (516) 661-5166

1997 ESA Partner

West Genesee Central Schools
Dr. Rudolph Rubeis, Superintendent
300 Sanderson Drive
Camillus, NY 13031
Telephone: (315) 487-4562
Fax: (315) 487-2999

1996 Governor's Excelsior Award

Pittsford Central Schools
Dr. John O'Rourke, Superintendent
42 West Jefferson Road
Pittsford, New York 14534
Telephone: (716) 218-1000

1995 Governor's Excelsior Award

Sewanhaka Central High School District
Dr. George Goldstein, Superintendent
555 Ridge Road
Elmont, NY 11003
Telephone: (516) 488-9800

1994 Governor's Excelsior Award

Pearl River School District
Dr. Richard E. Mauer, Superintendent
275 East Central Avenue
Pearl River, NY 10965
Telephone: (914) 620-3900

1992 Governor's Excelsior Award

Kenmore Town of Tonawanda
 Union Free School District
David Paciencia, Superintendent
1500 Colvin Boulevard
Buffalo, NY 14223
Telephone: (716) 874-8400

North Carolina

North Carolina does not have a state quality award program at this time.

Previous North Carolina Quality Leadership Award Recipients

1998:

Wake County Public School System
 Advancement—Large Education
Toni Patterson, Executive Director,
 Administration
P.O. Box 28041
Raleigh, NC 27611
Telephone: (919) 501-7935
Fax: (919) 850-8953

Craven County Schools Commitment—
 Large Education
Janet Furman, Director of Guidance/
 Communication
3600 Trent Road
New Bern, NC 28562
Telephone: (252) 514-6333
Fax: (252) 514-6351

New Hanover County Schools Honor Roll—
 Large Education
Dianne Avery, Community Relations Director
1802 15th Street
Wilmington, NC 28401
Telephone: (910) 254-4222
Fax: (910) 251-6079

Progress

Wake County Public School System
Craven County Schools
New Hanover County Schools
University of North Carolina – Wilmington
Moorseville Graded School District

1998 Advanced

Wake County Public School System
Toni Patterson, Executive Director, Admin.
P. O. Box 28041
Raleigh, NC 27611
Telephone: (919) 501-7935
Fax: (919) 850-8953

1998 Commitment

Craven County Schools
Janet Furman, Director of Guidance/
 Communication
3600 Trent Road
New Bern, NC 28562
Telephone: (919) 514-6333
Fax: (919) 514-6351

1997 Honor Roll
New Hanover County Schools
Dianne Avery, Community Relations Director
1802 S. 15th Street
Wilmington, NC 28401
Telephone: (910) 254-4222
Fax: (910) 251-6079

Ohio
Ohio Award for Excellence
Tom Casperson, Executive Director
Telephone: (937) 6556
E-mail: oe200001@ncr.com
Web site: www.oae.org

1995 Serious Commitment
Miami-Jackobs College

Oklahoma
Oklahoma Quality Award Foundation
P.O. Box 26980
900 North Stiles
Oklahoma City, OK 73126-0980
Mike Strong, Executive Director
Telephone: (405) 815-5295
Fax: (405) 815-5205
E-mail: mike_strong@odoc.state.ok.us
Web site: www.oklahomaquality.com

Oklahoma Quality Award
Award Levels: three

Oklahoma Quality Award – Achievement Level
Moore Norman Technology Center
   (Moore-Norman Vo-Tech)
(The first educational organization
   to win this award)

Oregon
Oregon Partnership for Excellence
Larry Sears, OPE Chair
Telephone: (503) 464-8547
E-mail: larry_sears@pgn.com
Web site: www.oregonexcellence.org

Oregon Quality Award
Award Levels:
   Certificate of Quality Commitment
   Certificate of Quality Achievement
   Oregon Quality Award
   Governor's Trophy

1996
Certificate of Achievement
Mountain View High School
Ed Tillinghast, Principal
2755 NE 27th Street
Bend, OR 97001
Telephone: (541) 383-6360
Fax: (541) 383-6469

Pennsylvania
No state award program in place; several regional programs:

Greater Pittsburgh Total Quality Award
c/o Greater Pittsburgh Chamber of Commerce
Three Gateway Center
Pittsburgh, PA 15222
J. Robert Graham, Executive Director
Telephone: (412) 392-4512
Fax: (412) 392-4520

Tri-State Regional Quality Award
Klein Plating Works
2020 Greengarden Blvd.
Erie, PA 16512
Michael P. Ricci, Quality Assurance Manager
Telephone: (814) 452-3793 x224
Fax: (814) 452-3531

Lancaster Chamber Business
Excellence Award
The Lancaster Chamber of Commerce & Industry
P.O. Box 1558
Lancaster, PA 17608-1558
Betty Rose, Assistant to the President
Telephone: (717) 397-3531
Fax: (717) 293-3159
E-mail: brose@lcci.com
Web site: www.lcci.com

Lehigh Valley Community Quality Award
Manufacturers' Resource Center
125 Goodman Drive
Bethlehem, PA
Tony Tlush, Manufacturing Extension Manager
Telephone: (610) 758-4596 or (800) 343-6732
Fax: (610) 758-4716
E-mail: tony@net.bfp.org

1990 Significant Progress
Millcreek Township School District

1992 Highest Achievement
Millcreek Township School District

1991 Significant Progress
Millcreek Township School District

Rhode Island
Rhode Island Race for Performance Excellence
80 Washington Street, Suite 208
P.O. Box 6766
Providence, RI 02940
Brian Knight, Executive Director
Telephone: (401) 454-3030
Fax: (401) 454-0056
E-mail: race@etal.uri.edu
Web site: www.rirace.org

RI Award for Competitiveness & Excellence
Award Levels:
    Bronze—Competitiveness Commitment Award
    Silver—Competitiveness Achievement Award
    Gold—RI Award for Competitiveness
        and Excellence

1995 Winner
Cranston Area Career & Technical Center,
    Cranston

1994 Winner
Community Prep, Providence

1994 Winner
Narragansett School System, Narragansett

South Carolina
South Carolina Quality Forum
c/o Advanced Training and Continuing Education
University of South Carolina Spartanburg
800 University Way
Spartanburg, SC 29303
Jeanette Reaves
Telephone: (864) 503-5990 or (888) 231-0578
Fax: (864) 503-5995
E-mail: jreeves@gw.uscs.edu
Web site: www.scquality.com

South Carolina Governor's Quality Award
Award Levels:
    Achiever's Award—Significant Progress
    Governor's Quality Award—Exemplary Quality
        Progress in Quality Management

Tennessee
Tennessee Quality Award
Tennessee Economic Development
333 Commerce Street
Nashville, TN 37201-3300
Marie B. Williams, President
Telephone: (800) 453-6474 or (615) 214-3106
Fax: (615) 214-8933
E-mail: tqa@bellsouth.net
Web site: www.tntech.edu/www/acad/acct/tqa/
    index.html

Award Levels:
    Quality Interest
    Quality Commitment
    Quality Achievement
    Governor's Award

2000 Quality Commitment
Greeneville City Schools
Greeneville, TN

Knox County Adult Literacy Program
Knoxville, TN

2000 Quality Interest
Chuckey Elementary School
1605 Chuckey Highway
Chuckey, TN 37641
Telephone: (423) 257-2108

Cumberland County Adult Education Program
Chattanooga, TN

Franklin Middle School
200 East 37th Street
Chattanooga, TN 37410
Telephone: (423) 209-5800

Gibson County Adult Education Program
Trenton, TN

Greeneville City Schools
Greenville, TN

Griffith Elementary School
Dunlap, TN

Hamblen County Department of Education
Morristown, TN

Henry County Adult Education Program
Paris, TN

Knox County Schools
Adult Education Program
1807 Martin Luther King Junior
Knoxville, TN 37915
Telephone: (865) 594-4411

Lenoir City – Loudon County
Adult Education Program
Lenoir City, TN

PI
Athens, TN

Rhea County Adult Education Program
Dayton, TN

Sevier County Adult Learning Program
Sevierville, TN

Smith County Adult Education Program
Carthage, TN

Vanderbilt University
Medical Center
1215 21st Avenue, South
Nashville, TN 37232
Telephone: (615) 936-2034

West End Middle School
3259 West End Avenue
Nashville, TN 37205
Telephone: (615) 298-6746

White County Adult Education Program
Sparta, TN

King College
Global Awareness
Bristol, TN 37620
Telephone: (423) 652-4333

Nashville State Technical Institute
Nashville, TN 37201
Telephone: (615) 353-3399

The Honors Course
Chattanooga, TN

1995 Quality Commitment
King College

1995 Quality Commitment
ETSU—College of Applied Science & Technology

1995 Quality Commitment
Roane State Community College

1995 Quality Commitment
Walters State Community College

1993 Quality Achievement
Belmont University

Texas
Texas Quality Award
P.O. Box 684157
Austin, TX 78768-4157
Telephone: (512) 477-8137
Fax: (512) 477-8168
E-mail: Qualtex@swbell.net
Web site: www.texas-quality.org

Award Level:
    Level 1
    Level 2
    Level 3

1998 Texas Quality Award
Brazosport Independent School District
Dr. Gerald E. Anderson, Superintendent
Mr. Mike Abild, Director of Business Services,
    primary contact
P.O. Box Drawer Z
Freeport, TX 77541
Telephone: (409) 265-6181
Fax: (409) 265-6802

1998 Texas Education Role Model
Amarillo Independent School District
Mr. Bob Morre, Superintendent
Dr. Gary Angell, Executive Director of Student
    Performance, primary contact
7200 Interstate 40 West
Amarillo, TX 79106-2598
Telephone: (806) 354-4300
Fax: (806) 354-4282

1998 Texas Education Role Model
Cypress Fairbanks Independent School District
Mr. Richard Berry, Superintendent
Ms. Susan Cory, Coordinator of Continuous
    Improvement, primary contact
P.O. Box 692003
Houston, TX 77269-2003
Telephone: (281) 897-4077
Fax: (281) 897-4149

1998
Rio Vista Independent School District
Dr. Sharron Miles, Superintendent
P.O. Box 369
Rio Vista, TX 76093
Telephone: (817) 373-2241 ext. 222

Greater Austin Quality Award
Contact: Jim Nelson
Telephone: (512) 322-5603
E-mail: jnelson@austin-chamber.org

Commitment

Anderson Mill Elementary School
Round Rock Independent School District

Bluebonnet Elementary School
Round Rock Independent School District

Braun and Butler Construction

Brushy Creek Elementary School
Round Rock Independent School District

C.D. Fulkes-Berkman Middle School
Round Rock Independent School District

Children's Austin Independent School District
Student Health Center

Deep Wood Elementary School
Round Rock Independent School District

Deerpark Middle School
Round Rock Independent School District

Forest Creek Elementary School
Round Rock Independent School District

Grisham Middle School
Round Rock Independent School District

Leona Doss Elementary School
Austin Independent School District

Popham Elementary School
Del Valle Independent School District

Wells Branch Elementary School
Round Rock Independent School District

Westlake High School
Eanes Independent School District

Progress

Baty Elementary School
Del Valle Independent School District

Berkman Elementary School
Round Rock Independent School District

Fern Bluff Elementary School
Round Rock Independent School District

Forest North Elementary School
Round Rock Independent School District

Hillcrest Elementary School
Del Valle Independent School District

Hornsby Elementary School
Del Valle Independent School District

Laural Mountain Elementary School
Round Rock Independent School District

Pond Springs Elementary School
Round Rock Independent School District

Rainbow Analysis Systems Group
Smith Elementary School
Del Valle Independent School District

Xenia Voight Accelerating Elementary School
Round Rock Independent School District

Highest Achievement

Gattis Elementary School
Round Rock Independent School District

1995 Commitment
Pease Elementary School

1995 Commitment
Reading is FUNdamental

1995 Progress
Barrington Elementary School

1994 Progress
University of Texas

1994 Commitment
University of Texas

1994 Commitment
Friends of Reading is FUNdamental

1994 Progress
Ortega Elementary

1994 Progress
Johnson High School

1994 Commitment
Eancs Independent School District

Utah
Utah Quality Council
P.O. Box 271367
Salt Lake City, UT 84127-1367
Telephone: (801) 825-3336
Fax: (801) 825-3337
E-mail: uqc@utahqualityaward.org
Web site: www.utahqualityaward.org

Utah Quality Awards
Award Levels:
    Governor's Quality Award
    Quality Progress Award
    Quality Improvement Award

Vermont
Vermont Council for Quality
Champlain Hill
1 Main Street
Winooski, VT 05404
Anne O'Brien, Executive Director
Telephone: (802) 655-1910
Fax: (802) 655-1922
E-mail: vcqual@aol.com
Web site: www.vermontquality.org

Award Levels:
    Governor's Award for Excellence
    Achievement
    Commitment

Virginia
Virginia does not have a state quality
    award program at this time.

Previous U.S. Senate Productivity and
    Quality Award Winners for Virginia

1995 Winner
Danville Public Schools, Danville

1993 Winner
Danville Public Schools, Danville

1993 Finalist
Portsmouth Public Schools, Portsmouth

Washington
Washington State Quality Award
P.O. Box 11669
Olympia, WA 98508-1669
Telephone: (800) 517-8264
Fax: (360) 664-4250
E-mail: wsqa@olywa.net
Web site: www.wsqa.wa.gov

Award Levels:
    Winner
    Achievement

Wisconsin
Wisconsin Forward Award
Department of Workforce Development
201 E. Washington Avenue
P.O. Box 7972
Madison, WI 53707-7972
Andrea Weiss, Executive Director
Telephone: (608) 663-5300
Fax: (608) 267-0330
E-mail: weiss@forwardaward.org
Web site: www.forwardaward.org

Wyoming
Wyoming State Quality Award
Herschler Building #1202
122 West 25th Street
Cheyenne, WY 82002
Jere Hawn
Telephone: (307) 777-7133
Fax: (307) 777-5840
E-mail: wsqa@missc.state.wy.us
Web site: www.commerce.state.wy.us/decd. wsqu

Award Levels:
    Diamond Award
    Jade Award
    Ruby Award
    Sapphire Award
    Amethyst Award
    Certificate

Glossary

Action Plans

Action plans drive action throughout the organization. They are based on the strategies necessary for organizational success. Action plans are tied directly to the strategic plan throughout the organization. They usually define the work to be done to achieve strategic goals and the measures to track progress against plan. Deployment might also require specialized training for some faculty/staff or recruitment of personnel.

An example of a strategic objective for an education organization might be to achieve student performance in the top quartile of the state's schools on a normalized test that is given annually. Action plans would likely entail determining which subjects have had the lowest scores, understanding skill deficiencies in those subjects, and developing curricula that enable students to master those skills. For higher education, a strategic objective might be to achieve student retention levels in the top quartile of comparable schools. Action plans may include determining chief causes of student dissatisfaction that lead to attrition by interviewing current, future, and potential students as well as those leaving the school. Then, specific actions to correct the problem would follow.

Active Learning

Active learning refers to interactive instructional techniques that engage students in such higher-order thinking tasks as analysis, syntheses, and evaluation.

Students engaged in active learning may use resources in addition to faculty, such as libraries, Web sites, interviews, focus groups, and primary source research projects. They may demonstrate abilities to perform higher-level tasks through projects, presentations, internships, practicums, independent study projects, and problem solving.

Align/Alignment

Alignment (to line up) refers to consistency of processes, actions, information, and decisions among business units, which need to support key organizationwide goals. Effective alignment requires common understanding of purposes and goals. It also requires the whole organization to use complementary measures and information to enable planning, tracking, analysis, and improvement. This means all parts of the organization and all people in the organization are pulling in the same direction in an effort to meet goals and objectives.

Analytical Tools

Tools for analyzing data may include brainstorming, Pareto charts, cause-and-effect diagrams, scatter diagrams, correlation and regression analysis, and histograms.

Analysis

Analysis refers to assessments and examination of facts and data performed by an organization or its units to provide a basis for effective decisions. Overall organizational analysis guides process management toward achieving key educational results and toward attaining strategic objectives.

Despite their importance, individual facts and data do not usually provide an effective basis for actions or setting priorities. Actions depend upon understanding cause-effect relationships. Understanding such relationships comes from analysis of facts and data.

Approach

Approach refers to how an organization addresses the Baldrige Criteria Item requirements—the methods and processes used by the organization. Approaches are evaluated on the basis of the appropriateness of the approach to the Item requirements; effectiveness of use of the approach; and alignment with organizational needs.

Benchmarking/Comparative Data

Benchmarking is the part of an improvement process in which an organization compares its performance against the best practices of other organizations or outside the educational community. It determines how those organizations achieved higher performance levels, and it uses the information to improve its own performance and to understand the current dimensions of world-class performance. The result of the process of comparing one organization against another produces comparative data. These data can be used to set goals to improve performance. In addition to benchmarks, other comparative data might include data collected by a third party, data on performance of comparable education organizations and competitors, and comparisons with similar organizations in the geographic area.

Continuous Improvement

This is the ongoing improvement of programs, services, or processes by small increments or major breakthroughs.

Cycle Time

Cycle time refers to time performance. This is the time required to fulfill commitments or to complete tasks from start to finish. Time measurements play a major role in the assessment because of the great importance of time performance to improving learning and organizational competitiveness. Other time-related terms in common use are design time, and response time to changing student needs.

Data Validity and Utility

Data are numerical information. They are used as a basis for reasoning, discussion, determining status, decision making, and analysis. Data proven to measure a particular construct or characteristic are valid data. Data utility (usefulness) is determined by the students, faculty, staff, and stakeholders; users of the data are the people who must use them.

Deployment

Deployment refers to the extent to which an organization's approach is applied to the requirements of a Baldrige Criteria Item. Deployment is evaluated on the basis of the breadth and depth of application of the approach throughout the organization. For further description, see the Scoring System on page 219.

Effectiveness

The extent to which a work process produces intended results.

Efficiency

The effort or resources required to produce desired results. More efficient processes require fewer resources than do less efficient processes.

Empowerment

Empowerment refers to faculty and staff having the authority and responsibility to make decisions and take appropriate actions. Empowerment results in decisions being made closest to the "front line," where work-related knowledge and understanding reside.

Empowerment is aimed at enabling faculty and staff to respond to student educational needs, to improve processes, and to better the organization's performance results. Empowered faculty and staff require information to make appropriate decisions; thus, an organizational requirement is to provide that information in a timely and useful way.

Faculty and Staff Involvement

A practice within a school whereby faculty and staff regularly participate in making decisions on how their work is done, including making suggestions for improvement, planning, goal setting, and monitoring performance.

Formative Assessment

This refers to frequent or ongoing evaluation during courses, programs, or learning experiences that give an early indication of what students are learning, as well as their strengths and weaknesses. Formative assessment enables diagnosis of student learning styles and strengths and weaknesses, as well as information on how well students are mastering course content so real-time improvements can be made.

High-Performance Work

High-performance work, a term used in the Item descriptions and comments, refers to work approaches systematically pursuing ever-higher levels of overall performance, including quality and productivity.

Approaches to high-performance work vary in form, function, and incentive systems. Effective approaches generally include cooperation between administration, faculty, and staff, including workforce bargaining units; cooperation among work units and departments, often involving teams; self-directed responsibility (sometimes called empowerment); individual and organizational skill building and learning; flexibility in job design and work assignments; an organizational structure with minimum layering (flattened), decentralized decision making where decisions are made closest to the front line/classroom; and effective use of performance measures, including comparisons. Some high-performance work systems use monetary and nonmonetary incentives based on factors such as school performance, team and/or individual contributions, and skill building. Also, some high-performance work approaches attempt to align the design of organizations, work, jobs, and incentives.

Innovation

Innovation refers to making meaningful change to improve educational and/or student services and/or processes and create new value for students, stakeholders and markets. Innovation involves the adoption of an idea, process, technology, or product that is considered new or new to its proposed application.

Successful organizational innovation is a multi-step process that involves development and knowledge sharing, a decision to implement, implementation, evaluation, and learning. Although innovation is often associated with technological innovation, it is applicable to all key organizational processes that would benefit from breakthrough improvement and/or change.

Integrated

Refers to the interconnections between the processes of a management system. For example, to satisfy students and stakeholders, an organization must understand their needs, convert those needs into designs, produce the offering or service required, deliver it, assess ongoing satisfaction, and adjust the processes accordingly. People need to be trained or hired to do the work, and data must be collected to monitor progress. Performing only a part of the required activities is disjointed and not integrated.

Interrater Reliability

The degree to which multiple raters, observing the same phenomenon, will give it the same rating. If they do, it has high interrater reliability; if not, it has low interrater reliability.

Leaders/Leadership System

Leaders refer to executives, administrators, and academic leaders. The Leadership system refers to how leadership is exercised throughout the organization—the bases for and the way that key decisions are made, communicated, and carried out at all levels. It includes the formal and informal mechanisms for leadership development used to select leaders and administrators, to develop their leadership skills, and to provide guidance and examples regarding behaviors and practices.

Measures and Indicators

Measures and indicators refer to numerical information that quantifies input, output, and performance dimensions of processes, products, services, and the overall organization (outcomes). Measures and indicators might be simple (derived from one measurement) or composite.

The criteria do not make a distinction between measures and indicators. However, some users of these terms prefer the term indicator: (1) when the measurement relates to performance but is not a direct or exclusive measure of such performance, for example, the number of complaints is an indicator of dissatisfaction, but it is not a direct or exclusive measure of it; and (2) when the measurement is a predictor ("leading indicator") of some more significant performance, for instance, a gain in student satisfaction might be a leading indicator of student retention.

Objective (Short-Term)

Objectives are usually considered subsets of goals. A goal may relate to financial success. One of the short-term objectives needed to meet this goal may be a monthly sales target.

Organization

This is a group of people with common goals and mission. The group may be any size, formal or informal, ad hoc or permanent.

Performance

Performance refers to output results obtained from processes and services. These permit evaluation and comparison relative to goals, standards, past results, and to others. Performance might be expressed in nonfinancial or financial terms. Three types of performance are examined by the criteria:

1. Student- and stakeholder-related performance refers to performance relative to measures and indicators of student learning, stakeholder, assessment results, perceptions, reactions, and behaviors. Examples include student retention, complaints, and student and stakeholder survey results.
2. Budgetary, financial, and mmarket performance refers to performance using measures of cost and budget, including expenditures, income, and expenses. Financial measures are generally tracked throughout the organization. Examples include instructional and general administration expenditures per student; income, expenses, reserves, endowments, and annual grants/awards; program endowments, scholarship growth, and percentage of budget for research and public service.
3. Operational effectiveness performance refers to performance relative to effectiveness and efficiency measures and indicators. Examples include safety, regulatory/legal and accreditation compliance, cycle time, productivity, and accomplishment of strategy. Operational measures may be measured at any level of the organization, such as whole organization, senior leader, key process, program, school, class, or individual.

Performance Excellence

Performance Excellence refers to work approaches systematically pursuing ever-higher levels of overall performance, including quality and productivity. Approaches to Performance Excellence vary in form, function, and incentive systems. Effective approaches generally include cooperation between administration and the workforce, including workforce bargaining units; cooperation among departments, often involving teams; self-directed responsibility (sometimes called empowerment); individual and organizational skill building and learning; flexibility in job design and work assignments; an organizational structure with minimum layering ("flattened"), where decision making is decentralized and decisions are made closest to the front line; and effective use of performance measures, including comparisons.

Prevention-Based

Seeking the root cause of a problem and preventing its recurrence (proactive posture) rather than merely solving the problem and waiting for it to happen again (a reactive posture).

Process

Process refers to linked activities with the purpose of producing a program or service for a student and stakeholder (user) within or outside the organization. Generally, processes involve combinations of people, machines, tools, techniques, and materials in a systematic series of steps or actions. In some situations, processes might require adherence to a specific sequence of steps, with documentation (sometimes formal) of procedures and requirements, including well-defined measurement and control steps.

For teaching, strategic planning, research, development, and analysis in education, process implies a general understanding of what constitutes competent performance such as timing, options to be included, evaluation, and reporting.

Productivity

Productivity refers to measures of efficiency of the use of resources. Although the term is often applied to single factors, such as staffing, machines, materials, energy, and capital, the productivity concept applies as well to total resources used in producing outputs. The use of an aggregate measure of overall productivity allows a determination of whether or not the net effect of overall changes in a process—possibly involving resource tradeoffs—is beneficial.

Refinement

The result of a systematic process to analyze performance of a system and improve it.

Results

Results refer to outcomes achieved by an organization in addressing the purposes of a Baldrige Criteria Item. Results are evaluated on the basis of current performance; performance relative to appropriate comparisons; rate, breadth, and importance of performance improvements; and relationship of results measures to key organizational performance requirements.

Root Cause

The original cause or reason for a condition. The root cause of a condition is that cause which, if eliminated, guarantees that the condition will not recur.

Senior Leaders

This refers to those with the main responsibility for managing the organization. Senior leaders may include administrators, department chairs, and faculty leaders. It includes the senior leaders (for example, president, superintendent, principal, and direct reports.

Stakeholders

This refers to all groups that may be affected by the organizations actions, success, and policies. Typically these include parents, parent organizations, faculty, staff, social service organizations, boards, alumni, partners, community agencies, businesses, employers, other schools, and professional societies.

Strategic Objectives

Strategic objectives refer to an organization's major change opportunities and/or the fundamental challenges the organization faces. Strategic objectives are generally externally focused, relating to significant students/stakeholders, market, service, or technological opportunities and challenges. Broadly stated, they are what an organization must change or improve to remain or become competitive. Strategic objectives set an organization's longer-term directions and guide resource allocations and redistributions.

Student and Stakeholder Interaction Process

This is the process by which an organization approaches, responds to, and follows up with students and stakeholders. It builds relationships and learns about student and stakeholder needs and expectations. The process of interacting can be by many methods, including phone, fax, e-mail, and face-to-face meetings.

System versus Process

A system is a set of well-defined and well-designed processes for meeting the organization's quality and performance requirements. For example, the leadership system refers to how leadership is exercised throughout the organization. Everything done in an organization is a process, but not all processes are part of a system, and not all processes are systematic.

Systematic Process

This is a process that is repeated and predictable, rather than anecdotal and episodic. A systematic approach to maintaining process consistency and ensuring student and stakeholder requirements are met would mean one could rely on it because it was tested and repeated.

Trend

For purposes of the assessment, it means that data have been collected over time, and when displayed (preferably on a graph or chart), they illustrate changes in a particular direction (positive/negative, increase/decrease). For example, the stock market trend as reflected by the Dow-Jones Industrial Average over the past few years has been positive (increasing). The federal budget deficit trend has also been positive (decreasing).

Value

This refers to the perceived worth of a program, service, process, asset, offering, or function relative to cost and other alternatives. Value considerations assist in determining the benefits of various options such as program and services to students and stakeholders.

Frequently, organizations need to balance value for students with those of other stakeholders, such as those businesses, faculty, staff, and the community, to deliver value to these groups.

Values

These are the principles and beliefs that guide/govern the behavior of an organization and its people toward the accomplishment of its mission and vision.

Clarifying Confusing Terms

Comparative Information versus Benchmarking

Comparative information includes benchmarking and competitive comparisons. Benchmarking refers to collecting information and data about processes and performance results that represent the best practices and performance for similar activities inside or outside the educational community. Competitive comparisons refer to collecting information and data on performance relative to comparable organizations or similar providers.

For example, a college that is community based generally recruits and retains students from its local area. Competitive comparisons require that the college know its primary competitors and find out how they are recruiting and retaining its students in an effort to attract and retain students.

Benchmarking would require the organization to find any types of organizations who carry out these recruitment and retainment processes better than anyone else and examine both their processes and performance levels. Such organizations may be large companies located elsewhere in the United States. Benchmarking seeks best-practices information. Competitive comparisons look at competitors, whether or not they are the best.

Student- and Stakeholder-Contact Faculty and Staff

Student- and stakeholder-contact faculty and staff are in direct contact with students and stakeholders. People who work in school or college offices such as admissions or student services are examples of contact people. They may be direct service providers or answer complaint calls. Whenever a student or stakeholder makes contact with a school, either in person or by phone or other electronic means, that person forms an opinion about the organization and its faculty and staff. Faculty and staff who come in contact with students and stakeholders are in a critical position to influence students and stakeholders for the good of the organization or to its detriment.

Student and Stakeholder Satisfaction versus Student and Stakeholder Dissatisfaction

One is not the inverse of the other. The lack of complaints does not indicate satisfaction, although the presence of complaints can be a partial indicator of dissatisfaction. Measures of dissatisfaction can include direct measures through surveys, as well as complaints.

Student and stakeholder satisfaction and dissatisfaction are complex to assess. They are rarely thoroughly dissatisfied, although they may dislike a feature of a program/offering or an aspect of service. There are usually degrees of satisfaction and dissatisfaction.

Data versus Information

Information can be qualitative and quantitative. Data are information that lend themselves to quantification and statistical analysis. For example, a faculty survey might reflect a percentage of the faculty dissatisfied with recognition programs. This percentage is considered data. These percentages add to the base of information about faculty satisfaction.

Education versus Training

Training refers to learning about and acquiring job-specific skills and knowledge. Education refers to the general development of individuals. A liberal arts education has its goal, education, whereas usually certification in computer networking is job-specific training. An organization might provide training in student counseling for its faculty, as well as support the education of faculty through an advanced degree program at a local college.

Empowerment versus Involvement

Empowerment generally refers to processes and procedures designed to provide individuals and teams the resources, tools, skills, and authority to make decisions that affect their work—decisions traditionally reserved for administrators.

Empowerment as a concept has been misused in many organizations. For example, administrators may pretend to extend decision-making authority under the guise of chartering teams and individuals to make recommendations about their work, while continuing to reserve decision-making authority for themselves.

This practice has given rise to another term—involvement—that describes the role of faculty and staff who are asked to become involved in decision making without necessarily making decisions. Involvement is a practice that many agree is better than not involving them at all but still does not optimize their contribution to initiative, flexibility, and fast response.

Operational Performance versus Predictors of Student and Stakeholder Satisfaction

Operational performance processes and predictors of student/stakeholder satisfaction are related but not always the same. Operational performance measures can reflect issues that concern students and stakeholders, as well as those that do not. Operational performance measures are used by the organization to assess effectiveness and efficiency, as well as predict satisfaction.

In the example of the school cafeteria, freshness of pizza is a key requirement. One predictor of satisfaction might be the length of time, in minutes, between cooking and serving. The standard might be 20 minutes or less to ensure satisfaction. Pizza standing more than 20 minutes would be discarded.

A measure of operational effectiveness might be how many pizzas were discarded because they were too old. The students/faculty do not care if the cafeteria throws out stale pizza, and therefore, that measure is not a predictor of satisfaction. However, throwing out pizza does affect profitability and should be measured and minimized.

Performance Requirements versus Performance Measures

Performance requirements are an expression of student/stakeholder requirements and expectations. Sometimes performance requirements are expressed as design requirements or engineering requirements. They are viewed as a basis for developing measures to enable the organization to determine, generally without asking the student/stakeholder, whether they are likely to be satisfied.

Performance measures can also be used to assess efficiency, effectiveness, and productivity of a work process. Process performance measures might include cycle time or error rate.

Support Services

Support services are those services that support the organization's programs and offerings. These services might include finance and accounting, library services, purchasing, management information services, software support, marketing, public relations, personnel administration (job posting, recruitment, payroll), facilities maintenance and management, research and development, secretarial support, and other administration services.

In the faculty/staff resources area (Category 5), the criteria require organizations to manage their human resource assets to optimize performance. However, many faculty and staff support services might also exist, such as payroll, travel, position control, recruitment, and faculty and staff services. These processes must be designed, delivered, and refined systematically according to the requirements of Item 6.3.

However, the details of developing work specifications, requests for quotations, and other aspects of the procurement process might be assigned to a procurement department. That department would be considered a support service that must design its own educational programs and services to meet the requirements of its internal customer and would be received as a support structure (6.3).

Teams versus Natural Work Units

Natural work units, such as departments, reflect the people that normally work together because they are a part of a formal work unit. For example, teachers who teach the same students in a middle school are a natural work unit, or those who all teach mathematics in a college environment.

Teams may be formed of people within a natural work unit or may cross existing (natural) organization boundaries. To design a science curriculum over the summer would usually require a temporary team.

About The Authors

Mark L. Blazey, Ed.D., is the president of Quantum Performance Group, Inc.—a management consulting and training firm specializing in organization assessment and high-performance systems development. Dr. Blazey has an extensive background in quality systems. For five years he served as a Senior Examiner for the Malcolm Baldrige National Quality Award. He is also the lead judge for the quality awards for New York State, Vermont, and the nation of Aruba and is a judge for the Wisconsin Forward Award. Dr. Blazey has participated in and led numerous site visit teams for national, state, and company-private quality awards and audits over the past 12 years. In 2000, Dr. Blazey was appointed to the National Workforce Excellence Network by the former assistant U.S. secretary of labor.

Dr. Blazey trained thousands of quality award examiners and judges for state and national quality programs, including: the Florida Sterling Award, Wisconsin Forward Award, Alabama Quality Award, Delaware Quality Consortium, New York State Quality Award, Pennsylvania Quality Leadership Awards, Illinois Lincoln Award for Business Excellence, Minnesota Quality Award, Vermont Quality Award, Nebraska Quality Award, Aruba National Quality Award, and the Costa Rica Quality Award, as well as managers and examiners for schools, health care organizations, major businesses, and government agencies. He has set up numerous Baldrige-based programs to enhance and assess performance excellence for all sectors and types of organizations.

Dr. Blazey has written many books and articles on quality, including the Quality Press best seller *Insights to Performance Excellence,* and co-authored *Insights to Performance Excellence in Health Care.* He is a member and Certified Quality Auditor of the American Society for Quality.

Karen S. Davison, Ed.D., received her doctoral degree from the University at Albany in 1981. She is the executive officer of Quantum Performance Group, Inc., where she advises private and public sector customers on performance improvement strategies and Baldrige-based assessments. Dr. Davison was a senior reviewer for the Empire State Advantage Award, and an instructor and mentor for the Aruba Quality Award. An educator since 1973, when she taught children with special needs in the Syracuse City School District, she has also directed gifted and talented education and served as chief of curriculum for the Maryland State Department of Education. Dr. Davison serves as vice-chair of the Board of Trustees of Finger Lakes Community College in Canandaigua, New York.

John P. Evans, Ph.D., is the Hettleman Professor of Business Administration at the University of North Carolina at Chapel Hill (UNC). He has been on the faculty of the Kenan-Flagler Business School at UNC for more than 30 years, during which he has served as the Interim Vice Chancellor for Finance and Administration and Dean of the Kenan-Flagler Business School. While dean, he served as president of the American Assembly of Collegiate Schools of Business, for which he chaired a task force that designed an entirely new accreditation process for business schools, introducing principles of modern quality management and improvement to this accreditation process. Starting in 1989, he served first as an examiner (1988–1989), then as a senior examiner (1990–1993), and then as a judge (1996) for the Malcolm Baldrige National Quality Award. He was the principal investigator on a research project sponsored by the National Science Foundation. In this project, with the participation of a number of organizations, he investigated the use of assessment of quality systems in the systematic improvement of organizations. Jack holds baccalaureate, masters, and doctoral degrees from Cornell University.

Index